The Life of Covenant

The Life of Covenant:

The Challenge of Contemporary Judaism

Essays in Honor of Herman E. Schaalman

Edited by Joseph A. Edelheit

SCJ

CHICAGO

ISBN 0-935982-22-1
Library of Congress Catalog Number 86-062848

Contents

Introduction

This *Festschrift* is a tribute of Torah to a rabbi whose rabbinate exemplifies Torah. A *Festschrift* provides an opportunity for a select community of scholars to honor a colleague through scholarship. Rabbi Herman E. Schaalman's contributions to Jewish life are reflected in the breadth and depth of the essays which are included in this volume. His presence and often his influence are reflected in the illustrious academy gathered in these papers.

The overarching theme of covenant has been the central core of Herman's own theological reflections. Covenant remains the descriptive context within which humans and God encounter one another. It is within the covenant that Torah and *mitzvot* have meaning. This is especially true for the modern-liberal Jew; the covenant provides a dynamic which stretches in time from Sinai until today. Herman Schaalman has taught this in his sermons, classes, and, most important, he has lived it as a Jew. It is for that reason that each of these essays is linked with and through the life of covenant—the challenge of contemporary Judaism.

Each essay's theme will be introduced individually with a description of the contributor and special attention given to his or her relationship with Herman Schaalman. The volume concludes, only coincidentally by way of the alphabet, with a unique reflection on Herman's rabbinate and his presence as a parent by his daughter, Susan Schaalman Youdovin. Susan, herself a rebbetzin, allows us a loving and intimate view of the man, the father, and the husband with his beloved Lotte, helpmate and wife of forty-five years. Susan's essay is a capstone of "family" scholarship. I have chosen to include an autobiographical reflection by Herman Schaalman. With the weight of profundity at the very core of this *Festschrift,* I did not want the vibrant and living presence of the volume's honoree to be forgotten. Coupled with his daughter's reflection, Herman's own ruminations add the fertile soil out of which all of the Torah which precedes it grows into a living Tree of Life.

Since the personal elements of his awesome rabbinate are conveyed by others, I as editor am allowed some room for my own reflections. I approached this idea and task long before the fates—and the various committees of deliberations—determined my future as the successor to Herman Schaalman. I speak therefore only for myself, though I am sure others would resonate with some of their own echoes, as I attempt to offer only some muted praise for my mentor, colleague, and good friend. Herman E. Schaalman is and always will be a role model as a rabbi. His rabbinate has had an overwhelming influence on me and many others. Consider Herman's presence in the lives of those from Emanuel Congregation who have become rabbis: Joseph Weinberg, Washington Hebrew Congregation, Washington, D.C.; David Leib, Temple Beth El & Center, San Pedro, California; Jay Sangerman, Brooklyn, New York; and Fred Reiner, Sinai Temple, Washington, D.C. Then there were his "students": Bennett Greenspon, Temple Beth Emet, Pembroke Pines, Florida; Marc Berkson, Temple Judea Mizpah, Skokie, Illinois; and Michael Weinberg, Sinai Temple, Michigan City, Indiana; all of whom attended Beloit College and later became rabbis. There is Richard Ettelson, who studied Torah with Herman on Shabbas morning and was guided by him into the rabbinate. Add to these who were directly influenced, those who were honored to have worked with Herman Schaalman as assistants when their rabbinates were still emerging: David Mersky, Joseph Edelheit, John Friedman, and Michael Weinberg. This is another group that will continue to represent his presence throughout their rabbinates. Who knows how many students at Olin-Sang-Ruby Union Institute went on to become rabbis, Jewish professionals, or Jewish lay leaders because of Herman's role and influence in their lives. I can say for myself, and also for others, that Herman E. Schaalman's rabbinate is rooted in the opening lines of *Pirke Avot:* "*V'Haahmidu Talmidim Rabim*" (Raise up many disciples).

Herman E. Schaalman's vanguard efforts in programming for Jewish youth, Jewish camping, and adult education are models still worth repeating. His efforts in the areas of mixed marriage and Jewish identity will all stand on their own record for generations. His influence regionally and nationally, in various Jewish institutions, will be felt long beyond his active rabbinate. All of these factors reflect Herman E. Schaalman's rabbinate, yet it is most aptly, and maybe most profoundly, captured in his own words. As a student of texts, I am obligated to honor my teacher by going to his text, to let his words convey his presence. This is particularly true of his addresses to the Central Conference of American Rabbis during his presidency.

The theology and vision which best describe this rabbi are articulated in his first presidential address to the CCAR: "Our vocation [as a people], that to which we were called is to be the *'am berit*, the Covenant people. No other definition is legitimate. No other definition is worthy either in view of our past or our future vision." While Herman clearly refers to *the people* as being *called* to respond as a *covenanted* community, it is clear that he sees this as the charge of the rabbinate. He has tried to teach and to warn that a *professional* rabbinate cannot be a role model to a community which seeks a response to the possibility of holiness. The covenant is that way of describing the relationship and the vision which *calls* both the rabbi and the people. Later in this same address in New York, in 1982, he concludes his charge to his colleagues with the following: "The risk is radical, but so is the existence and destiny of *am Yisrael*. Torah, the giving and receiving, our effort at 'hearing' the Divine Word is our vocation and thus our commitment." Again he teaches us that both the people and rabbis must be open to the risk of the challenge of covenant. More important, he reflects the all-important dialectic within the covenant: "the giving and the receiving." He has often said that there can be no *Matan Torah* (giving Torah) without *Kabalat ha-Torah* (accepting Torah). This same dialectic is central to his view of the rabbinate. One of his first lessons to me was, "You can only be a rabbi to the degree that the congregation lets you be their rabbi." Again, the covenant: the constant flow of giving and receiving which has kept Judaism so dynamic.

In his second presidential address to the CCAR in Los Angeles in 1983, he again reaffirmed the Jewish people as a covenantal community which should remain, essentially, united. Given these assumptions, he continued his probing of the role of the rabbi. He carefully reviewed the rabbinate as a calling in which various historical contexts have emphasized the prophetic, priestly, and counseling roles. Herman E. Schaalman once again proved what his colleagues have come to know for years: he won't settle for anything less than the sacredness of the rabbinate. He concluded his analysis of the rabbi's roles with an explication of Lev. 10:3: "*Bikeroveay ekadesh*, by becoming and being rabbis, we seek to be near to God. We undertake to be the ones who dare and risk such nearness. We need to know of holiness, and bring near to others—sacred moments, sacred times, sacred places, sacred acts." Herman E. Schaalman is a rabbi who has lived Torah as a response to the Shoah. In the face of radical evil, he teaches the holy—he lives a life called to covenantal responsibility. As a rabbi there is no single role he has chosen, but rather, an all-inclusive synthesis of roles which allows for his ability to help others, to teach Torah, and to draw others closer to God. While few will deny that his standards for the rabbinate are exacting, all will have to accept that those same standards have always been exacted with even greater severity and intensity on himself.

I have no way of proving it, but I sense that the intensity with which Herman Schaalman has pursued his rabbinate is rooted within that extraordinary sensitivity of a refugee from Germany in 1935. I traced this to his remarks in Jerusalem in 1981 upon his assuming the presidency of the CCAR. He mentions the "sheer miracle" of standing for a scholarship from the Hebrew Union College which was awarded to "five students at the *Lehranstalt* in Berlin." He reflected on his refugee status from Nazi Germany and said (though it was not recorded in the written document in the CCAR yearbook): "He was a brand plucked from the fire." There is a tragic and little-known footnote to the reported story of the "five students"—there was a sixth student. As I have heard the story from among the "five Germans"—Herman Schaalman, Gunther Plaut, Alfred Wolf, Wolli Kelter, and Leo Lichtenberg—there had been six invitations offered, but only five arrived with the necessary and life-saving scholarships. Dr. Elbogen, president of the *Lehranstalt* in Berlin, ushered the students into his office, and then "choices" were made that changed history. There was a sixth student who perished—literally one one-millionth of the *Churban*. I am sure that for Herman E. Schaalman, and maybe for the others of the five students, there has always been another whose rabbinate has become mystically intertwined with theirs. Herman E. Schaalman is the youngest of the five, the last to retire and the first to reach the position of president of the Central Conference of American Rabbis. With his retirement, it is now time to tell this story, so that Herman's disciples can now assist their teacher by adding to their rabbinates an extra element—for the one who was called to be a rabbi, but who perished among his people. Herman E. Schaalman's rabbinate is an eternal response to this story, confirming the life of covenant, especially for those whose lives now are only fading memories.

This *Festschrift* would not have been possible without the gracious patronage of many people whose admiration and love for Herman E. Schaalman are now tangibly made real: Elliot and Naomi Blumberg, Robert and Terri Cohn, Arthur and Kay Dickholtz, Larry and Jane Gelman, Joseph Gidwitz, Howard and Barbara Gilbert, Ronney and Rose Harlow, Robert S. and Terri Jacobs, Elliot and Frances Lehman, Harry and Ruth Lebeson, Dr. Jerome and Felice Mehlman, Stanley and Bea Owens, Melvin and Pearl Post, Karen Pritzker, the Pritzker family, Joseph and Sylvia Radov, Audrey Ratner, Ilse Ries, Sidney R. and Frances Robinson, Burton and June Ruby, Jack M. Ruby, William and Helen Schindler, and Joe and Jeanne Sullivan.

I want to further acknowledge the help and support of Deenie Kohn, my secretary while at Sinai Temple, Michigan City, and Barbara Miles and Harvey Plotnick, secretaries at Emanuel Congregation. All of them aided this project in various and critical ways. Herman and Lotte Schaalman's children, Susan Schaalman Youdovin and Michael Schaalman and their spouses, have been sources of support and encouragement and added labor when I needed it. Dr. Howard Sulkin, president of Spertus College of Judaica in Chicago, has seen in this volume a vital statement of scholarship, an important avenue of tribute for Herman E. Schaalman, and a project worthy to carry the *Haskama* of Spertus College.

On behalf of all those listed and all the contributors whose essays follow, I thank Herman E. Schaalman for allowing us to take this opportunity to return to him only a portion of what he has given to so many. May this volume of Torah honor Rabbi Herman E. Schaalman by adding a measure of knowledge that will aid another generation to live their lives within the covenant and accept the challenges of contemporary Judaism.

Joseph A. Edelheit
Rabbi
Emanuel Congregation
February 20, 1986
11 Adar 1, 5746

An Autobiographical Reflection: Herman E. Schaalman

Herman Ezra Schaalman was born in Munich, Germany, in 1916, the oldest of three male children of Adolph and Regina Schaalmann. I lived there throughout my childhood and adolescence, leaving Munich in May 1935 for Berlin. I attended grammar school at the Maximilian Gymnasium in Munich, from which I graduated in late spring of 1935. In addition to academic studies, I was a passable musician and a fairly good athlete. I received special training in Hebrew and was only the second young boy in the history of the *Liberale Gemeinde* to chant the entire sidra for Bar Mitzvah. I functioned as a boy cantor in the big liberal synagogue in Munich on a number of occasions such as Chanukah services, and often was asked to participate in the chanting of services in an orphanage where my father frequently functioned as a lay cantor. The family divided its attendance at services between this orphanage and the great liberal synagogue, which later was destroyed on special orders of Adolf Hitler because it was opposite the Kuenstler Haus and thus blocked the view from this artists' club.

Particularly memorable during these early years were the summers which the family spent in a cottage on a farm at Starnberger See. These weeks on the farm and at the shore of the lake were intense family events, filled with hiking, swimming, learning with each other, and the cultivation of deep ties between the three brothers and the parents. Both on vacations and at home, every Saturday afternoon was devoted to Bible study. The Buber-Rosenzweig translation was used to elucidate the Hebrew text. It was an unfailing weekly family event, which took precedence over any other activity. The Schaalmann home was intensely observant in *kashrus*, daily prayers, and the observance of Sabbath and all Holy Days. From Bar Mitzvah onward, I would join my father in the early morning recital of the daily prayers, as well as donning the *tephilin*.

I was a good student in the Gymnasium, with perhaps better than average aptitude for Latin and Greek. During the early thirties, the rise of Nazism, with all the attendant disturbances in personal relations among the peer group, was an ominous anticipation of what was to happen later. There were only two Jewish students in the Gymnasium. Both were in the same class. My Jewish friend, Franz Weil, was beaten up so regularly that he transferred to Switzerland to complete his studies. My father, Adolph Schaalmann, engaged the services of a retired police captain to teach me jujitsu. After a couple of incidents in which I applied this newly acquired martial art, I was left strictly alone, and even though I was the next to the smallest in a class of about thirty, there were no major incidents of personal attack and violence.

After graduating from the Gymnasium, I enrolled in the *Lehranstalt fuer die Wissenschaft des Judentums* in Berlin. I entered the so-called preparation course together with perhaps fifteen others. During the early weeks of this course, the school received an offer from the Hebrew Union College in Cincinnati, Ohio, to grant scholarships for studies leading to the rabbinate to five students of the *Lehranstalt* to be selected by the faculty. After a cumbersome and, at times, most painful selection process, I was one of the five who were chosen. In August of 1935 I set sail for the United States and Cincinnati.

The six years which I spent at the Hebrew Union College in Cincinnati were a period of intense learning both of the English language and of the many Jewish subjects, several of which I had not touched except for my few weeks in the Berlin school. At the same time, I had to enroll as an undergraduate at the University of Cincinnati because I had no university degree from Germany. The transcript of the Gymnasium courses and grades induced the heads of the various departments to grant enough credits to amount to a bachelor's degree. Inasmuch as I had no English language training to speak of, the University insisted upon freshman English. Since, however, the accumulated credits established senior standing, I was asked to choose a major and a minor as well. Taking the easy way out, I chose German as the major and then by a fluke enrolled in the Philosophy Department as my minor, thus discovering what would become a lifelong preoccupation. I came under the influence of Professor Roloefs, who combined philosophic learning and religious commitment to a remarkable degree. Roloefs's impact on me as a young student left a permanent mark. Roloefs was also particularly helpful when, within a few years of my arrival in the United States, my father was placed into the Dachau Concentration Camp in 1938 as part of the *Krystallnacht* action against Jewish leaders in Germany. Professor Roloefs was also instrumental in offering and obtaining for me a graduate fellowship in philosophy at the University of Cincinnati, leading toward an M.A.

During my stay at the Hebrew Union College, together with the four others who came at the same time from Berlin, I experienced the painful transition from one culture to another, one language to another, one religious life-style to another. Particularly when it came to the wearing of a *kipa,* the recital of the *birkas hamozon* after meals, and similar matters, I felt impelled to cling to the practices of my earlier life, at times under great stress and attempts by the administration of the College to dissuade me and others from these traditional leanings and practices. I formed lasting friendships with some of my non-German classmates, foremost with Lou H. Silberman, Malcolm Stern, and the late Dudley Weinberg. There were also several members of the faculty, such as J. R. Marcus, Sheldon Blank, and the late Zvi Diesendruck, Sol Finesinger, and Samuel S. Cohon, who smoothed the path of the "greenhorn." None, however, was more helpful or effective than the matron of the dormitory, Lillian Waldman-Lieberman, whose friendship and humanity were so profound as to make life more bearable time and again.

Graduation from Hebrew Union College and ordination took place on May 24, 1941, followed on May 25 by marriage to Lotte Stern, whom I had come to know the preceding fall. Lotte had emigrated from Germany and, after a short residence in Danville, Illinois, moved with her mother, Augusta, to Cincinnati where we met.

During our honeymoon, we were informed that the congregation in Cedar Rapids, Iowa, was interested in interviewing a young rabbi as a possible occupant of the pulpit. Interrupting our honeymoon, I went to Cedar Rapids, conducted services and preached, and to my great joy was engaged the same night. We stayed in Cedar Rapids, beginning in late August of 1941, through the war years, until 1949. Two children, Susan (born in 1943) and Michael (born in 1948), completed the circle of our family. The Cedar Rapids years were years of intense growth for a young rabbi, who had been totally unacquainted with the American small town scene. There followed much participation in public life, teaching at Coe College, Cornell College in nearby Mt. Vernon as a Jewish Chautauqua lecturer, a permanent radio program, and involvement in the life of that part of Iowa as a frequent public speaker. I have always felt a very special gratitude for Temple Judah and its people for their encouragement and support, not the least in 1945 in the aftermath of our automobile accident, the recovery from which took nearly a full year.

In late spring of 1949, the Chicago Federation of the Union of American Hebrew Congregations, at the instigation of the then President of the Union, Rabbi Maurice Eisendrath, called me to be its regional director. I followed the late Rabbi Phineas Smoller as the second in that function, and served as regional director from 1949 to 1955. My single most important achievement was to propose, find, finance, and finally direct what later became known as the Olin-Sang-Ruby Union Institute at Oconomowoc, Wisconsin. During my tenure, I was instrumental in helping four or five new Reform congregations come into being and in introducing the principle of committee structures into various congregations in the area. Special emphasis was laid upon ritual and adult education activities.

In 1955, Emanuel Congregation, preparing itself for the retirement of Rabbi Felix A. Levy, approached me as a possible successor. After mutual agreement had been reached and a congregational vote in October 1955, I assumed partial duties in October, and was installed on January 6, 1956, as Rabbi of Emanuel Congregation. During the early part of 1956, I also still functioned as part-time director of the Chicago Federation of the Union, until my successor, Rabbi Richard G. Hirsch, could assume his duties at the beginning of the summer.

Emanuel Congregation had a well-deserved reputation as a great congregation, in large measure due to the work of my predecessor, Rabbi Felix A. Levy. The development of additional programs, particularly in adult education, renewed emphasis on worship, on youth activities, and the like, were readily accepted by the Congregation. Efforts were also made to develop a well-functioning system of committees, each charged with the responsibility for major aspects of congregational life. In this fashion, dozens of people were drawn into the work of the Congregation, a process that has continued at a high level.

During the better than thirty years of my tenure at Emanuel, I enjoyed the help and collegiality of four young rabbis, David Mersky, Joseph Edelheit, John Friedman, and Michael Weinberg, each of whom brought outstanding gifts of mind and heart to the work of the Congregation. One of them, Rabbi Edelheit, is the successor designated to assume my post in July of 1986.

Emanuel Congregation always provided a challenging field of many-sided endeavors for me. There was a continuous appreciation of scholarly work and the communication of its results to many study groups, as well as in sermons. There was an unceasing call on my time for attention to those personal events in an expanding congregation's life which are natural to the calling. The Congregation grew to include about 900 families and never experienced the major fluctuations in rise or decline of membership which were typical of congregations in the metropolitan Chicago area. Some of the outstanding lay leaders, both men and women of the Jewish community in Chicago and in the country, found a stimulating Jewish home in the Congregation. It was also both expected and accepted with pride that I injected myself into the life of the Jewish and non-Jewish community in a variety of different areas, local, national, and international. At one time or another, I served on the boards of the Jewish United Fund of Metropolitan Chicago, the American Jewish Committee, the Chicago Board of Rabbis, the Chicago Association of Reform Rabbis, the Union of American Hebrew Congregations, the Synagogue Council of America, the Israel Bonds organization, American Friends of the Hebrew University, Jewish Council on Urban Affairs, and many others too numerous to detail here. Work in the field of television as well as production of scholarly essays likewise were part of my activity during this period.

During our years with the Congregation, Lotte and I were able to celebrate the Bas Mitzvah of our daughter Susan, the Bar Mitzvah of our son Michael, the confirmations and the marriages of both children. Our household included Lotte's mother, who injected the traditions and values of her German past until she was laid to her final rest in 1977.

On two or three occasions, my mother, Regina Schaalmann, who lives in São Paulo, Brazil, visited the Congregation and established her own ties with members of Emanuel. This was likewise true of my two brothers, Ernst and Manfred, who live in Brazil and Israel, respectively.

One of the signal achievements of my life was the founding in 1951 of the first camp of the Reform movement at Oconomowoc, Wisconsin. To this day, I take a keen interest in the Olin-Sang-Ruby Union Institute, serving on its board and teaching faculty, as well as taking groups of people from the Temple on retreats over stated weekends.

In 1966, I was awarded a Doctor of Hebrew Letters degree from the Hebrew Union College—Institute of Religion. Earlier, I had been honored as one of the outstanding citizens of foreign birth residing in Chicago by the Immigrants Service League.

I am active as a lecturer at Garrett Evangelical Theological Seminary, at DePaul University, and have read papers at Chicago Theological Seminary, at North Park Theological Seminary, and at many other educational institutions throughout the country.

The single most coveted honor that has come to me was my election as president of the Central Conference of American Rabbis in 1981. My installation took place in Jerusalem at the annual meeting of the CCAR. I served until 1983. Previously I had served as chairman of the Committee on Mixed Marriage and as chairman of the Patrilineal Descent Committee. I am currently chairman of the Committee on Ethics as well as chairman of the ad hoc Committee on Rabbinic Standards.

I am the proud grandfather of Johanna, Keren, and Jeremy Schaalman, the children of Roberta and Michael Schaalman, who reside in Milwaukee. My daughter Susan is married to Rabbi Ira Youdovin, currently in St. Petersburg, Florida. These are the special blessings for which I give thanks daily to the *borey olom*.

Suzanne Basinger was born and raised in Chicago and is the daughter of the late Rabbi and Mrs. Felix Levy. Rabbi Levy was the rabbi of Emanuel Congregation for nearly five decades. She is a graduate of Ohio State University and did graduate work at the University of Chicago and Loyola University. In 1971, she was the delegate to the White House Conference on Aging. She is past president of Emanuel Congregation, the first woman to serve in that position. She has been either president or served on the board of directors of several major Jewish organizations, from her congregation all the way to the national level. She has been involved with Rabbi Herman Schaalman for more than three decades, and has worked closely with him in his rabbinate at Emanuel Congregation, as well as on the regional Union of American Hebrew Congregations level. She brings a very important vision of a congregation in Judaism, born within her deep commitment to the covenant and the Jewish people.

Suzanne Basinger raises the issues of the contemporary Jewish woman and the commitment to preserve Jewish tradition. Basinger brings her own insights as a Jewish lay leader into the focus of the life of covenant, which challenges tradition to respond to modernity. Her demand for a new model of the Jewish woman in Jewish schools is a way to expand our views. We need to preserve our understanding of that revelation at Sinai, which offered a way of life to each person, regardless of gender. One cannot allow the covenant to become an issue of gender. Suzanne Basinger forces us to ask these questions.

Preserving the Covenant—a Challenge for Jewish Women

Suzanne Basinger

At the turn of the century, Dr. Jacob Lazarus said, "The wonderful and mysterious preservation of the Jewish People is due to the Jewish woman. This is her glory; not alone in the history of her own people, but in the history of the world." Dr. Emil Hirsch noted, "The opportunities for the Jewish woman today to reform her own home are many. What the synagogue now needs is intelligent enthusiasm. It is the woman who possesses this gift. Let her place her new culture in the service of her old faith and the winters of indifference will yield to springtides of young and hopeful life. At home let her be the priestess of the ideal, abroad the prophetess of purity and refinement, and through her will Judaism and the Jewish name be exalted to heights never before attained."[1]

Rabbi Emil Hirsch was one of the leaders of classical Reform Jewry and for him to support study and learning for women in our movement and to realize that women are the motivators of Judaism, in themselves and in their husbands and children, gave support for women to be equal to men in our movement. Women in the Reform movement have equality. The early leaders of the Reform movement in Germany wanted to give women equality. Abraham Geiger wrote, "Let there be from now on no distinction between duties for men and women, unless flowing from the natural laws governing sexes." While the qualification at the end left open the possibility of continued differentiation in religious roles, the importance of the claim that men and women should be considered as fully equal in religious obligations cannot be denied. In the Reform movement women sit together with the men, they are counted in a *minyan*, they have

1

aliyot. A *get* is not required, but if a woman wants one she can have it. Women have equal access to study, they can perform all *mitzvot*, and, more recently, they serve on congregational boards as presidents of congregations and have been ordained as rabbis and invested as cantors. There are no real studies as to *where women really* are in the Reform movement, but it is clear that they do have access to full participation alongside the men. As women study more, become students of Bible, they will be able to participate in all aspects of religious life.

In the Conservative movement at this time there is a struggle to give women greater equality with men. Here too they sit in the pews with the men, they have recently decreed that women can be counted in a *minyan* and can be ordained as rabbis, and they are looking into the *mitzvot* that women can perform, such as wearing a tallit.

There has been much legal discussion by the great early scholars of women's rights within the synagogue. Rashi maintained that women fulfilling positive time-bound *mitzvot* (from which they are normally exempt) are violating the prohibition against adding to the commandments. Rabbi Samuel Edels said that this is debatable. Rashi did not respond to the Babylonian Talmud's assertion that Michal, daughter of King Saul, used to wear teffilin, and the wife of the prophet Jonah would go to Jerusalem on the festival pilgrimages. Rashi's chief opponent on the issue of women performing positive time-bound *mitzvot* was Rabbenue Tam. There were several commentators who have compelling arguments in favor of women performing *mitzvot*. Rabbi Asher ben Yechiel (the Rosh) states explicitly that women may perform any positive time-bound *mitzvot*, and the Vilna Gaon declares, "We permit women to lay their hands on a sacrifice," seeming to imply that women may perform any positively stated time-bound commandment.

For example, the Rama said we do not permit a woman to put on teffilin because women are not careful about keeping clean. Teffilin, frowned upon by the authorities, is the very commandment whose performance by a woman is specifically permitted in the Talmud.

Incidentally, early archaeological digs of ancient synagogues reveal that there was no separate seating. It is believed that during Purim festivities men and women were separated because of the imbibing and carrying on of the men, and this was later extended to all other services.

Although Reform Jewish women have had the freedom of choice, one of the problems has been that it *has not been* out of knowledge. In order to really know what women's rights should be, we have to know what we have been given and what has been denied to us, and the reasons for it.

We must be able to understand the needs of those women in both the Conservative and Orthodox branches, and we must in some way try not to offend either. Orthodox Jewish women have a much more difficult lot because *Halakhah* controls them, and until the men are willing to reevaluate *Halakhah* and offer opinions in light of today's society and culture, there can be little change. However, the women in the Orthodox movement can themselves be the movers for change.

"There is a striking parallel to our concern with the status of women under *halakhah*. Referring to the bringing of the first fruits, the Mishnah says that a proselyte has to bring them but he may not recite the appropriate formula (Deut. 26) because he cannot say, "The land which the Lord swore to our ancestors to give us."[2] The Yerushalmi contradicts our Mishnah and rules that he *is* obligated to recite the formula. The proof text is God's promise to Abraham, "For I have made you the ancestor of a multitude of nations," which is interpreted to mean that henceforth Abraham is considered to be the father of all the nations. Every convert, therefore, is a direct descendant of father Abraham. This difference of opinion about the status of the convert persists down through the centuries. Rabbeinu Tam is opposed to granting him full equality. The Ri favors it. So does Maimonides. The Mishnah would deny him the privilege of saying "God of our Fathers" when he prays by himself. He must say, "God of the fathers of Israel." Some of the later authorities would keep him from leading the congregation in prayer or even in leading *birkat hamazon*. Others permit him to say and do everything like any other Israelite. The halakhic controversy rages around the meaning of texts, but one would have to be naive to believe that all this discussion is more than pretext. The basic problem is one's attitude toward converts. Those who wished to extend full equality to them were content to quote Yerushalmi's interpretation making Abraham the father of all peoples. Those who were not happy with converts would not have accepted this text or any other text. Surely when one prays to the "God of our Fathers," the word "our" means the collective Jewish people, and not the assemblage of individuals united at any one prayer service. The problem is not the individual texts but the convictions and the prejudices of those who sit in judgment, which means all of us.

The same difference prevails about our attitude toward the status of women. Surely the "covenant which Thou has sealed into our flesh" refers to the collective flesh. No one excludes a man who is forbidden by the *Halakhah* to be circumcised from the mitvah of *birkat hamazon*.

Texts are important. We cherish them. They are part of the glory of our heritage. But we should not become prisoners of the past. The time has come for modern halakhists to admit that, reflecting an evolution which covers almost 4,000 years, the vehicle of the *Halakhah* occasionally has paused to take on unnecessary baggage at various stations along its difficult and often tragic journey into the present. Today it is overloaded and therefore finds itself almost incapable of movement.

Jewish men must recognize the fact that the *Halakhah* often has been unfair, ungracious, and discriminatory toward our women. We cannot undo the past, but we can measure up to the needs of the present by granting full equality to Jewish women under the *Halakhah*.[3]

The women in the Conservative movement have made strides and are vocal within their movement to gain greater equality. They no longer want to be peripheral Jews but want to be in the mainstream of the Conservative movement, and those of us in the Reform movement who think we are more in the mainstream than are the Conservative women had better take a closer look.

Women in the Reform movement have had the freedom to grow in relationship with God: to experience and respond, to perform all the *mitzvot*, to have the same access to study and learning—but do we? Leonard Fein of Brandeis University has said the most radical thing happening in the non-Orthodox American Jewish community is that people are talking about God and theology. But nobody is doing that which is most radical: talking *to* God. Women do have equality in their access to God in the Reform movement, and the responsibility is ours to keep this equality; we must be in the vanguard for equal rights for all Jewish women. But we must first become as knowledgeable as we can. For example, a problem with which Reform women are not confronted—and believe me, it is more out of ignorance—is *tum'at nidda*. In other branches of Judaism the women are separated from direct enjoyment of much Jewish ritual because of *tum'at nidda*, the period of time when the woman is considered "impure." Rachel Adler says that "*tum'at nidda* was distorted when pathology entered halacha and the state of nida for women became a monthly exile."[4]

"Whereas *tum'at niddah* had been a way for women to experience death and rebirth through the cycle of their own bodies, it became distorted into a method of controlling the fearsome power of sexual desire, of disciplining a mistrusted physical drive . . . the state of *niddah* became a monthly exile from the human race . . . women were taught disgust and shame for their own bodies . . . the *mikveh*, instead of being the primal sea in which all were made new, became the pool at which women were cleansed of their filth and thus became acceptable sexual partners once more."[5] With Rachel Adler, I think this taboo is un-Jewish, and even though Reform women are not confronted with this problem they should work side by side with other Jewish women for a modern interpretation, not a sexist one.

I think that we have to remember that our sources do permit women to accept the commandments as an obligation. *Mitzvot* are not a sometime obligation or undertaking, but women who accept the *mitzvot* with seriousness and devotion may very well herald the day when men and women will participate equally in the world of Jewish observance.

In order to accomplish any kind of equality, we have to begin at birth. This is true for the Reform movement as well as other branches. For the male there is the *Brit Milah,* the establishing of a covenant. There should be a ceremony establishing covenant at the time of the birth of a girl. This can be done at the time of naming the baby, with a meaningful ceremony. Such a one has been written by Rabbis Sandy and Dennis Sasso and is called "Brit B'not Ysrael," the Covenant for the Daughters of Israel. This would be a good way to begin putting females in a covenantal relationship and give them a sense of belonging to the Jewish people on an equal footing.

In our religious schools today girls have the same opportunity for learning. They go to Hebrew school as well as religious school and can be Bat Mitzvah, which is all to the good, but they do not learn in religious school much about the role that women have had in Jewish history. They are not given any heroines or models to emulate. Susan Rosenblum Shevitz suggests the following steps:

1. Provide a viable and wide-ranging choice of female role models in textbooks and life situations.
2. Present the options of available Jewish life-styles for women.
3. Depict Jewish society in copy and illustration without traditional sex-role differentiation.
4. Portray evolving roles of Jewish women in different societies as a function of changing social, economic, and cultural factors.
5. Encourage the student to use publicly the skills she has been taught.
6. Present different modes of religious expression (and not only the traditional) to her without transmitting the feeling that it is unnatural or unfeminine for a girl to want to develop her religious sensitivities.

It is very important that girls know that their religious and spiritual development is taken seriously, and the above steps must be taken for the successful education of the female student, to give her the means with which to identify and to fulfill herself in Jewish life.

Jewish women certainly have been affected by the women's liberation movement and consciousness raising, and that is one of the moving factors in reassessing our position and role in Jewish life. For me, and I can speak only for myself, it has to be done with understanding. In our past the Jewish family has been very important. In the past the Jewish home was where the father was king and the mother queen on Shabbat, regardless of the oppression of the outside world. The family has been the place where humane values were salvaged and nurtured, where peculiarities and uniqueness could thrive. What does family mean to us today? Is it important for us to maintain family strengths, or does liberation mean freedom from all the old traditional roles? Personally, I think not; to be truly liberated we must have freedom of choice, and in freedom of choice we can take those obligations and commitments that give meaning to our lives. So we have to find in our heritage those values—the force of a covenantal relationship that was accepted at Sinai—to make a positive Jewish way of life. Choices are never easy because with them comes the yoke of commitment. When we accept this commitment we should know that we must study. We must learn Torah for the sake of Torah. If we are to have aliyot, it should be because we are in the pursuit of knowledge, and on this there should be no regard for sex. This will not come easily, but we can begin. If women become talmudic scholars like Judy Hauptman, if women become rabbis, then they can begin to write books about great Jewish women, help to make *Halakhic* interpretations and have a voice in the changes necessary to give us equality in Jewish life. Being on congregational boards or becoming congregational presidents will not make these changes; these are administrative positions to which we bring a lot of expertise from our other organizational activities, but input in the learning and study programs—becoming scholars in our own right—will give us representation where we have not had it before. I would hope in the years to come that women will be astute enough not to jump in and take over but will be very conscious of the fact that for so long we did not have a voice, and now that we do, we will present our position and work for each and everyone, male and female, to have acceptance in the sight of God, man, and woman, and that women will maintain the strengths that they have had throughout the centuries of making their home their Temple and working for equality in their synagogues with the help of the men.

Then it can truly be said that the wonderful and mysterious preservation of the Jewish people is due to the Jewish woman. This is her glory, not alone in the history of her own people, but in the history of the world, and for all tomorrows.

Notes

1. Bikkurim 1:4.
2. Report by Rabbi Aaron H. Blumenthal, Emeritus, of Emanuel Jewish Center in Mount Vernon, New York, to the Law Committee of the Rabbinical Assembly, June 10, 1974.
3. Rachel Adler, "The Jew Who Wasn't There: Halachah and the Jewish Women," *Response*, no. 18 (Summer 1973).
4. Susan Dworkin, "A Song for Women in Five Questions," *Moment* (May/June 1975).

Eliezer Berkovits is the one leading Jewish theologian with a commanding voice in the moderate Orthodox community. Rabbi Berkovits was professor of Jewish philosophy and Jewish thought at the Hebrew Theological College in Skokie, Illinois, until he made Aliyah *several years ago. He is noted for his theological treatise in especially the areas of contemporary thought as they face traditional* Halakhah. *He is particularly noted for his book,* Faith after the Holocaust. *He has lectured several times at Emanuel Congregation and is a long-time personal friend of Herman Schaalman, with whom he has worked many years to bridge the gaps between the Reform and the Orthodox communities.*

Eliezer Berkovits provides us an encapsulated critique of Judaism in a period of great devastation and rebirth. Berkovits, one of the most thoughtful theologians of our age, traces the vitality of the covenant as rooted in a historically evolving community of religious faith. Jews understand that faith means a covenantal responsibility, which in turn means to act and not simply believe. The Jewish people, in its own state, now realizes its ultimate challenge of the covenant. Berkovits poses for us, not only the theological questions, but the key covenantal questions.

Judaism: After the Holocaust, in the Age of Statehood

Eliezer Berkovits

I

The Holocaust has been the ever-present experience of our generation. It has confronted us with innumerable pressing problems. The very purpose of Jewish existence has been questioned. Especially for the religious Jew, it has become the most serious challenge to faith. This preoccupation is well justified. Though the confrontation is trying and depressing, yet it would be an ethical-spiritual tragedy if we allowed the meaning of the Holocaust and its memory to sink into soothing oblivion. As to the world at large, only in a state of darkened values could it contemplate its trivialization.

However, this is not enough. The unavoidable confrontation is only one aspect of the challenge. Unfortunately, its other aspect, perhaps the even more important one, has been almost completely overlooked. It is the question, What now? A third of our people has been destroyed. Where do we go from here? How to continue?

In the course of our history, we have sustained a long series of national catastrophes. We have survived because we always succeeded in responding to major catastrophes in a creative manner. After every major catastrophe an old-new form of Judaism came into being. Therein lies part of the secret of Jewish eternity. After the destruction of the First Temple in Jerusalem, the Synagogue was waiting to take its place. The Synagogue was a revolutionary transformation of the divine service.

During the decline of the Second Temple period, the Tora She'ba'al Peh, the oral Torah, flourished. About one hundred years after the second destruction, the codification of the oral tradition had been completed in the Six Orders of the Mishnah and became the basis of Jewish unity and continuity.

There was no longer a Jewish state, but another structure was ready to take over. After the decline of the Center in the Jewish land, Babylonian Jewry came to new vitality. The Babylonian Talmud was created, a unique spiritual, ethical, social, and scholarly achievement, the sustaining life well of Jewish identity for ages to come. After the tragic disintegration of the Babylonian Center, Spanish Jewry came into being and established its Golden Age of Jewish learning, philosophy, poetry, science. Then followed the catastrophe of 1492; but the Central European Jewry had already been functioning in their own Ashkenazic style, whilst the centers of Kabbalistic schools were flourishing, especially in Zefat.

In response to the Black Death Massacres in Central Europe, the vital centers in Eastern Europe came into being. In addition, Hasidim and the Hasidic movement were leading the way to new, healing understanding of Judaism of the Ages.

So, again, in our generation the Jewish people stands before the question of destiny. How to rebuild? What is the next phase of Judaism going to be? Before anything else we have to understand the situation in which we find ourselves. What is it that happened to us? What is its meaning? The uniqueness of our present situation is not determined by the Holocaust alone, but by the sequence of two events, dialectically opposed to each other. The one is the annihilation of European Jewry, the greatest disaster that has befallen the Jewish people since the destruction of the Temple in 69/70 of the C.E. The other is the fulfillment of the most exciting promise, the tradition of an expected G'ula, Redemption: the rise of the State of Israel, the restoration of Jewish sovereignty in the land of our Fathers, an event to which the Jewish people has been looking forward—rather irrationally—during the entire course of its exile.

Radical destruction of the past, followed by the elevating opening of the gates into the future. Heaven forbid to suggest that we accept the Holocaust as the price that had to be paid for the rise of the State. Yet, for the future history of the Jewish people and of Judaism, for the believing Jew, the interrelatedness of the two events represents one of the great miracles of Jewish history. He sees in it a special act of divine providence. Maimonides, in his discussion of the possibility of miracles, makes mention of a midrashic opinion, according to which a miracle need not mean the suspension of a law of nature. The *timing* of the event is essential, that is, that it occur when it is most needed. As if we would say that the dividing of the waters of the Red Sea happened as the result of some natural event; yet it was a miracle because it occurred at a time when, without it, the children of Israel could not have been saved from the armies of Pharaoh. Similarly one might say that as the extent of the Holocaust was being absorbed by Jewish consciousness, the Jews might have been overwhelmed by despair of the possibility of a Jewish future. Only one event could have redeemed them from such radical despair, the one that actually happened, the rise of the State of Israel. The only event to inspire us with new hope, that could become the source of new energy and faith in the future, was indeed the realization of the age-old vision— the Return.

However, independently of the faith of the religious Jew, both events are intrinsically related to each other in what they mean in the continuing history of the Jewish people. We often hear it argued that the Holocaust surpasses all human imagination in its meaninglessness. Yet it is essential that we master sufficient moral courage to contemplate its meaning for our generation. We usually refer to the six million Jewish victims. Actually, an entire culture and civilization was destroyed. We are accustomed to speak of the Ghetto, of the *Stetel*, with a sense of modern superiority.

But surely, now is the time to recall the heroic creativity and achievements of the *Galut* Jewries. For many centuries Jews, in conditions of oppression and deadly persecution, lived in *K'hillot*, in self-organized communities. They maintained their own law courts, *Beth Din*, whose decisions were accepted and followed. They had a general educational system that embraced the children from all social and financial strata centuries before the idea had ever been conceived by anyone in the Western world. The social and welfare services were continuing a tradition from talmudic times. There was the *Hekdesh* and the *Tamhui*; communal kitchens, care for the poor, the stranger, and the sick. All expenses were covered by communal taxes and charitable donations. The system was functioning without state authority, without police or military enforcement. It was a society of self-rule, based essentially on a freely accepted internal discipline, sustained by commitments to values, beliefs, and faith. Everywhere these *stetl* Jewries created a vast literature of Jewish law, biblical commentaries, ethical works, poetry. In most continents they somehow transformed the language of the host country into their own, gave it a style of their own, a literary quality of their own. The life experience of centuries was preserved in a living tradition that was passed on from generation to generation. Often it was preserved in pithy sayings that were the repositories of a characteristically Jewish wisdom and humor. All this, an entire culture and civilization, is gone, never to rise again. Conditions, political, social, economic, cultural, have changed so fundamentally that what was will never be retrieved. A great heroic chapter of Jewish history is closed. An entirely new chapter has to be started, new in relationship to the one closed by human hatred and barbarism; and yet, one of continuity in the comprehensive history of the

11

Jewish people, in faith, values, and meaning. What might be the nature of the new chapter? Where will it be decisively enacted? A great deal of original creative thinking is needed, new and yet old. Where is it to come from?

II

A second meaning of the Holocaust indicates the direction that we have to follow. This second meaning is the moral bankruptcy of Western civilization that rendered the Holocaust possible and perpetrated it. Jews do not like to dwell on this universal moral aspect of the tragedy as it affected especially the Jewish people. True, millions of others were also killed. But the subject is not numbers, but the annihilation of an entire people, its culture and civilization, the destruction of its human status. All that for the only reason that they were Jews; that they existed. In a sense nothing fundamentally new happened, only the technology was new. In essence, the Holocaust was the continuation of a tradition of hatred, practiced upon the Jewish people and Judaism. It could never have happened without the ocean of inhumanity that preceded it. Jews do not like to acknowledge it, because if the Jewish people have been singled out for hatred and persecution, no matter for what reason and purpose, then Jews must represent something different, maybe even unique. Such a truth would threaten the basis of assimilatory emancipation. They wish to continue as before, being integrated into the same world and worldly culture as before the Holocaust. But that world collapsed morally. These are the words of the historian Arnold Toynbee on the subject of Nazi Germany: "A western nation, which for good or evil, had played so central a part in Western history since the first emergence of a nascent Western Civilization or a post-Hellenic interregnum, could hardly have committed these flagrant crimes if the same criminality had not been festering foully below the surface of life in the Western world's non-German provinces. The twentieth-century German psyche was like one of those convex mirrors in which a gazer learns to read a character printed on his own countenance through seeing the salient features exaggerated in a revealing caricature. If the twentieth-century German was a monster, then, by the same token, the twentieth-century Western civilization was a Frankenstein guilty of having been the author of this monster's being."

The Holocaust was the testing ground, history's challenge to the ethical authenticity of the Western world; the demand to make a stand on fundamental humanitarian issues. As such, it was a unique opportunity for moral and spiritual recovery. The failure to respond to the challenge found its expression partly in active cooperation with Nazi Germany, partly in indifference, a form of nonconcern that was encouraging the

Germans in its effects. Ever since, the Western world has been experiencing a process of decadence of values and is being enveloped in a major spiritual crisis. Camus once called totalitarianism the passion of the twentieth century. It may be more to the point to say that this century is characterized on the one hand by a permissive shallow liberalism; on the other, by that passion for totalitarianism of which Camus wrote. The result is an all-embracing insecurity. The basic mistake of modernity has been revealing itself: scientific-technological advance was confused with humanitarian progress.

Is it a mere coincidence that after the Final Solution intended for the Jewish people the Western world has maneuvered itself to the brink of the possible Final Solution for all humanity?

This, then, the moral bankruptcy of Western civilization, is the second meaning of the Holocaust. It holds a twofold significance for the new chapter of Jewish history into which we have to enter. Having been singled out for destruction is the end of assimilationist emancipation. At the beginning of the struggle for emancipation a friend of the Jewish cause declared in the French parliament; to the Jews as human beings everything; to the Jews as Jews, nothing. Jews accepted the formula and even gave it a phrasing in Hebrew that said: Be a Jew in your tent and a human being as you leave it. The Holocaust has turned the Jew back upon himself; it calls him back to himself. The spiritual decline, darkening of values, the moral decadence of the West, turns the Jew back upon himself not only in the ethnic-political sense, but even more so into his own Jewish spiritual dimension.

III

What we have called the second meaning of the Holocaust indicates the direction that the new phase of Jewish history has to take. It links the Destruction to the other revolutionary transformation in our time, the establishment of the State of Israel. The turning-back upon ourselves in the ethnic-political as well as the moral-spiritual sense in the present circumstances can only be done naturally in a Jewish State. In this context a few words have to be said on the basic nature of Judaism. There is an essential difference between what is normally understood by the term "religion" and Judaism. Religion addresses itself to the individual. It is a kind of personal relationship between an individual and the God he believes in. No matter how many adherents a religion may have, be they even in the hundreds of millions, it is always the individual who faces his God. Nations as nations do not stand in any relationship to God. But Judaism did not commence with a prophet but with "Abraham Avinu," with our Father Abraham. From the beginning it is a people, a nation, with which God is concerned. The call to Abraham contains a promise: "And I shall make you into a great nation." The same promise is repeated to Moses when God, after the sin of the Golden Calf, wants to reject the children of Israel and make him the father for a new beginning. The Prophet Isaiah lets God say: "This people I have formed for myself . . ." Yet, nothing could be more mistaken than to see in this a form of racism or exclusiveness. The gates are forever open. Anyone who wishes may enter if he does so out of conviction. He becomes a son or daughter of our Father Abraham. He becomes a Jew in the full sense of the word, no matter what his racial characteristics may otherwise be. In addition, all humanistic universal ideals have their source in Judaism. Not only does the Torah teach us to love one's neighbor as one's self, but in the very same passage it is commanded to love the stranger. Then, again, there shall be one law for the stranger and the citizen: "Justice, Justice, thou shalt pursue"; "Thou shalt not hate the Edomite! He is your brother," and numerous other universal ideals. All universal ideals reach the world from Judaic sources. The vision of the millennium of peace was conceived by Isaiah: "Nation will not lift up sword against nation; nor will they learn the art of war any longer." Of more contemporary political significance are the prophet's words about the day when Israel will be a third partner to Egypt and Assyria, "a blessing in the midst of the earth. For the Eternal of Hosts blessed him saying: Blessed be my people Egypt and the work of my hands Assyria and my inheritance Israel."

Notwithstanding all these universalistic ideals, Judaism is about the life of a people in relationship with God. The individual is responsible, he is to walk in the presence of God; but he is Jewish because he is within the collective system of responsibility, the people's covenant with God. This is essential to Judaism.

Judaism's chief concern is not with ideals, but with their realization in life. Idealistic self-sacrifice is laudable and often unavoidable—God knows we Jews are familiar with it—but decisive is the realization of the ideal in daily life. The deed of realization, however, is always public; it has to take place within society. "Thou shalt not kill" addresses itself not only to the individual. The Torah demands a social order from which violence between a man and his fellows is eliminated. "Justice, Justice, thou shalt pursue" requires a society based on justice. "You shall have one law for the stranger and the citizen" could be fulfilled only within a comprehensive judicial system of equality. For this reason, within Judaism from its inception the obligation and the responsibility have been placed upon the national entity.

Mankind as unity, brotherhood, and equality is a noble idea. But unfortunately, it does not exist. As reality, mankind is a biophysical psychic entity of inequality, disunity, intolerance, and hatred. The decisive requirement for the realization of the ideas of peace and brotherhood in the world is that nations as nations strive for its fulfillment. The instrument for the realization of humanitarian ideals in history is the comprehensive society, the national entity. Thus, the natural implementation of Judasim is by a Jewish people, living in its own land, in control of the conditions of its existence, so that it may work for the realization of those responsibilities that derives from its covenant with God and from its life in the sight of God. This does not mean retiring from the world into a new kind of self-erected ghetto. It does demand that the Jewish people take a stand in the world in Jewish ethnic as well as spiritual authenticity. All this, however, is hardly possible in the Diaspora. Outside of their own land, not only the people are in exile, Judaism too is exiled from its natural habitat. .

The consequences over the centuries gradually changed the character of Judaism. The area of the possible application of the teachings shrinks more and more. At certain times, Jews may play an important part in the political life of any country, as individuals. The Jewish people in exile live in communities, but not in the national dimension. Jews as individuals are responsible to deal honestly in the economic sphere; but there is no possibility for the establishment of a Jewish economic system. Again, the Jew as an individual may serve in all kinds of humanitarian causes. But entire systems of Jewish civil and criminal law, family law, and social ethics have no possibility of implementation. In history, there were times of wide areas of Jewish internal autonomy in various countries of dispersion. But more and more the extent of such autonomies became reduced. Thus, wide sections of Jewish teaching became enclosed in heavy Talmudic volumes. Regularly, Judaism was forced out of the public domain into the private one, from national existence to communal organization. Finally, especially in our own days, it had to move from the community structure into congregations. Thus, the way of life of the people was reduced to mere religious observances by individuals; a comprehensive national culture in the presence of God became, finally, a mere religion.

IV

This final phase was reached mainly in the Western countries of assimilationist emancipation. Apart from that, as indicated earlier, the achievements of *Galut* Jewries were heroic. We have every reason to be proud of them. All that, however, is now over forever. The Ruin itself points to the direction in which to progress. Jewish destiny of our day provides the possibility.

Once again Judaism is moving into the public domain of national existence. It is regaining its original direction in history. It is true, we are

15

confronted with entirely new challenges, new problems, new responsibilities. How to establish a spiritual, religious Judaic order in a State in the final phase of the twentieth century? Indeed, not how to establish a State of Jews, but a Jewish State. At this time, for instance, there exists not a single Talmudic scholar who knows how to manage a Jewish state in accordance with *Halakhah;* how to apply Jewish civil and criminal law within a modern state structure. As to the secularist camp, especially in Israel, nothing could be more tragic and more farcical than at this hour, when we are called upon to start a new phase in the history of Jewish national life and culture, we should fall victim to the temptations of a morally and spiritually disintegrating Western civilization.

We have no previous experience for the present task. Yet, this alone is the way; this—the future. We need intellectual courage to understand the radically new situation. We must beware of transferring Galut-condition ideologies, interpretations, and application of Judaism into the age of Statehood. We have to return to our spiritual sources and listen to the Word of God addressed to this hour. Beyond all ideological division, we must strive for mutually supporting unity. Finally, with the courage of a faith, tried in the furnace of universal history, we must not fail to hear the call of the historic destiny of our people.

Eugene B. Borowitz is one of American Jewry's leading thinkers and an outstanding proponent of covenant theology. A rabbi, he serves as professor of education and Jewish religious thought at the New York School of the Hebrew Union College, Jewish Institute of Religion. He is the founder and editor of Sh'ma: A Journal of Jewish Responsibility. *He served on several faculties, including the Jewish Theological Seminary of America, and is the author of eleven books. Eugene Borowitz was one of the group whom Herman Schaalman brought together at Oconomowoc in the 1960s. This was the so-called Group of Covenantal Theologians. Borowitz has lectured several times at Emanuel Congregation and has been an important personal friend throughout Herman Schaalman's rabbinate.*

Eugene Borowitz brings his keen, liberal mind to an analysis of contemporary ethics within a "Jewish context." Borowitz demands that we respond to tradition, which roots our consciousness within the covenant. He also provokes us to remain open to, and choose from, our responses to tradition, thus ensuring that the covenant remains dynamic. Borowitz, a leading covenantal theologian, aids us in finding how to think about contemporary Jewish issues within a covenantal tradition which is open to modern thought. His case in point is a classic study of traditional *Halakhah* as a valuable resource for contemporary standards in an always-expansive covenant.

Hillul Hashem:
A Universalistic Rubric in Halakhic Ethics

Eugene B. Borowitz

The need to rethink the theory of modern Jewish ethics arises from the loss of the meaning the liberals assigned to the words "Jewish" and "ethics." For Hermann Cohen and the many who utilized his ideas, the neo-Kantian definition of ethics determined the meaning of the word "Jewish." Today, the several competing versions of philosophic ethics all operate under a cloud of uncertainty, as Alasdair Macintyre's widely discussed *After Virtue* (Notre Dame: University of Notre Dame Press, 1981) makes plain. Thus, one mode of reestablishing a compelling theory of Jewish ethics involves studying contemporary options in ethics and applying the most appealing of these to Judaism.

An alternate path explores the independent meaning the term *Jewish* should have in such a theory. Self-respect demands that it be given at least equal weight with Hellenic or Germanic philosophy, specifically, that they not be allowed to dictate what Judaism properly understands to be "the good and the right." From this perspective, mediation between Judaism and ethics begins from the Jewish side and does so in terms of authoritative Jewish teaching, namely, with concern for the *halakhah*.

Orthodox and postliberal Jews can easily share this approach to Jewish ethics though they are likely, in due course, to come to different conclusions about contemporary Jewish responsibility.[1] In doing so they must face the continuing difficulty generated by this procedure: how to reconcile a particular people's legal system with the sense of goodness available to all human beings.

This study arises as a continuation of my interest in this approach,

19

evidenced recently by a response to Aharon Lichtenstein's much-discussed paper, "Does Jewish Tradition Recognize an Ethic Independent of *Halakha*?"[2] There I pointed to the ambiguous and subordinate status of the "ethical moment" in *halakhah,* thus impugning the commanding power of Jewish ethics. Here I propose to study a specific halakhic provision which illumines Jewish law's relation to universal human moral judgment, namely the category *hillul hashem* insofar as it shapes Jewish duty in terms of gentile opinion.

An inner theological dialectic lies behind the legal tension to be explored. God has given the Torah to one particular people, the Jews, and its rules distinguish between those who do and those who do not participate in the system. The same Torah indicates that God stands in a similar relationship, if a legally less demanding one, with all humankind, the children of Noah. Hence they may be said to have a legitimate basis for judging Jewish conduct.[3] The potential tension between what the Torah permits to Jews and a harsh evaluation gentiles might make of it creates the subset of the laws of *hillul hashem* to be studied.

While the term *hillul hashem* does not occur in the Bible, its equivalents are found in several biblical books, with heavy concentrations in Leviticus and Ezekiel. The *peshat* of these texts may be classified as moving from concrete acts of profanation, to those which directly or indirectly cast aspersions on God, and finally to an abstract sense of *hillul hashem.*

Since the book of Leviticus pays considerable attention to cultic acts which sanctify God—to the extent that various items can be called God's "holy things"—so, by extension, mishandling them profanes God. (Thus Lev. 21:6, 22:2, 32; Mal. 1:12; and perhaps Ez. 20:39.) Idolatry—specifically, sacrificing one's child to Moloch—is a desecration (Lev. 18:21, 20:13). Ezekiel accuses certain women prophets of equivalent sacrilege (Ez. 13:19). The theme also encompasses noncultic violations, of which swearing falsely by God's name is a similarly direct profanation (Lev. 19:12). And it includes unethical acts like a father and son having sexual relations with the same girl (Am. 2:7) and the Jerusalemites reneging on their solemn pact to free their Jewish slaves (Jer. 34:16). Ezekiel envisages this notion abstractly and four times, in consecutive verses, proclaims God's determination to sanctify the Divine name which the people of Israel has profaned through its sinfulness (Ez. 36:20–23).

The social dimension of several of these acts of profanation deserves particular attention. The heinousness of the sacrilege derives as much from what the act says about God to others, a public, as from its intrinsic profanity. The biblical authors consider God's social, corporate acknowledgment even more important than the equally indispensable private faith of individuals. The political term, king, so often used to refer to God, testifies to this social understanding of God's reality. Hence acts which imply that there is no God or which as good as do the same by testifying falsely to God's nature or commands, profane God's "name," that is, our understanding of God or, equally, God's reputation. Much of rabbinic teaching in this area derives from this social context.

A direct line runs from the Bible to the Talmud's teachings about *hillul hashem*.[4] Thus, since Jews are enjoined to sanctify God's name by martyrdom rather than commit murder, idolatry, or sexual offenses, failing to give up one's life then profanes God's name. So does rebelliously transgressing commands of the Torah. This identification of God with God's commands results in a significant rabbinic expansion of this theme, namely, that "important people," scholars being the chief case, must live by a higher standard than ordinary folk. People take rabbis and other such dignitaries as models for proper behavior. They therefore ought to avoid acts which the Torah otherwise permits but which, done by them, might lead to a lowering of communal standards and, in turn, to lesser sanctity in God's people, thus profaning its God.

A motif of particular importance for this investigation emerges from this preliminary survey. The concept of *hillul hashem* has extraordinary power.[5] When properly invoked, it can, so to speak, change the contours of Jewish duty. It does so by overriding a previous permission granted by the Torah and negating it, thus determining duty anew.

The *halakhah* contains such a possibility because its piety emphasizes the corporate dimension. Here the individual's "prior" options are limited to enhance the community's religious life and to safeguard it from sin. (With the Bible, the rabbis consider leading others to sin a qualitatively worse level of iniquity than is private transgression.) While the rabbis occasionally refer to the possibility of *hillul hashem* in private (*betzinah* or *beseter*)—of which the most notorious example is the advice to one overcome by lust to satisfy himself where he is not known—their overwhelming attention is given to acts in public (*befarhesiya* or *berabim*).[6]

Recognizing the cosmic importance the rabbis attached to the Jewish community and its practice of the Torah, the imperative, internal, social quality of *hillul hashem* seems quite logical. But considering the general corporate (as against individual) denigration of the gentiles, the *umot haolam* or *goyim*—who are usually identified as "wicked," and thus deserving of God's judgment—it comes as something of a surprise to discover that the same process operates in relation to them. The rabbis prohibit certain acts to Jews, not because the Torah proscribes them, but because of what doing them might lead gentiles to think or say.[7] In such cases, potential gentile opinion leads to a change in the "prior" contours of Jewish duty: hyperbolically, in some cases the gentiles "make" Torah.

In itself, this concern for the religious judgment of idolators is worthy of note. It testifies to the universalism implicit in *halakhah*. Of even greater interest, these prohibitions take precedence over Jewish economic loss, which the rabbis normally avoid in keeping with their principle, *hatorah hasah al memonam shel yisrael,* "the Torah has compassion on the funds of Jews." This unusual aspect of *halakhah,* with its intriguing parallels to recent ethical thinking about the universalizability of ethical judgment, deserves investigation.

Before proceeding, an important disclaimer must be made. In each instance to be studied, the majority of sages say Jewish law directly prohibits the act involved. They then rule that it carries a double opprobrium because it also constitutes *hillul hashem.* Here we are interested in the well attested if minority usage of *hillul hashem* which some sages invoke to prohibit Jewish acts toward gentiles which they otherwise consider permissible. (It would also be of great interest if historians of the *halakhah* could elucidate the socio-temporal circumstances to which the rabbis may have been responding in these rulings.)

We may group the sixteen specific applications of *hillul hashem* we are studying into three categories: (1) the prohibition of acts directly disparaging God's honor or doing so by dishonoring the Jewish people; (2) the prohibition of possible stealing from gentiles whether direct or indirect; and (3) the prohibition of acts, national or individual, that might be perceived as deception.

Three acts fall into the first category. Only one is explicitly described as a direct affront to God: taking law cases to a gentile court.[8] This might be seen as testimony to the superiority of the gentiles' god or, with homiletic license, as indicating the denial of the God of Israel.[9] The other two cases dishonor the Jewish community: publicly taking charity from gentiles[10] and permitting gentile contractors to work for Jews on the Sabbath when it is clear that they are working for Jews and gentiles do not permit work on their own Sabbath.[11]

The remaining cases, the overwhelming majority, concern thievery and deception. For *halakhah,* then, gentiles become a decisive factor in shaping the law mainly in ethical matters. The editors of the *Talmudic Encyclopedia* consider the most embracing category of this theme *gezel hagoy,* "the robbery of gentiles." They not only treat it as the leading instance of the invocation of *hillul hashem* relative to gentiles[12] but they devote a substantial independent article to the topic.[13]

The problem is most easily confronted via a Tanaitic tradition cited in Y. B. K. 4.3. Two Romans, sent to learn all about Judaism, commented after having studied it that they admired Jewish law save for the provision that Jews are permitted to rob gentiles (perhaps, more narrowly, that Jews may keep what has been stolen from gentiles).[14] Thereupon Rabban Gamaliel prohibited the robbery of gentiles because it involved *hillul hashem.* Here not only do we have gentile opinion shaping Jewish duty (to the economic loss of Jews) but an indication that the permission once operated and the prohibition was instituted later. In any event, Jewish law proscribes the robbery of gentiles, whether because intrinsically forbidden by the Torah and doubly abominable as *hillul hashem,* or, according to some authorities, forbidden only under the latter rubric.

That would seem to settle the matter. Yet the robbery of gentiles arises in other specific matters which, for the sake of greater specificity, I consider below under the rubric of potential deception. A further set of problems arises probably because human cupidity is strong and Jews have been steadily persecuted. Thus, some authorities acknowledge that acts considered the robbery of gentiles might not become known, thus removing them from the prohibition of *hillul hashem.* But this means permitting such acts according to those sages who do not consider them intrinsically prohibited.[15]

Two prohibitions may be said to have been instituted to avoid even a gentile perception of Jewish theft. In the first instance, though Jews in the home of a Jewish owner may eat of that with which they are working, that practice is forbidden when the owner is gentile. He might conclude that Jewish laborers steal from their bosses.[16] In the second instance, a synagogue menorah which is the gift of a gentile may not be exchanged for anything else, even to perform a commandment, though that is possible for one donated by a Jew. And the sages explicitly note that invocation of *hillul hashem* is to prevent the gentile complaining about Jews appropriating his gift.[17]

Five cases, most of which traditionally are connected to the notion of *gezel hagoy,* seem to me better considered as forms of interpersonal deception. Thus, one may not lie to a gentile[18] or mislead him in negotiating to buy his slave.[19] A particularly intricate case involves *hafkaat halvaato,* the abrogation of a gentile's loan. In the original case, the loan was made by one gentile to another who then became the lender's slave until the loan was paid off. A Jew who purchases that slave should normally pay off the loan, but some authorities say that Jews are not obligated to repay loans to gentiles.[20] Thus, Rashi, commenting on the talmudic text, says that this is not really *gezel hagoy,* only the refusal to give him back his money.[21] Sages following this legal line allow for keeping gentile money but consider this form of doing so less troubling a matter than outright *gezel hagoy.*

Hafkaat halvaato also arises analogously to other cases, described below (and, as we shall see, remains a living consideration for contemporary halakhic practice). The editors of the *Talmudic Encyclopedia* seem sensitive to the ethical problems involved in this issue. They therefore conspicuously feature an opinion that restricts this option, namely that of the Meiri, perhaps the leading traditional liberalizer of Jewish law regarding gentiles. In sum, once again the sages divide between those who hold *hafkaat halvaato* intrinsically forbidden and also a *hillul hashem,* and those who proscribe it only when it leads to a profanation of God's name.[22]

Two other forms of interpersonal deception are forbidden because of possible detrimental gentile opinion. One involves making a private condition when swearing an oath to a gentile under coercion, thus rendering it invalid.[23] The other concerns taking advantage of an error made by a gentile in the course of a negotiation.[24]

The five remaining cases seem more social in focus and if not prohibited might lead gentiles to consider Jews untrustworthy. A Jew may not oppress a gentile,[25] or keep something he has lost,[26] or deny him the testimony he seeks, even if this involves a loss to another Jew,[27] whenever such an act might lead to a profanation of God's name.

Perhaps the most troublesome of these issues is the avoidance of taxes imposed by a gentile government. While it is clear that "the law of the [gentile] country has the force of [Torah] law," a body of opinion clearly holds that in certain cases avoidance is permitted—but not if it might involve *hillul hashem*.[28] Finally, as the case of the Gibeonites made clear to the rabbis, the Jewish people may not break a treaty it has made with another people, even if false pretenses are involved, should that act result in the disparagement of the Jews and thus the profanation of God's name.[29]

One can therefore say about these sixteen instances that the evidence abundantly demonstrates that in certain cases, mainly ethical ones, gentile opinion can be a decisive, overriding factor in determining, even altering, *halakhah*. It would be of the greatest interest to know what constitutes the necessary warrants for invoking *hillul hashem* in a given case and what limits there are to its uncommon power. Nothing in the literature studied touches directly on the theory of the utilization of *hillul hashem*. Indeed, we do not find it characteristic of any given sage and it seems, on the surface, to be used with as much randomness as consistency.

So much is classic *halakhah*. To see how this motif might be of help to us in clarifying the nature of Jewish ethics today, it will help to take a brief look at its contemporary employment. A search made by the Institute for Computers in Jewish Life through the responsa program of the Bar-Ilan Center for Computers and Jewish Studies provided the necessary data. It generated a list of sources in which the term *hillul hashem* appeared in close association with either *goy* or *akum* (literally, "idolator"; legally, "non-Jew"—though hardly a happy association). In the works of three eminent respondents of our time, Yechiel Weinberg (*Seridei Esh*), Moshe Feinstein (*Igrot Moshe*), and Eliezer Waldenberg (*Tzitz Eliezer*), seventeen possible *teshuvot* dealing with our topic occurred.[30] Of these, only eight were relevant to this study, the others either could not be found, had no reference to this topic, or related only to *hillul shabbat*.

Yechiel Weinberg is best represented in this sample, as five of his *teshuvot* deal with *hillul hashem* in relation to gentiles. He uses the term *hillul hashem* in these texts only in the citation or summary of the traditional dicta. The case topics are: (1) martyrdom (*Seridei Esh,* vol. 2, no. 79), (2) teaching gentiles Torah, where he adduces the case of the Romans (*Seridei Esh,* vol. 2, no. 90), (3) selling a synagogue seat to satisfy a debt, where the sale of synagogue property is discussed (*Seridei Esh,* vol. 3, no. 63), and (4) the robbery of gentiles (*Seridei Esh,* nos. 74–75—in the latter, beware of the misprint at the top of page 254 which indicates that this is responsum no. 57 rather than no. 75).

Only two responsa of Moshe Feinstein are relevant to this study. Both involve the issue of *gezel hagoy* with one merely mentioning the classic opinions (*Igrot Moshe, Yoreh Deah,* vol. 1, no. 103). The other is somewhat more interesting since it seems to be the only instance of this concept being used in a fresh application as against the citation of classic precedent (*Igrot Moshe, Hoshen Mishpat,* vol. 1, no. 82). He suggests that the sages did not absolutely require the return of a gentile's lost article because while voluntarily doing so can lead to sanctifying God's name among gentiles, having to do so might, on occasion, lead to *hillul hashem.* It should be noted, however, that this unique example of a contemporary creative use of the concept of *hillul hashem* occurs in a theoretical discussion of the law of the rabbis living among idolators.

The one relevant *teshuvah* of Eliezer Waldenberg has special interest since the questioner proposes a new application of *hillul hashem.* Quite conscious of the concept's special power, he suggests that wearing his *tzitziyot* so that they are visible, rather than obscured by being under his other clothes, may lead gentiles to set inordinately high standards for his behavior (since most Jews are not this pious). This might lead to what he ingeniously calls *avak hillul hashem,* "a hint [literally, "the dust"] of a profanation of God's name" (*Tzitz [sic] Eliezer,* vol. 8, no. 3). Hence he inquires whether, since this does not involve either giving up the practice or altering it to avoid gentile mockery, he may wear his *tzitziyot* obscured. To which the answer is a firm negative, with the possibility of *avak hillul hashem* apparently of so little substance that Waldenberg never discusses it.

From this sample, limited in authorities and to the questions they have chosen to answer and publish, some tentative conclusions may be drawn. Apparently the major *poskim* of our time use the concept of *hillul hashem* only in the cases and contexts in which it came down to them. They do not seem to apply it to any new situations or in terms of any different perception of gentile opinion. Insofar as they are indicative of the broad sweep of contemporary *halakhah,* we may say that Jewish law internally recognizes that in certain instances, largely ethical, it should be governed authoritatively by gentile reactions to Jewish behavior or their perceptions thereof, if the sages, by standards and methods remaining obscure, deem such fresh legal determinations warranted.

At this point, liberal (and postliberal) Jews demur. For these authorities the Emancipation has changed nothing, and gentile opinion is still thought of as if there were no Jewish political equality amid functioning democracies. By the very grant of full civic status to Jews and the continuing effort to overcome the powerful vestiges of fifteen hundred years of legally established anti-Semitism, gentiles and their ethical opinions are worthy of very much more consideration than they were in pre-Emancipation times. The appeal to Jews of the Kantian insistence on the universalization of ethics rests on this intellectual-social basis. Rabbinic Judaism understood that "a decent respect to the opinions of mankind" can mandate Torah law. The changed behavior of gentiles toward Jews, and the continuing realities of Jewish equality, demand greater concern with and respect for the ethical judgments of those who are not Jewish.

The liberal concern with ethics stems from this religious perception. The search by postliberal thinkers for a new understanding of Jewish ethics may involve rejecting the liberals' insistence that Jewish obligation be universalizable. However, the new particularism does not invalidate the essential truth that Jews today must sanctify God's name in significant part by attending to universal, that is to gentile as well as Jewish, moral opinion.

Recent Jewish suffering at gentile hands bolsters rather than refutes this affirmation about the significance of gentile understandings of ethics. True, the Holocaust ended Jewish liberals' messianic enthusiasm at gentile goodwill. And the continuing manifestations of anti-Semitism must keep Jews wary, not only of our enemies but of our own wishful thinking. Such bitterly won realism does not constitute reason to deny that the Emancipation radically changed relations between Jews and gentiles. It raised universalism from a largely neglected human theoretical notion to an ideal which continues to exert powerful political pressure on much of humankind. If particularistic standards of ethical behavior are to be restored to supremacy, it will be difficult to argue that the German people had no right to do what it did; or, of equal significance today, that all humankind should have stood up to protest the barbaric German violation of fundamental human rights. More, if democracy cannot be trusted, not only is most of world Jewry unsafe but so is the State of Israel, whose survival depends on the continued health of free nations.

Let me illustrate the divergence of these two Jewish views of attention to gentile ethical judgments by showing how they affect or might affect one aspect of contemporary Jewish ethical responsibility, namely, a Jew's religious obligation to pay taxes to a non-Jewish government.

Herschel Schachter, professor of Talmud at Yeshiva University, devotes half of a recent study to this issue.[31] One might assume that the well-known talmudic principle *dina demalkhuta dina*, "the law of the country is [Torah] law," applies to taxation, a civil matter. The question is not that simple, and Schachter clarifies the background and substance of a significant difference of opinion on a gentile government's right to levy taxes. He writes, "This dispute . . . is not just a hair-splitting technicality. Upon the resolution hinges the major question of whether a Jew living under a non-Jewish government has to consider the laws of the land as legitimately binding [in Jewish law] upon him or not . . . It is not necessary at this point to follow through to the end of the technical dispute; suffice it to record that practical halakhah generally accepts that the ruler does have certain legitimate powers over the individuals under his control, and that to some extent, as part of keeping the Torah, Jews must accept these restrictions or guidelines." (Note the qualification, "generally accepts," which allows a loophole that will grow at the next level of the discussion.)

Schachter then continues with a discussion of the sages' differing opinions as to the extent of the government's right to levy taxes.[32] Since the matter remains unresolved, he can only continue the discussion "Assuming that the government has the legal right to levy taxes, and that the citizens are obligated to pay these taxes, *like any other debt that any individual owes to someone else*"[33] (emphasis added, as it returns us to the rabbinic notion of the Jew's right not to pay back a gentile loan). He then goes on to ask, "What would be the status [in Jewish law] of one who does not pay his taxes; or does not pay the full amount that he should legally be paying?"[34]

The difficulties now deepen. "If however it is a non-Jewish government to which one owes taxes . . . The Talmud clearly forbids 'gezel akum' stealing from a nochri [sic], but 'hafka'as halva'oso' is allowed. That is to say that although theft from a nochri is forbidden, *not paying back* a debt which one owes to a nochri is not considered an act of gezel (theft). If this be the case, then the non-Jewish government has all the legal right to levy just and fair taxes; still, what is to forbid the individual from failure to pay his taxes on the grounds that 'hafka'as halva'oso' (non-payment of a debt) of a nochri is allowed?"[35]

Schachter apparently cannot bring himself to translate the term *nochri*, which means "gentile" (literally, "stranger"). Reading the paragraph without the euphemism of the Hebrew term changes its ethical impact, precisely the question of gentile opinion (and perhaps that of poorly informed Jews as well who assume that Torah law is generally ethical and not discriminatory).[36]

He further notes that with the proliferation of small businesses the issue is a real one, but the sages do not definitively settle it. He continues, "To the question of whether it is permissible to operate a store and not collect or not pay sales tax, we find a mixed response."[37] He then explicates different views on this topic. He indicates, in one sentence, that the Vilna Gaon and "other Poskim" (though only *Kesef Mishneh* is cited in his note) permit nonpayment. Since there is no further citation, it is he who adds that "if one might possibly create a situation of 'chilul hashem' by not paying taxes, there is no doubt that the 'heter' [permission] of 'hafka'as halva'ah' [not repaying a gentile loan] of akum [here not 'nochri' but the old legal term for gentile, 'idolator'] does not apply. In the *rare instance* where (a) there is no question of signing a false statement, and (b) there is no possibility of causing a chilul hashem, this group of poskim does not consider it forbidden."[38] He then continues with a discussion of the opinion of those who insist on payment and, tellingly, raises the further issue of patronizing such an establishment, recording a statement of Rabbi J. B. Soloveitchik that it is forbidden.

To the postliberal Jewish ethical sensibility appropriate reverence for the teaching of prior generations has here been carried too far. Almost every authority cited in Schachter's discussion lived under conditions of political inequality and discrimination, as well as in an economy of scarcity. Like the three contemporary respondents cited above, nothing in his discussion takes cognizance of the Emancipation and of the radically changed relations of Jews and gentiles.

Suppose, following the story of the Talmud of the Land of Israel, that gentiles, long told they cannot truly understand Judaism unless they understand *halakhah,* come to study it. And they learn that devout Jews in America are still guided by their sages to consider whether the American government does or does not have religious validity, does or does not have the right to tax them, and whether they, in turn, do or do not have an obligation to pay taxes, or, indeed, to pay back gentile loans (if, of course, in the exercise of *halakhic* creativity they can be reasonably certain of not being detected and avoid *hillul hashem*)? Should not some contemporary Rabban Gamliel, indeed the *halakhic* community as a whole, rise up and decree that the very discussion of these matters in these terms, much less acting upon them, constitutes a *hillul hashem?*

But why wait for such a discovery and thus allow a grave sin to occur? Why not admit that in our changed situation, we ought to broaden our appreciation of human ethical opinion and, giving it greater scope than it once had in the life of Torah, allow it to override such elements of civil discrimination and inequality as have come down to us? The task of mediating between *halakhah* and ethics remains a difficult one for postliberals. But the fresh will to be guided by classic Jewish teaching must not be allowed to wipe out the truths of universal ethics on which, in fact, we build our Jewish existence day by day.

Notes

1. I use the term "postliberal" to distinguish those non-Orthodox thinkers who consciously distance themselves from the earlier liberal equation of Jewish ethics with universal ethics (generally formulated in a neo-Kantian structure) and who thus gave inadequate weight to the *halakhah's* independent striving for the good. The postliberals seek to remedy this by treating the classic Jewish legal sources with at least equal dignity.

2. Lichtenstein's paper is found in Marvin Fox, *Modern Jewish Ethics* (Columbus: Ohio State University Press, 1975. My response, "The Authority of the Ethical Impulse in Halakhah," appeared in *Studies in Jewish Philosophy*, vol. 2, and in somewhat different form in Jonathan V. Plaut, ed., *Through the Sound of Many Voices* (Toronto: Lester and Orpen Dennys, 1982). For the view that ethical considerations per se play no part in halakhic decisions, see David Weiss Halivni, "Can a Religious Law be Immoral?" in *Perspectives on Jews and Judaism*, ed. Arthur Chiel (New York: Rabbinical Assembly, 1978).

3. See the admirable study by David Novak, *The Image of the Non-Jew in Judaism* (New York: Edward Mellen, 1983). I am not fully persuaded that the sources bear out the philosophical underpinnings that Novak finds in the origin and development of the category of Noahide law, but he has made a most impressive case for a considerable if implicit rationality in these laws.

4. This study of the *halakhic* sources on *hillul hashem* is based on the relevant articles in *Entziklopediyah Talmudit*, 17 vols. (Jerusalem: Talmudic Encyclopedia Institute, 1955–), henceforth ET, namely, *"goy"* (vol. 6), *"gezel hagoy"* (vol. 6), and, particularly, *"hillul hashem"* (vol. 15). My independent check of a number of the sources cited indicated that, other than what a historical-critical hermeneutic might add, the articles faithfully and intelligently represented the texts cited. For ease of reference, I shall therefore cite the rabbinic materials underlying my analyses by reference to the apposite encyclopedia column or footnote, all from the article *"hillul hashem"* unless otherwise specified.

5. ET, col. 347ff., the subsection on the "important person."

6. In keeping with the methodology of this study, I forebear from citing the many *agadic* passages which testify, with the usual hyperbole, to the seriousness with which the rabbis deplored the sin of *hillul hashem*. See the collection in ET, col. 356ff.

7. ET, col. 344.

8. Many sages are quite explicit about this and make such statements as, "lest the gentiles say, 'The Jews have no Torah,'" (n. 160), "or they might say, 'Why did God choose thieves and deceivers to be His portion'?" (n. 161), or it might lead them to cast aspersions on the Jewish religion (n. 163).

9. ET, col. 347.

10. ET, n. 91.

11. ET, col. 356; cf. *"goy,"* vol. 6, col. 310.

12. ET, col. 355. The only *teshuvah* of David Hoffmann dealing with *hillul hashem* involved this sort of case (*Melamed Lehoil*, pt. 1, *Orah Hayyim* 35). We shall encounter another one below in our consideration of contemporary *teshuvot*.

13. ET, col. 351.

14. ET, vol. 6, col. 487ff. The article has nine columns of text with 134 notes in the usual condensed style of ET.

15. There are several variations of this story with the Romans making somewhat different complaints in them, e.g., *Sifre Deuteronomy*, ed. Louis Finkelstein, p. 401. The issue of the robbery of gentiles occurs only in the Talmud of the Land of Israel. Corroborative material, however, may be found in the discussions cited in B.M. 111b.

16. The issue of the robbery of a gentile becoming known is raised repeatedly by the sources cited in the article on *gezel hagoy*.

17. ET, col. 353, nn. 174–75.
18. ET, col. 355, nn. 209–15.
19. ET, nn. 160–61.
20. ET, nn. 167–68.
21. ET, n. 169, but see the extended treatment in the article *"gezel hagoy,"* col. 493.
22. Ibid., nn. 97–98.
23. Ibid., nn. 102–3.
24. ET, *"hillul hashem,"* col. 353.
25. ET, n. 169, and see the long discussion in the article *"gezel hagoy,"* col. 494f., and see particularly n. 127 which is the case we are discussing.
26. ET, n. 170, and the discussion in the article *"gezel hagoy,"* nn. 108–11. The usual understanding of this is failure to pay one's debts. It may thus only be another way of putting the issue of *hafkaat halvaato,* but I have adduced it here for the sake of completeness.
27. ET, n. 169, and the discussion in the article *"goy,"* col. 359, nn. 153–57.
28. ET, nn. 216–17.
29. ET, article *"dina demalkhuta dina,"* vol. 7, col. 301.
30. ET, cols. 353ff.
31. I do not know what to make of the following statistical anomaly: though more *poskim* spoke of *hillul hashem* in relation to *goy* than to *akum* (six pages of printout to four), the bulk of the classic respondents used the former, less derogatory term while a much higher proportion of modern *poskim* (arbitrarily, those later than the Maharsham—Shalom Mordecai Shvadron, 1835–1911) used the latter term. In our sample, sixteen of the seventeen responsa were listed in the *akum teshuvot,* and the one indicated with the usage *goy* (though it did not appear in the cited sentence) could not be located due to a difficulty with the printout at that point (*Igrot Moshe,* possibly *Hoshen Mishpat,* vol. 3, no. 3).
32. "Dina De'malchusa Dina," *Journal of Halacha and Contemporary Society* 1, no. 1 (Spring 1981, Pesach 5741): 103ff.
33. Ibid., 107–11.
34. Ibid., 111.
35. Ibid.
36. Ibid., 112–13.
37. Ibid., 113.
38. Ibid., 113f.

Emil L. Fackenheim is University Professor and Professor of Philosophy Emeritus at the University of Toronto and Fellow of the Institute of Contemporary Jewry at the Hebrew University of Jerusalem. He was ordained a rabbi in 1939 in Germany. After serving a congregation for five years in Canada, he pursued an academic career for more than four decades. He has written several important works and is considered one of the most important Jewish thinkers living today. His focus on issues regarding the Shoah *is regarded as seminal. This focus is particularly noticeable in his last work,* To Mend the World. *His relationship with Herman Schaalman spans an entire lifetime. One can find a dedication in one of his books to his friendship with Herman Schaalman. Herman brought Fackenheim to Oconomowoc when the Covenantal theologians were brought together. Emil spoke several times at Emanuel Congregation. This is not only a scholarly and professional common vision, but a personal relationship that goes beyond description.*

Emil Fackenheim, himself a refugee from the *Shoah,* brings his philosophical insights to an issue of contemporary redemption: Ethiopian Jewry. He raises questions about liberal Judaism's vitality as a bearer of the covenant and its relationship with the modern state of Israel. The ingathering of *Beta Israel* is a remarkable example of a contemporary exodus. Liberal Judaism's open and critical mode of thinking allows for an acceptance of *Beta Israel's* identity without "Orthodox" preconditions. Fackenheim once again brings us a sense of the immediacy within the covenant's challenge to all Jews, especially to those of *Beta Israel* who have been brought to the land of their ancestors, modern Israel.

Two Types of Liberal Judaism: Reflections Occasioned by the Israeli Rescue of the Beta Israel

Emil L. Fackenheim

In 1960 I read a paper entitled "Two Types of Reform" at the annual convention of the Central Conference of American Rabbis. Twenty-five years later I find myself writing an essay with a similar title in honor of Herman Schaalman, one of the most distinguished and dedicated members of that organization, on the occasion of his retirement. And it is exactly fifty years ago that I first heard Herman, my oldest friend among the living, expound the opening sentences of the Bible to a group of his friends of whom I was one. After all these years, I have forgotten precisely what Herman said. What has remained unforgotten is the way in which he did his expounding. He made the text speak to us as if it were written *for* us, here and now. He was far removed, however, from the modernistic superiority that at once condescends to the text and reads into it what is not there. ("Isn't it marvelous how Genesis anticipates Einstein," or, according to taste, "how the prophets anticipate Jefferson and/or Marx," and the like.) Herman read the ancient text *reverently*, quite naturally assuming that much of it would be dead but *listening* to what, in the text, though ancient, *was alive*. Herman read the biblical text in the spirit of the best of Liberal Judaism.

I

My subject in 1960 was an encounter between Reform Judaism and Hasidism, an encounter well prepared by, if not yet underway in, the work of Martin Buber.

My subject now, in the year of the heroic rescue of the Ethiopian Jews by the State of Israel, is an encounter, as yet unprepared, between Liberal Judaism and the Beta Israel. ("Beta Israel" is the term to use, since "Falashas," strangers, was a derogatory label pinned on them by their enemies and persecutors, whereas "Beta Israel" is the term they apply to themselves.) As for my present preference of the word "Liberal," this is very largely, though by no means entirely, due to the fact that I have moved to Israel. I wish to include Conservative and even Orthodox Jews in my account, providing that the latter are broadminded enough to admit pluralism into Judaism.

Twenty-five years ago I spoke out against the kind of romanticism which might cause a modern Jew to overlook, or in extreme cases even accept, elements in Hasidism past and present such as lapses into superstition, a near-idolatrous submission to miracle-working rabbis, and in general a flight into an antimodernist obscurantism. Today I must make, at least in passing, mention of a possible romanticism that is caused by an improper wish to escape from the prospects of the twenty-first century. Even though rightly inspired by the marvelous steadfastness of the Beta Israel for no less than two millennia, such romantics would seek refuge, understandably but vainly, in a world long vanished before the twenty-first century could be imagined. Liberal Judaism must, for better or worse, be *in* the modern and postmodern world even though, being Judaism, it ought never to be entirely *of* it.

Moreover, it must be and remain of the modern and postmodern world at its best as well. And that democracy *is* the modern world at its best is more evident today than it was twenty-five years ago, when many of us were still naive enough to believe that the World War II victory over Nazism had made the world ripe for democracy. Today the democracies are few and embattled, and it behooves Liberal Judaism to be firmly on their side, by no means only because of the political exigencies of the day, but also because Liberal Judaism is liberal. That it was always wrong for Liberal Judaism to view Orthodox Judaism, condescendingly, as a dead relic from a medieval past has been proved, decisively, by the simple fact of a vital orthodoxy within the modern democracies. A vital orthodoxy, however, is one thing, a medieval-style orthodox fanaticism that would impose its will on dissenters is quite another; and nowhere is the difference as clear and painful as in the State of Israel when fanaticism is able to use the power of the state to its own ends. The battle for democracy, then, is incumbent on Liberal Judaism not only in its relations with the world at large, but also within the realm of Judaism itself.

In recent years Liberal Judaism has shown its own vitality nowhere more far-reachingly and profoundly than in the battle against male chauvinism. It is most far-reaching because, arguably, male chauvinism is as ancient in Judaism as Judaism itself. The battle is also most profound, and for this reason not to be won by a glib resort to doctrines and ideologies fashionable in our time. Only when the ancient texts are read with the reverence Herman Schaalman brought to them fifty years ago, can Liberal Judaism cope with the question of how, if at all, in terms other than those of the text itself, to address the God of Israel.

In the quest for an encounter with the Beta Israel, however, all this needs to be said merely in passing, for whereas here and there a modern Jew, in flight from modernity, may have become the follower of a Hasidic guru, it can safely be predicted that no such person will become part of the Beta Israel even if he tried. In this context, it is important to stress, not the virtues of the alliance of Liberal Judaism with modernity, but rather its vices. Liberal Judaism originated in the nineteenth-century age of progress, in which it was a virtually unchallenged dogma that the historically later is ipso facto the morally and religiously better. And this dogma led to the frequent confusion, in liberal ranks, Jewish as well as general, of the best with the most up-to-date. The nineteenth-century German rabbi S. R. Hirsch was right in at least one respect, his refusal to make modernity, or what called itself modernity, the standard of a viable Judaism; and Hirsch was the founder of neo-orthodoxy. This particular stance on Hirsch's part should long have been shared fully and without hesitation, by Liberal Judaism also, if only because the nineteenth-century dogma of necessary progress has long been smashed by twentieth-century catastrophes. Still there are those in our midst—one must suppose that assimilationism, overt or covert, is the cause—who continue to confuse the best with the latest. By that standard, or indeed even if modernity as such is the standard, an encounter between Liberal Judaism and the Beta Israel would be neither necessary nor possible. We would, of course, welcome them in our midst, for we are after all not racists. But we would view them as coming to us from the Stone Age.

II

From whatever age they have arrived, they are here. And their coming has been made possible and actual by the fact of a Jewish state, and by the further fact that it has remembered its sometimes forgotten but most essential vow; the ingathering of the exiles from the four corners of the earth. True, vigorous efforts to save the Beta Israel were made in the Diaspora also, especially when it became known that they were threatened with literal, physical extinction. (The threat still hangs over the thousands left behind.) However, no one can argue that such efforts could ever have gotten off the ground without a Jewish state; and the rescue by that state of the Beta Israel should suffice to make an end to such remnants of "classical reform" anti-Zionism as here and there still survive. As for Israel

35

itself, it is hard to find words to describe the joy and exhilaration that gripped the whole people when the Beta Israel arrived. That the Israeli condition is troubled these days need not be stated, for one reads about it, and the nature of the troubles, in the newspapers. But then the Beta Israel came, and all Israel was uplifted and reassured. "Now at last," the collective Jewish ego in Israel seemed to be saying to itself, "I know again why I am doing and suffering all this. And now I know I have faith that the enterprise will prevail." Already the Beta Israel have given to Israel more than Israel can give in return.

III

But it is not the Jewish state and its Zionist convictions alone that made their coming possible and actual. Far more basic and profound was something in the Beta Israel—a fidelity to the Land of Israel, to Jerusalem, to the Jewish Book that has no parallel anywhere in history, not even in Jewish history. The Beta Israel were cut off from the rest of the Jewish people for two millennia, so much so, for long periods of time, as to believe that they were the only Jews left in the world. Even so they remained faithful through centuries of humiliation, oppression, and murder. This is an age of little fidelity and less faith. If only the world understood, the Beta Israel would be *Time*'s Man of the Year. (Or would it be "Person" or "Persons"?) But then, when it comes to matters Jewish, the world rarely understands.

Do Jews themselves understand? Doubtless the fidelity of the Beta Israel is admired, and since their arrival some of the qualities that go with it—their honesty, their eagerness to learn—have already become legendary. But can secularist Israelis understand the grounds of their fidelity? Nor, from what has thus far transpired, does such an understanding come easily to Jewish orthodoxy in Israel. And within the general exhilaration the few voices of dissonance have come from the orthodox establishment. "They are Jews," this establishment seems to be saying, "but not quite 100% Jews, so that this or that ceremony is still needed to make up for the missing percentage." Much to its credit, the Beta Israel rejects this demand with dignity and indignation. From its own point of view, Orthodox Judaism can rightly object that the Beta Israel possesses only the "written" but not the "oral" Torah, this latter being, in the Orthodox view, revelation given to Moses on Mount Sinai verbally, and passed on from generation to generation until it, too, was finally committed to writing in Talmud, Midrash, and Shulchan Aruch. But the primary response that ought to follow from this fact is the awe-inspired query, addressed to the Beta Israel, how, if the "oral" Torah is indispensable, they managed to live in faith and faithfulness without it. Instead, for the time being at least, fanaticism seems by and large to have its way.

This is not to say that this fanaticism does not, on occasion, feel unsure of itself and in consequence lapse into apologetics. Thus, on one recent occasion, a representative of the Orthodox establishment referred to orthodoxy not as in possession of oral as well as written Torah, but as "normative Judaism." This, as is well known, is the term invented by Conservative Judaism in its effort to set limits to legitimate change within Judaism, and what is articulated by the term "normative" is of course not merely where to draw the line but also by what standards to draw it. Here the reappearance of the Beta Israel in the mainstream of Jewish history gives rise to the question whether age and fidelity might not be the best of all standards. If so, the Beta Israel might well be entitled to provide standards that set norms for all Judaism.

IV

It is in this situation that Liberal Judaism in Israel ought to come on the scene. Liberal Judaism has, in any case, a task in Israel that, for the most part, still lies ahead. From the beginning, there has been a split in the country between *Dati'im* ("religious"—Orthodox) and *Lo-Dati'im* ("non-religious"—everyone else, from the most vociferously secularist to Conservative Jews approaching Orthodoxy); and to the mind of any fair and well-informed judge there was no way of avoiding it. One might have hoped, however, for a gradual narrowing of the split, caused by ideals shared and defended. Instead there has been an unfortunate widening, without doubt largely caused by what is no mere "siege mentality" but an actual siege forced upon the country by neighbors whose hostility shows few signs of weakening. Liberal Judaism ought to try to become a mediating force, fighting for its rights vis-a-vis the *Dati'im* even as it demonstrates the genuineness of its Jewish credentials, while offering a Jewish message to the *Lo Dati'im* many of whom, one may be sure, have a deep longing for what to them could be a viable Judaism. In the modern West, Liberal Judaism has always had to fight the temptation to degenerate into mere assimilationism. In Israel this temptation is minimal; and Liberal Judaism has a task, not yet fully recognized, which could be vital for Israel as a whole and hence also for all Judaism everywhere.

In this context, there arises the possibility of an encounter between Liberal Judaism and the Beta Israel. Only a bigoted Liberal Judaism—a contradiction in terms but a possibility because of the widespread arrogant belief in the superiority of all things modern over all things ancient—will dismiss the Beta Israel as a remnant from the Stone Age that should hurry up and become modern. A genuinely Liberal Judaism—that is, one that is both genuinely Jewish and genuinely liberal—will inquire of the Beta Israel, with a sense of awe and in a spirit of genuine quest, how they managed to live so long, carry on so long, be faithful so long. Liberal Jews, in short, will be prepared to listen and learn as well as to speak and teach. And in such an encounter, if it will take place, they ought to consider themselves as acting on behalf of all Judaism, Orthodoxy included. For them the listening and learning is easier than for their Orthodox brethren; while by no means dismissing the oral Torah, they are unencumbered by the Orthodox belief that access to the written Torah is impossible without it.

VI

What will emerge from such an encounter, it is impossible to predict. One cannot even predict that an encounter of the sort we have envisaged can and will take place at all. What encourages the attempt is a fact known to us all and surpassing all others in significance: the ancient Beta Israel and the liberal of Liberal Judaism possess the same Book. This crucial fact takes me back to the incident of fifty years ago which I mentioned at the beginning. A group of young Jews in Berlin, all in search of a vital Judaism, sat in a circle, opened the Book, and Herman Schaalman expounded for us its first page. And the Book, stemming from then and there spoke to us here and now. Should the same not be said for the Beta Israel, for these many centuries? Could they have endured in fidelity without such a reading? It would be presumptuous for us not to try to find out.

Back in 1935, of course, Herman was not alone in his reading and his exposition. He had simply learned it before the rest of us. And the greatest teachers in our time were Martin Buber and Franz Rosenzweig. When in the twenties, Rosenzweig opened the Frankfurt *Lehrhaus,* he said in his opening address, "that those Jews for whom the new school was intended were all at the periphery of Judaism, for they were alienated both from the Book and from each other, but that in reading the Book together, ready to listen to what is alive in it, they would find their way back to the center." The return of the Beta Israel into Jewish history lends a new life to Rosenzweig's words. Our best hopes for a future Judaism are confirmed whenever Jews of different or even mutually antagonistic views make an effort to read together the Book that belongs to them all.

Joseph B. Glaser is the executive vice-president of the Central Conference of American Rabbis. He directs the operation and activities of more than 1,400 Reform, Liberal, and Progressive rabbis throughout the world. He has done postdoctoral work at the Hebrew University, as well as at Oxford. He is known as one of the most prominent voices on the national and international Jewish scene. His relationship with Herman Schaalman is extensive, as the latter served in national offices in the CCAR. During the two years of Herman's vice-presidency, and the following two years of Herman's presidency at the CCAR and beyond, Herman and Joseph Glaser continued their personal as well as their professional relationship.

Joseph R. Glaser had a unique position during the last decade. He has watched as the Central Conference of American Rabbis struggled internally with issues of mixed marriage, outreach, and patrilineal descent, while at the same time he attempted in good faith to be a part of *K'lal Yisrael*. His questions are not rhetorical; his message is an urgent one. The covenant has historically bound the people into at least a sense of unity, but today's demands for, and the realities of, a radical pluralism of Jewish goals and agendas challenge that historic possibility. Joseph Glaser has often worked behind the scenes to keep the unity intact. His essay raises important questions about the future of the covenant and the possibility of one Jewish people.

Will There Be One Jewish People?

Joseph B. Glaser

This is a subject that has been close to the heart of Herman Schaalman all of his life. I have never known it to be out of his consciousness for a moment. It is not by accident that he has been in the eye of the hurricane on matters pertaining to *Ishut* which have absorbed the Central Conference of American Rabbis during the past two decades. He was, wisely, appointed chairman of the CCAR Committee on Mixed Marriage and then some years later was appointed chairman of the Committee on Patrilineal Descent. During his term as president of the Conference, that issue came to a climax, and following his presidency, he was appointed chairman of the Committee on Rabbinic Standards, the mandate of which was to address the problem of ecumenical ceremonies in connection with marriage.

In carrying out these volatile mandates, he demonstrated his profound commitment to *K'lal Yisrael,* which was known to be mediated by his well-thought-out sense of Reform integrity and personal honor. It was because of this commitment that such great trust was placed in him.

I was privileged to observe at first hand Herman Schaalman's struggle with what appears to be the virtually inevitable deadlock of these two countervailing forces. It is at such an agonizing time that a person is truly tested. Whatever the outcome, and history has yet to judge, the honesty, the probing intellectual capacity, the loyalty to principle and tradition, and the warming goodwill of a unique man and an exemplary rabbinic spirit will have shone through as a lasting blessing.

41

Will there be one Jewish people?

This question is being asked increasingly and, in spite of my natural tendency to resist making predictions, I find myself saying, "Yes, of course. Why do you ask?" (A good question—we will deal with it later.)

Why am I so sure of the answer? I base it on my knowledge, both instinctual and historical, of the Jewish people. Hillel's famous dictum, *Im lo neviim hem, benai neviim hem* (If they [the Children of Israel] are not prophets, then they are the children of prophets), is what guides my instinct that *amcha* deeply wants one Jewish people and always will. As one woman put it to a panel of an Orthodox, a Conservative, and a Reform rabbi, addressing this subject recently in a Conservative synagogue, "You rabbis work it out!" And she spoke, quite properly, in impatient, even angry tones. The Orthodox rabbi, sitting next to me, muttered, "Interesting." We should remember that, all through Jewish history, with rare and then miraculous exception, the will of the people has been the paramount determining force.

Let us also remember the *Iggeret Temen,* Maimonides' letter to the Yemenites: "It is your duty, our brethren of Israel, who are scattered over the whole earth, to strengthen one another." Those Yemenites, like others in the Levant, having lived apart from their Ashkenazic fellow Jews for millennia, and from many other Sephardim as well, are now living in unity with them in Israel. What of the Soviet Jews who have migrated in recent years to Israel, who are mixed married, nonhalakhically divorced, uncircumcised, and converted, if at all, without *mikveh?* They are now living in "unity" with the rest of the Jews in Israel—and here.

A far more dramatic and compelling example of the insistence of the Jewish people on unity, on inclusion rather than exclusion, is the rescue and absorption of the Ethiopian Jews, not only in the fact of ecclesiastical hairsplitting, but also the racial possibility. The Ethiopian Jews, black, have lived in isolation for three thousand years, unable for all those three millennia to participate in the talmudic tradition or Jewish culture, yet are drawn lovingly into the unity of Jewish peoplehood by that *magnet* at the core of the Jewish people which answers that strange, almost foreign question being asked about whether or not there will be one Jewish people.

Yes, there will be one Jewish people, notwithstanding dire predictions to the contrary, which run the danger of becoming self-fulfilling prophecies. I wish the Irving Greenbergs and the Reuven Bulkas would tone down a bit. Their questions are useful, because we do have a problem, but we should not allow ourselves to be whipped into a hysteria which could produce either mindless, unprincipled action, on the one hand, or further polarization on the other. Too many expressions of such hysteria are being heard in the graceless, angry blasts of grandstanding rhetoricians on both sides, who embarrass, diminish, and further confuse us. Solutions can be found, but not in the glare of publicity, and they must be the result of true mediation and not the "answers" emanating from a third power base purporting to be the peacemaker.

In discussing the specifics of what currently divides us—at least Orthodox from Reform—it is important, indeed imperative, to bear in mind that both sides are sincere, are deeply devoted to their particular form of commitment, and, except for the lunatic fringe of each, regard each other with warmth, if not respect, and a yearning to bridge somehow the theological and *halakhic* (if such a term can be used in this context) gap. Neither wants to "read out" the other.

Conversion

While it is true that, theoretically, the Orthodox and some Conservatives have not accepted certain Reform converts, this was never a major issue on either side until it became tangled with the Law of Return of the State of Israel. I use the word "tangled" advisedly, as it raises the issue of church and state in America and elsewhere, the experience of which can illuminate the instant discussion. While we cannot presume to apply the constitutional safeguards of the United States to the uniquely Jewish State of Israel, it is instructive to remember that the Knesset of Israel is a secular body, legislating secularly with the votes of avowed atheists, Moslems, and anyone else who qualifies by virtue of citizenship and electoral support for membership in the Knesset. In the 1985 attempt to amend the Law of Return, most of the Arab members of Knesset voted against the amendment. Had that Arab vote been reversed, the amendment would have passed. *Non-Jews would have decided the question of who is a Jew.* What utter nonsense! It is an open secret that the Orthodox, including the *Agudah* in Israel, are well aware of this anomaly, and really don't want this divisive and mischievous issue coming up again and again, but they point the finger at the "gentleman from Brooklyn" and lament that when he forces the issue periodically, how can they not at least appear to be in favor of *al pi halakhah*, "according to the law"? With all of the noise and tumult, this is not a harbinger of "two Jewish peoples."

Mamzerut

A more serious problem arises from the Reform policy of not requiring a *get* (bill of divorce) before the performance of a religious marriage ceremony of a civilly divorced woman. This, according to *halakhah*, makes the issue of such a marriage *mamzerim* (illegitimate). They can only marry each other, not any other Jew. This, of course, brings into play the whole problem of *aguna,* the "chained" woman, who cannot remarry either because of a missing husband who cannot be proved dead or because of a spiteful and/or avaricious separated husband who refuses to give a *get.* Reform Judaism, mindful of the palpable injustice involved, and aware that the origin of the *get* arose out of the same need to which contemporary civil law of divorce is addressed, decided to extend the principle of *dina malchuta dina* (civil law takes precedence over rabbinic law) to the divorce question. Although we make no apologies for it, Reform rabbis are sensitive to the personal problems that can ensue and act accordingly in many cases. Golda Meir, while prime minister of Israel, was once asked if something could be done for the hapless *agunot.* She replied that when there were great rabbis, there were no *agunot,* as great rabbis were always able to find a way. She went on to lament, quite candidly, that there were no great rabbis today. A similar judgment can be made on the subject of *mamzerim.* I heard the astonishing story from a Dutch Liberal rabbi of a Dutch Orthodox rabbi who, when he returned to Holland at the end of World War II, as his very first act, went to the secret place where he had hidden his records of *mamzerim* and was "back in business." A "great" rabbi he wasn't. But the majority of rabbis during the European experience were more enlightened. When they saw a strange young man sitting in the back of the synagogue, they had a pretty good idea that he might be a *mamzer* from another town. They didn't ask any questions when they introduced him to an eligible young woman in their community. These were "great rabbis." They had *sechel* (understanding) and *rachmonus* (compassion) and did not allow themselves to be tied up in the inhumane knots of the *chumra* (restrictive measure). Such should also be the attitude in confronting the subjects of autopsy and women's rights and privileges.

Women Rabbis

As one who for decades has been in the forefront of the movement to ordain women rabbis, I must confess that I still understand the discomfiture experienced by the Orthodox and many Conservative Jews at this new phenomenon. Yet I also comprehend that it is a cultural, psychological hurdle for them, and not primarily a *halakhic* one. All of the arguments I have heard are secondary and/or derivative. In the argument over women military chaplains, for instance, it finally boiled down to: "How can you expect an Orthodox boy, whose gut reaction would be horror, to accept the rabbinic services of a woman, when, because of the military situation, he has no choice? It isn't fair. In civilian life, he just wouldn't belong to that *schule*." In sum, the woman rabbi is a nonissue, except within the movements of Judaism themselves, and should not be produced as "further evidence" that we are moving in the direction of an inevitable split. It is at this point that I must introduce the wistful comment of an Orthodox rabbi, who said of all of this: "I wish we could go back to the old days when we ignored each other. We got along so much better, and were able to get together on the really important things." Amen.

Theology and Liturgy

Interestingly, not much is said about these subjects, although they simmer, and surface here and there. One would almost welcome good, vigorous debate of this nature, rather than haggling over the more exasperating and non-intellectually oriented, ethnic matters of *ishut*. A perhaps rather extreme example of the diffidence that exists is found in an experience I had in publishing our new High Holyday prayerbook, *Gates of Repentance*. I first approached an Israeli printer who agreed to set the type, but the next day he telephoned me that he couldn't sleep all night and, in the morning, asked the chief rabbi if it was all right to take the job. He was told in no uncertain terms that it would be a sin to set this text. The printer, with deep regret, backed out of his agreement. Fearful that we could be similarly sabotaged anywhere along the line if I continued my quest for an Israeli-based publication, I retreated to the shores of America, where I was led to a Hassidic printing house, with firm assurances from the middleman who so directed me that there would be no problem. Nonetheless, I sat down for a face-to-face confrontation with the Hassid in charge and told him I didn't want any surprises. No surreptitious changes of text; no sudden pangs of conscience and visits to the Rebbe in the middle of the project. He looked deep into my eyes and, with a hint of a smile, said: "Rabbi Glaser, if you were Rabbi Kelman (Rabbi Wolfe Kelman is executive vice president of the Rabbinical Assembly) coming to me with this text, I might have a problem. But the *epikursis* of the Reform is so well known, I don't have any trouble with it." And he was as good as his word. A gentleman and a scholar! Yet more seriously, behind what really amounts to toleration in these matters among our people lies the knowledge that our liturgy has never been fixed and that our theology, if ever taken very seriously as a subject, has never acquired dogmatic status, but for the belief in One God, and on that we all agree. As far as prayer books are concerned, the general feeling has been. So if you don't like it, don't use it.

Patrilineal Descent

For some reason, which I have never quite been able to fathom, the passage of the resolution by the Central Conference of American Rabbis on patrilineal descent triggered an explosion which has led directly to the question of Jewish unity being raised in alarm. Logically, it should be far less of an issue than *mamzerut*, about which nothing can be done since it is an irreparable disability, whereas a "flawed-incomplete" Jew can easily be converted *al pi halakha*. Maybe it was the proverbial straw that broke the camel's back; maybe it was all the attendant publicity; maybe it was the feeling that we were "rubbing their faces in it" when everyone knew that most Reform congregations had been accepting de facto patrilineal Jews all along, and few were making an issue of it. Whatever it was, it seemed to mobilize all the anxieties, as, frankly, I feared. In expressing my own reservations about taking such an action, I had counseled my colleagues that we might, indeed, be striking a blow against Jewish unity, which I consider to be of paramount importance. I pointed out that we were doing it anyway. Why raise a red flag? To this I received the retort that the Orthodox and some Conservatives don't recognize Reform conversions anyway, and therefore, however we decide to confer Jewish status was unacceptable to them. In 1983, following the passage of the resolution, when I was upbraided by an Orthodox colleague, I conveyed this to him. He had no answer. I had other reservations about patrilineal descent, too, but I did not oppose it because I do believe that for our time it is right. I am still not sure we needed a resolution, and there are many problems ahead, not only for Jewish unity, but for the Reform movement and for the individuals affected, but in terms of the substance of the issue, *halakhically,* sociologically, and psychologically, patrilineal descent makes sense and, I hope, will be good for the Jewish people.

The Real Issues

Now let us get to the real issues, the mishandling of which could, indeed, threaten Jewish unity. These are: *political control, rabbinic authority,* and *halakhic mode*. They are all of a piece. Harold Schulweis put it well in *Sh'ma*: (15/296)

> The issues surrounding the character of Conservative Judaism are not simply intramural disputes. It is not the purported viability of the Conservative movement which is being debated. What is at stake is the relationship among the Jewish religious movements and the threat of sectarianization. Are we in effect headed towards a *de facto* delegitimiz-

ing of Jewish schools of thought we disagree with? Are we turning each other into Karaite sects? . . . Acceptance amd recognition of others does not mean an end to the effort to persuade the other, but it means an end to that form of pan-halachic arrogance which claims that there is one mode of *halakhah* or but one way to arrive at a religiously authentic decision.

Schulweis also calls on the Jewish laity to pressure its rabbinic leadership

to meet together, without the distracting lights of publicity, so as to return Jewish life to the arena of public trust. The laity cannot stand idly by. The character of its life is at stake. *Its children's lives are being affected.* (Emphasis added)

Schulweis further states:

Years ago Abraham Joshua Heschel warned of "pan-halakhism," that orientation which reduces all Jewish living and thinking to the citation of halakhic precedent. Pan-halakhism is intolerant of arguments drawn from the *aggadah,* Jewish ethics and philosophy. Anxious for the *p'sak* (decision) it wields a threatening sword of "halakhah" over every issue. Pan-halakhism is impatient with the notion of modes of *halakhah,* with arguments which question the validity of a cited precedent or the moral value of an inherited law or the ethical and social consequences of a position. Such arguments are dismissed as merely "modern, non-halakhic, ethical, relativistic, extra-halakhic." That many of the arguments are weighted with economic, political and psychological considerations is ignored.

The utilization of this mind set, so deplored by Rabbi Schulweis, to exert political control in Israel, as well as in other countries where there is the concept of the established "church," has led to enormous frustration and bitterness on the part of those victimized by it, and is largely responsible for the "revolt" which one might call such actions as the passage of the patrilineal resolution by the CCAR.

In essence, the perennial battle over the Law of Return is not so much a question of who is a Jew as it is: Who is a rabbi? It is basically a question of rabbinic authority, and when it comes down to that, one must remember the angry woman in the conservative synagogue who told the rabbis to "work it out." Yet, when rabbinic authority is challenged, the authenticity of a whole movement is likewise challenged, and thus we have the makings of *Kulturkampf.* It wasn't always thus in Jewish life. Hillel and Shammai lived side by side, and Shammai even allowed their children to marry those of Hillel in spite of the dispute over *halitza* (Leverite marriage). Joseph Caro's *Shulchan Aruch* needed *Moses Isserles' Maph.* Clearly, the importance of these issues which divide our movements is arguable. Some are crucial to one or the other side, and some are not. But

Jewish history is replete with such controversies, and the general principle of unity has almost always, somehow, mediated the differences. To depart from this principle, *or even to set up such a possibility by proclaiming its inevitability, and thus virtually justifying it,* is to bring down on one's head an awesome, historic guilt.

All of these issues, and the attendant "fall-out," must be considered against the monumental backdrop of Jewish unity and the compelling reasons for it: *Israel,* that embattled, endangered state, invested with our love and resources, seen at the center of our very future, wherever we Jews may reside, depends upon that quintessential bulwark of her defense, a united American Jewish community; *our own security,* made insecure by a new, virulent breed of anti-Semite loose ranging from the Posse Comitatus and the Liberty Lobby and among others stirring suspicion about the Jews among the desperate farmers of the Midwest, to Louis Farrakhan filling Madison Square Garden and other auditoriums around the country with tens of thousands cheering at his vile, obscene hatred of Jews and Judaism; and finally, whatever became of *ahavat Yisrael, the love of one Jew for another*? Could there be a more basic tradition in Jewish life? *K'lal Yisrael* (the whole of the peoplehood of Israel) implies inclusion, not exclusion; it calls for the strengthening of the bond between Jews of all stripes and claims. The sound of the shofar calls Jews *together,* and it is therefore a wanton perversion for anyone to use the imagery of the shofar in advising Jews to stay away from Reform and Conservative synagogues on the High Holydays. *Amcha,* the Jewish people, understand all this and resonate to it. They will stick together; they will figure out a way, even if it means rejecting their leaders.

Let us not be so tense, so desperate. It is not helpful to have advertisements in the Jewish press likening this problem to the loss of the ten tribes. It is not an accurate historical parallel, to begin with, and it tends to border on a hysteria we do not need as we try to pick our way objectively through this. At this point, I am not sure it is possible any more, but I prefer the slightly whimsical, and wistful, formulation of the Orthodox leader who said: "I wish we could go back to the old days when we ignored each other." In disunity, perhaps, there is unity.

Let me make it clear that I share Irving Greenberg's concern and, indeed, respect it. I only differ with him in regard to the tone and the framing of the issue, and in one other important respect: as much as he calls for felicitous, open dialogue, it always seems that the onus is on the Reform and the Conservative ultimately to do the yielding. If such a reading is correct, all such efforts will lead into a blind alley. I wish, instead, that Rabbi Greenberg would address his admirable capacity for agonizing over the future of the Jewish people, and his truly brilliant intellect, to solving Orthodoxy's problems of *aguna* and *mamzer* and pan-halakhism and narrow rigidity, and thus help Orthodoxy be with the times, as rabbis and Jews ought to be, and really, until only relatively recently, always have been. I have utilized Jewish references, but would end by quoting from Thomas Jefferson, who always struck me as a *Yiddische kop* of the first order, who said in 1816:

> Some men look at constitutions with sanctimonious reverence, and deem them like the ark of the covenant, too sacred to be touched. They ascribe to the men of the preceding age a wisdom more than human, and suppose what they did to be beyond amendment. I knew that age well; I belonged to it and labored with it. It deserved well of its country. . . . Laws and institutions must go hand in hand with the progress of the human mind. As that becomes more developed, more enlightened, as new discoveries are made, new truths disclosed, and manners and opinions change with the change of circumstances, institutions must advance also, and keep pace with the times.[1]

Notes

1. Paul L. Ford, ed. *Writings of Thomas Jefferson,* 2:11–12.

Alfred Gottschalk is the president of the Hebrew Union College, Jewish Institute of Religion, and professor of Bible and Jewish Thought. He has a Ph.D. from the University of Southern California, has written numerous scholarly essays, books, and translations, and participates in several scholarly anthologies. He lectures widely and has been a cutting edge of Jewish academics and the expanding field of interfaith higher education. Rabbi Gottschalk's relationship with Herman Schaalman spans nearly two decades, as Herman has become more involved in the national scene and his relationship with the College-Institute has increased, as he has served on the Board of Governors of HUC-JIR. Alfred Gottschalk and Herman Schaalman, both refugees from Germany, have a common prophetic vision of the covenant.

Alfred Gottschalk raises up the great prophetic ideals for a contemporary society in which these prophetic ideals are the goals and goads. Judaism and Christianity have always drawn upon the prophetic ideals as *the* ethical standards of their respective faith communities, whereas, in our all too often crass, narcissistic, and competitive society, we seldom find the prophetic ideals of which Alfred Gottschalk writes. If the covenant was sustained by the prophetic challenge to a morally corrupt society of the past, then surely Alfred Gottschalk's contemporary essay raises the question of a covenantal demand that challenges our own moral laxness.

Prophetic Thinking in the Nonprophetic Society

Alfred Gottschalk

Today in the world of theology there is a preeminent concern with the updating and modernization of religious life. The motivation which animates this concern is often very difficult to pinpoint and varies within each religious tradition. If one may generalize, at least with regard to the positive aspects of this motivation, there surges to the forefront the overwhelming need to highlight the relevance of the ancient and time-honored truths of the Judeo-Christian heritage. We feel we have something eternal and positive in our religious faiths which responds to a crisis-stricken world, and that we search our respective religious traditions to find that hidden spark that will reclaim adherents to our beliefs. Revolutions within religious thought, reformations of its beliefs and practices, "updating" and adjustment to the times, are not new to the thoughtful student of the history of religion. There is therefore nothing unique in the dynamics of religious reform, even though the particular phases of its development, and the changes that it brings about, often leave us awestruck by their seeming novelty.

For example, Josiah's great religious reform of 621 B.C.E. undoubtedly left his contemporaries breathless. This religious reform stimulated the monumental book of Deuteronomy, with its emphasis on the binding nature of the moral covenantal requirements, all of which had been espoused two centuries earlier by the Hebrew prophets. The religious reform which Josiah effected brought to the apex the synthesis of the prophetic movement, and this changed the matrix of Jewish communal religious life. The genius of any great reformation of thought

51

or belief lies in its contention that it is really not a reformation at all. Josiah, if Deuteronomy is an index to his thoughts, claimed to teach nothing more than the basic tenets of the ancient covenant entered into by the people of Israel at Sinai. Amos, a century or so earlier, surveying the religious cults of his day, asked rhetorically, "Did ye bring unto Me sacrifices and offerings in the wilderness forty years, O house of Israel?" (Am. 5:25). Did God require the noise of song, or the solemn assembly, the burnt offerings and the meal offerings, the sin offerings and the many variations of tithes, as manifestations of faith? Certainly not! Speaking for God, the prophet replies in God's name, "I hate, I despise your feasts, And I will take no delight in your solemn assemblies. Yea, though ye offer me burnt-offerings and your meal-offerings, I will not accept them, Neither will I regard the peace-offerings of your fat beasts. Take thou away from Me the noise of thy songs; And let Me not hear the melody of thy psalteries. But let justice well up as waters, And righteousness as a mighty stream." (Am. 5:21–24). With the sounding of that note a revolution in religious life of monumental importance was initiated, the impact of which has reverberated throughout the generations. Yet Amos did not claim to be innovating. He was only reiterating the basic truth of the Sinaitic tradition as he understood that tradition.

Other ruptures with long-standing and revered religious traditions proceeded with similar claims. The Protestant Reformation, which was espoused by many great and diverse voices, claimed to be a return to the true meaning of the Scriptures. If one can draw a tentative general conclusion about the Second Vatican Council, especially *Nostra Aetate* (October 1965), its "Guidelines and Notes," its direction, it would have to be charted along similar lines of thoughts of Hans Küng: "With Pius XII's encyclical *Mystici Corporis* (1943), [and] . . . During the twenty years since, Catholic theology has concentrated more and more on the Church as the 'people of God,' the 'community of believers,' and has thus begun to think out afresh, for theology and for life, starting with the New Testament, this most important and most ancient concept of the Church . . . "[1]

Whether the start in the reformation of our religious traditions originates in the covenant at Sinai, or more generally in Scriptures—both Hebrew and New Testament—the essential quality remains the same. It is an attempt to get to the demythologized *kerygma,* the essence of revelation severed from the barnacled traditions and ritual acts that have obscured the inner meaning of that revelation. This tendency or motivation which is the positive aspect in any meaningful reform I should like to call the capacity for "prophetic thinking." In Jeremiah's words, it corresponds to the need "to root out and to pull down, And to destroy and to overthrow; To build, and to plant" (Jer. 1:10).

The fact that from time to time the capacity for prophetic thought and action manifests itself is the greatest index of the fundamental richness and vitality of the Judeo-Christian tradition. Jews and Christians often retreat from its demanding truth and fall into nonprophetic action and thought. This unfortunate entity constitutes the greatest challenge to both of our religious missions.

During periods of reformation when there is a restructuring of the means and forms which bring us into closer and more immediate confrontation with God's commandments, another set of motivations, negative in character, manifest themselves. These motivations, unlike the positive ones, prevent us from effecting a true and complete reformation and frustrate our ultimate goals. Born of the desire to maintain the nonprophetic society, these negative motivations abort the reformation by stopgap and superficial measures. These so-called reforms conspire to keep us from hearing the commands for social justice which are the hallmark of prophetic teaching. Often these are seen when we concentrate on ritual, with questions like: Shall this prayer be said in Hebrew, Latin, English, or German? Shall we shorten the service by abbreviating the liturgy? Shall services start at ten A.M. or ten-thirty because of the additional half-hour of discomfort it may give to the parishioner? Shall the preacher deliver a sermon, or is a sermonette more appropriate?

There are some religious-minded people who need to be in communion with God, while there are others who need to remain estranged from God, to eclipse Him from their lives. Recently, we have discerned clearly the emergence of both groups of religious-minded people, one group enamored of prophetic thinking and the other of thinking profit. The latter group wants religious reforms to be accommodated to its comfort while the former seeks to create a measure of discomfort. One group is sick of conscience, the other sick with conscience. Estrangement from God seems to require only some anemic form of religion in which lip service replaces the service of the heart. Characteristically, such a religion becomes a palliative, an opiate, and a substitute for the demands that are made upon us by the prophet, "To do justly, love mercy and walk humbly before God" (Mic. 6:8).

I

It was Thomas Carlyle who more than a century ago proclaimed in his *Heroes and Hero-Worship* that "Universal History, the history of what man has accomplished in this world, is at bottom the history of great men who have worked here." In agreeing with Carlyle we give emphasis to that orientation of history which gives just due to those heroes of culture, those unusual and singular personages who found strength in times of turmoil to bring light into a world beset with darkness and truth to the dark and obscure corners where ignorance and hatred held sway. The hero-image of Judaism, the prototype of the religious culture bearer, is the *prophet*. Around this image Judaism built its vast ethical and religious system. So deeply did the prophet leave his impress upon Jewish consciousness, that Moses was depicted as chief of the prophets; that the Messiah according to rabbinic tradition is understood as a prophet (San. 93b). The medieval Jewish commentator Saadia described the messianic age as one in which "prophecy will reappear in the midst of our people so that even our sons and slaves will prophesy" (*Emunot V-deo't* 8:6). We can learn more about prophetic thinking by looking closely at prophets and observing their mission as the prophets meshed with the power structure of their day and the evils that beset their society.

Let us define who is a prophet. The word "prophet" is a translation of the Hebrew, *Navi*; a word whose meaning is still not firmly fixed. *Navi* may mean "one who is called," "one who proclaims," or "one who shouts." The English connotation of "prophet," derived from the Greek, furthers the impression that the prophet is a teller of fortunes and futures. This is part of the prophetic personality, but more than being a foreteller or seer, the authentic prophet is a forth-teller, that is, a commentator on what *is* happening, a *Roeh*, a seer. The prophets themselves had criteria for true and false prophecy, and the fortune-telling aspect was a relatively minor concern in determining who was "true" and who was "false." What was crucial in this determination was whether the prophet told the truth or not; whether he abdicated his moral obligation or not.

Micah gives us an apt example of a false prophet. "Thus saith the Lord concerning the prophets that make my people to err; That cry: 'Peace,' when their teeth have anything to bite; And who so putteth not into their mouths, They even prepare war against him" (Mic. 3:5). The prophetic group was a complex one. There were prophets who were ecstatics, who were priests, and who claimed they were not prophets at all. Saul, the first king of Israel, naked and in an ecstatic state prophesied before Samuel (1 Sam. 19:24). Jeremiah and Ezekiel, among others, were priests as well as prophets. Amos denied the title, claiming that he was neither a prophet nor a prophet's son (Am. 7:14). The institution of *Neviut*, prophecy, underwent change, which is clear from the literature itself. Jeremiah was the first among the literary prophets to willfully designate himself as a *Navi* (Jer. 1:5). By his time, those whom we now call literary prophets hardly ever used the ecstatic state per se for the purposes of divination. No longer did true prophets travel in bands, or accept hire for their forth-telling. What really came to distinguish them from the ordinary seers was not their vocation, or the way in which they said God spoke to them, but the very nature of their message, *Devar Adonai* (the word of the Lord), which they claimed to speak.

This is also true of some of the preliterary prophets, men of whom we know by virtue of what is said *about* them in Scriptures. Their words ring true to us in what they attempted to teach as the clear demands of conscience. Samuel, who anoints Saul king, also breaks him as king when Saul arrogates to himself the right to violate the requirements of the prophetic word (1 Sam. 13:13–14). Nathan confronts King David when the latter has the loyal soldier Uriah exposed to sure death so that he might take Bath-Sheba (2 Sam. 11–12). The accusation of guilt with Nathan's words "Thou art the man" (2 Sam. 12:7) has reverberated throughout the history of human conscience. David confessed his wrong, and Nathan left the court unharmed. This early narrative of the book of Second Samuel indicated that the king was not above the law. An Israelite king was bound by a firmly established code, already deeply ingrained in the conscience of the people of Israel by the time of the monarchy. There was a tradition of egalitarianism, to which all who were descendants or were witnesses to the bondage and burden of Egypt, and the Exodus and the wilderness wandering, were heir. The formal consolidation of the state and an established priesthood, the ecclesiastical shield of that state, often obscured these early traditions. Kings such as Solomon, who opened the commonwealth to foreign influences, often tended to forget these traditions.

This was particularly true with King Ahab, who wantonly attempted to repudiate the ancient tradition that a man could not be severed from his patrimony against his will. The prophet Elijah confronted the king with the charge of illegal appropriation and was persecuted for his efforts. Elijah appeared on the horizon of history as a reminder that God's law had been broken and a human being, namely Naboth, unjustly treated. Samuel, Nathan, and Elijah were remembered by the chroniclers of the history of their period because of their commitment to *Torat Moshe,* the "law of Moses."

There were early traditions among the Hebrews of what we today call *basic human rights.* These rights when violated lead to revolutions and reformations of thought and institutions. The racial revolution which we are still witnessing, and I use the word "witnessing" decidedly in its theological sense, is but one further example of this process. The Reverend Dr. Martin Luther King, among others, chose to wage this revolution along prophetic lines of thought. Quotations from Amos, Isaiah, Micah, and Jeremiah relating to the early formulation of these very ideas are common parlance today. The words seem to live again as they once did in the streets of Jerusalem and on the hilltops of Galilee, on the heights of Mt. Carmel, and the barren beaten wadis of the deserts of ancient Israel. The courage to defy wrong, to pluck it up and tear it down, is prophetic courage, but that is not enough. One must also plant anew and prepare the way for greater society. Prophetic thinking in our nonprophetic society makes us aware of these wrongs and should propel us into the forefront of the battle for human rights.

The prophet's vision means that he looks at the world with a concern for eternity. It is not just the *glaring* social wrongs which occupy his thought, but the *entire spectrum of human conduct.* He is concerned with the totality of the quality of life; each and every aspect of it is important to him. In this context of prophetic concern, let us attempt to "listen" to the words of Amos as he trudges the rock-strewn roads from Judah to Israel to deliver his message. As we "listen" we must ask, What was wrong in this land that God could not bear? From outward appearances the reigns of King Uzziah of Judah and Jeroboam the son of Joash were prosperous and secure. The markets were at their all-time highs. There was wealth and plenty in the land, and the people were pious. They brought more than the required sacrifices and said all of the proper liturgy and thronged to the altars of worship. The foreign policies of these kings had pushed their kingdoms into some preeminence and had led them to restore their historic boundaries. Outwardly nothing seemed amiss.

Amos began to pry the lid of his society open. He pointed first to the transgressions of Israel's neighbors and with sure and ruthlessly logical arguments showed that they were guilty of acts of genocide. Damascus had "threshed Gilead with sledges of iron." Tyre had sold all their captives to Edom. Moab had burned the king of Edom until his bones turned into lime. These were clearly acts reprehensible to the human conscience. Judah's sin was that it rejected God's law and Israel's; in the midst of great plenty, it was rife with social injustice. The rich exploited the poor; virtuous people were demoralized; the poor were oppressed; the needy walked the streets hungry while the wealthy classes, removed from it all in their vacation spas, thrived. With power and the courts on their side, the rich took all they could from an exploitative economic and political system. The vulnerable elements of society—the fatherless, the widows, and the orphans—were unprotected and manipulated. On the surface all seemed well, but to the eyes of the prophet the rotten core of his society was evident.

It is characteristic of "prophetic thinking" to be radical. To this end, prophetic thinking is given to extremism. The prophet is an absolutist in truth telling, and his own life epitomizes truth in action. He stands for the ideal society based upon absolute righteousness in which ideals are uncompromised. Dire consequences are usually attendant to this kind of expression and can be amply demonstrated from history. Amos was exiled, Jeremiah imprisoned, Jesus crucified, Bruno burned at the stake, and Dr. Martin Luther King, Jr., assassinated. Yet such consequences of prophetic action are irrelevant to the prophet. It is not that he does not care what happens to him. He does! But he cannot control his impulse for truth telling. It is, as Jeremiah says, "a fire pent up in the bones." He must speak. The prophet from his humanness often laments that his life is abnormal. He gives up home, wife, children, and position to carry out his mission. He is possessed of an irresistible drive to right wrong, undo the yoke of the bound, "let the oppressed go free." He sees himself as an instrument of God's will and as a mouthpiece of God's word. This is a somewhat frightening sort of man. The prophet and his thinking make us uncomfortable, and in truth we try to avoid them both. Prophetic thinking is based upon ancient truth, and yet is revolutionary in the way that it must be applied in every age to the nonprophetic society. The prophets in their wisdom, aware of human frailties, signaled the millennium *Ba-aharit ha'yamim,* "at the end of days." They realized that as long as human society exists, their programs and their ideals will always need to be rediscovered. We hope that at each threshold of the advancement of human civilization more of the prophetic program is fulfilled and the millennium brought that much closer. But the troughs and the regressions of human civilization are always there to renew the call for prophetic thinking and prophetic effort.

We need to be reminded of some of the indispensable qualities in prophetic thinking. All of the prophets believed that they were agents of a living God who made requirements of man. They required no further proof of God's existence and Providence than their experience of His closeness. This experience is lacking by and large in the life of modern man. There is, in Martin Buber's words, "an eclipsed God" who confronts us. We treat God as an object in the same way we treat people as objects: an "it" to be manipulated and not a "thou," a subject, to be confronted. There was a time when we used things and loved people. Now we use people and love things. The prophets confronted, held dialogues, and disputed with God. Yet with it all they fully understood what was required of them. When people are eclipsed from God, no relationship of positive significance is possible with the deity or the requirement of prophetic action.

The question must by now be forming in our minds: Can we become prophets? I think not, for prophets are chosen; they can will to be nothing other. We can, however, engage in "prophetic thinking." This will not be an idle pious pastime but a vigorous surge to action and to deed. The Jew calls this *mitzvah* and the Christian "works." We saw more prophetic thinking in the revitalization of the Judeo-Christian heritage through united interfaith and interracial participation in the recent struggle for human rights, than in all of the theological papers on the subject laid end to end. If Amos could have been here today, he would not have felt as lonely as I am sure he felt at Beth El. There are other issues on which prophetic thinking remains to be applied. There is still the problem of war and peace, of physical and spiritual genocide, of nuclear disarmament. Most of our world is still poverty stricken, and there are too many hungry children. There are still those who are ground under the heel of oppression, exploited and hopeless, who look to us for some measure of deliverance. The revival of the social gospel and of the prophetic mission represents the greatest opportunity for a meaningful reformation of contemporary life. And our own age is still reflected in the plea of the prophet Isaiah (1:18–20):

> Come now, let us reason together, Saith the Lord;
> Though your sins be as scarlet, They shall be as white as snow;
> Though they be red like crimson, They shall be as wool.
> If ye be willing and obedient, Ye shall eat the good of the land;
> But if ye refuse and rebel, Ye shall be devoured with the sword;
> For the mouth of the Lord hath spoken.

Blu and Irving Greenberg are dear friends and great admirers of Herman Schaalman. Blu is the author of On Women in Judaism *and a scholar in Jewish studies who has written and lectured extensively on feminism and Judaism, as well as on the Jewish family and the Jewish community. Irving "Yitz" Greenberg is the president of CLAL—The National Jewish Center for Learning and Leadership. He was formerly director of the President's Commission on the Holocaust, and chairman of the Department of Jewish Studies at City College of the City University of New York. He is one of the first major theologians of the* Shoah *to articulate the importance of theology as a subject for an intra-Jewish dialogue. Yitz was among the Orthodox covenantal theologians who joined Herman and other Reform and Conservative theologians in summer sessions in the sixties. He has worked tirelessly with Herman, both from within his congregation and nationally, to broaden the common vision of Reform and Orthodox leaders.*

Blu and Irving Greenberg raised the central issues of the covenant, the land, the people, and God. Both of these critical thinkers have forced the tradition to respond to the pressing issues of contemporary Jewish identity. Their analysis reflects the Greenbergs' deep commitment to a covenant rooted in Jewish tradition, but always dynamic in its awareness of a people acting in history. This essay is an important addition to the covenantal school of theology, which continues to view Jewish thought in a dialectical tension. For Blu and Yitz Greenberg, the eternal triangle of God, Torah, and Israel when lived through a life of covenant is always encouraging the most creative Jewish response.

Land, People, and Faith: A Dialectical Theology

Blu Greenberg and Irving Greenberg

I. The Land Is Central in a Natural Existence Rooted in God

In the beginning God created the people and the faith. And the land was included from that very beginning in the covenantal relationship—as a gift of the Lord, as symbol and guarantor of the covenant, as fruit of God's actions in history.

One of the earliest liturgies of the Israelites, a primal confession of faith which has been called "the heart of the Pentateuch"[1] is the following:

> A wandering Aramean was my father: and he went down into Egypt and sojourned there, few in number: and there he became a nation, great, mighty and populous. And the Egyptians treated us harshly, and afflicted us, and laid upon us hard bondage. Then we cried to the Lord the God of our fathers, and the Lord heard our voice, and saw our affliction, our toil, and our oppression: and the Lord brought us out of Egypt with a mighty hand and an outstretched arm, with great terror, with signs and wonders: and He brought us into this place and gave us this land, a land flowing with milk and honey. And behold, now I bring the first of the fruit of the ground, which thou, O Lord, hast given me. (Deut. 26:5–10)

It is neither accident of sacred history nor primitive nationalist need that makes the land so central. From the beginning, the centrality of the land flows from the very structure of existence as conceived and articulated in Hebrew Scriptures.

The biblical claim is that human existence, natural existence, is rooted in God. The flow of life and direction of history orient toward the Lord. All of human existence takes place on two levels, that of daily interhuman relations and that of orientation to God which sustains, guides, and redeems the other. In moments of revelation, call, or redemption, humans learn this truth. If they respond properly, this revelation guides all that they do. A person who lives a life motivated only by power, wealth, status—all the calculated considerations of "secular" existence—ultimately ends up practicing idolatry, that is, absolutizing that which is only partial. Yet the secular life, properly lived, is the locus of encounter with God and movement toward redemption. Secular life is the basic activity and way of humans. Taking life seriously, living it responsively, without giving absolute allegiance to its mundane dimensions is the biblical prescription for human life.

Such life, however, is lived not merely as an individual but as part of a larger unit—a family, a people, humankind.

II. The Covenantal Relationship Binds God, People, Land

A central biblical affirmation is that knowledge of God and of the true nature of existence will be a blessing for the nations. Therefore, God called his covenantal people into existence to serve as paradigm and witness to the true nature and destiny of human life, to human value, to relationship to God, to ultimate redemption. This calling, this responsibility could only be lived out in history, in the human realm, in everyday life. Were it not so, those called to serve as paradigm and as witness would be unable to speak to humankind in its lot. Thus, the people which is rooted in God and serves as proof that existence in God is ultimately the only assured existence must simultaneously live in the world. This people needs land, security, health; it is affected by war, drought, death; it must meet the challenges and temptations of existence as best it can. In these experiences, it must be conscious of and faithful to its Lord. By their very nature, then, all aspects of the religious life are dialectical, oriented both to the world and to God.

The call that initiates Jewish faith and peoplehood contains an exquisite dialectic, incorporating Israel's rootedness in God and in the land: "The Lord said to Abram: Go forth from your land, your kindred, your father's home—to the land that I will show you" (Gen. 12:21).

The patriarch's first act involves an uprooting, a transfer of the center of gravity from the natural ground to life in the Lord. But he does this by going to a new land—to found a people. *The act of living in God does not eliminate the natural life; it illuminates it.* The natural life is not repudiated in following God; rather, it is enriched, and quite literally so: "And I will make you a great nation: I will bless you, I will make your name great. And you will be a blessing" (Gen. 12:1).

To deepen the dialectic: the destined land is not identified ahead of time. Going there will take faith in God and willingness to set out on roads unknown which lead one knows not where. It is not a land which is self-evidently holy, a paradise or sacred ground so full of divine forces that the worshiper can only submit to it. It is "a land that I will show you." Only God's election and the believer's actions will reveal its holiness.

And to complete the dialectic: the acts of creating a people and looking to a land—acts so particular, so involved in turning inward—are accompanied by the promise that they are of universal significance. Abraham is told, "in you, the nations of the earth will be blessed" (Gen. 12:2).

Even as Abraham begins to settle the land, he experiences it as the gift of God. "Lift your eyes from the spot on which you stand and look North and South, East and West. All the land that you see I will give to you and to your seed forever . . . " (Gen. 12:3).

When God and Abraham enter into a covenant, the land becomes the actual substance of that covenant. The extraordinary biblical claim is that God, too, is bound by the covenant. God self-obligates to give Abraham the land. The divine understanding is expressed by symbolically passing between the pieces.[2] (N.B.: God is bound first.) Later, a complementary covenant is made. Abraham and his seed will uphold the covenant to be God's people, marking it in their very flesh with circumcision. In turn, God will be their God and will give the land to Abraham and his seed forever, in fulfillment and sign of that covenant (Gen. 17:1–14). Thus, the land is the very essence of the covenant.

III. Promise and Fulfillment: The Dialectic

Another layer of meaning can be found in the land's covenantal symbolism. The land is not actually given to Abraham. It is promised to him. Many of Abraham's life experiences, in fact, dramatize that he is not yet rooted in or in possession of the land. The quarrel with Lot (Gen. 12), the war with the kings (Gen. 14), the quarrel over the wells (Gen. 21), and the burial of Sarah (Gen. 23) all underscore the fact that Abraham is essentially an outsider in the very land promised to him. The promise of possession is constantly contradicted by actual events which demonstrate that Abraham is landless. Thus living by the promise is in itself education for and expression of faith. The anticipated possession of land, the classical model of establishment and security in the world, becomes the constant instruction and symbol that, after all, Abraham lives rooted in God alone, sustained by God's promises.

The possession of the land sets up the promise-and-fulfillment model which is one of the central modalities of biblical faith. The believer lives by God's promises, even though those who live by the world's standards might sensibly scoff or doubt the likelihood of these improbable assurances ever being realized. When the promise is fulfilled, it is confirmation to both believer and nonbeliever alike of God's existence and power. It is demonstration that God's promise is indeed more reliable than those worldly vectors by which most people measure probability of realization.

The promise and fulfillment motif weaves through the central experiences of the Jewish people and faith and is a striking feature of biblical history. The land and the people's existence are repeatedly linked. The promise to the fathers that their children will be numerous and that the land will be theirs is fulfilled in the Exodus narrative; the children's redemption from Egypt shapes them into multitudinous people and moves them toward the promised land (Gen. 50:24). The land promised at the Exodus is given to the next generation in conquest, thus enabling the people to flourish (Josh. 13, 14, 24). Much later, after several generations have lived on the land, they are expelled; however, the exile is terminated by the promised restoration to the land, and the survival of the people is assured (Jer. 32:6–44; Is. 40ff.). In each case, the fulfillment is decisive testimony to Israel that the Lord is God and the Lord guides history. The experience of living by the promise (with fulfillment coming much later) also served in good stead in the period of extended exile when Israel lived in anticipation of its restoration.

There are additional links between covenant and land, both in the patriarchal and Exodus narratives of the Torah.

The renaming of the patriarchs expresses this theme. In biblical symbolism, to give a name is to define the essence. The change of name from Abram to Abraham and from Jacob to Israel (e.g., the person becomes the covenanted one) occurs in conjunction with a renewed promise of possession of the land (Gen. 12:4–8, 35:10–12).

Similarly, possession of the land symbolized rightful succession to the spiritual patrimony. He who inherits the land is also the progenitor of the covenant line; Ishmael goes to live in the desert and Keturah's sons are sent eastward by Abraham so that Isaac remains the clear and unquestioned heir. When Abraham sends Eliezer to find a wife for Isaac, indicating to him that the blessing will be passed to Isaac (Gen. 24:6–8), he warns, at the same time, that Isaac is not to be taken out of the Promised Land. Note again the subtlety of the dialectic. It is not the original, biological birthplace, but the Promised Land that is now the ancestral home. And Abraham is supremely confident that the Lord who took him from his home and promised him the land will ensure that a suitable wife will be found to guarantee the continuity of the family (Gen. 24:5–8).

This theme is repeated in the conflict between Jacob and Esau to succeed their father Isaac in the chain of covenant. Even after the trickery is discovered, Isaac still confirms that he willingly chooses Jacob as the true successor by passing the patriarchal blessing to him: "May He give *you Abraham's blessing*, to you and your children, *that you will inherit the land you live in*, the land which the Lord gave to Abraham" (Gen. 28:4).

The indissoluble link of promise, land, and people fittingly closes the patriarchal cycle. As its last living figure, Joseph, prepares to die, he asserts his confident faith that the Lord will remember Israel and bring them to the land He promised to the fathers. Indeed, he asks that his bones be taken along to be reburied there (Gen. 50:24–25).

In the Exodus cycle, which is the core of the Five Books of Moses,[3] we find the same intimate union of land, people, and faith. Here again the link is a consequence of the very structure of the biblical conceptions of history and human destiny. God has entered into history by establishing a special relationship to humanity through an elected part of the human race. But this people must be free if it is to be able to worship the Lord properly (Ex. 5:1–4). "Let My people go, that they may worship Me" is the leitmotif of the exodus (Ex. 4:23, 5:1–3, 7:26, 8:16, 9:1–13, 10:3). When the Jews are so totally oppressed, they cannot hear or grasp God's concern (Ex. 6:9). Conversely, when they are redeemed, they will know (e.g., experience directly) that the Lord God exercises the primary claim on their loyalty (Ex. 6:7, 20:2). Their redemption will be the most resounding testimony to the Lord's name and power (Ex. 7:5, 9:15, 11:8, 15:14–19, 18:1, 8–11). In turn, that act of redemption will be completed by bringing the people to their land (Ex. 6:8, 13:3–5, 11:16). In one Exodus pericope the connection is made through the fulfillment of the promise to the fathers:

> And I have also established My covenant with them to give them the land of Canaan, the land of the sojourning in which they sojourned. And I also have heard the groaning of the children of Israel kept in bondage by Egypt and I have remembered My covenant. Therefore . . . I am the Lord and I will bring you out from under the burdens of Egypt and I will redeem you . . . and I will take you to Me for a people and I will be to you a God and you shall know that I am the Lord your God . . . and I will bring you into the land which I swore to you to Abraham, Isaac and Jacob and I will give to you for a heritage: I am the Lord (Ex. 6:4–8).

65

Elsewhere in Exodus the role of security and rootedness in the land is made the background and basis of the central rituals of the people. The events of the Exodus are to be retold and reenacted when Israel settles in the promised land (Ex. 13:3–16). This injunction might appear to emphasize the extreme dependence of the people upon the land—as if the land were the only place where these events could be relived in memory and reexperienced in ritual. Yet in this very central moment of Jewish faith and history, the subtlety of the dialectic of the people's relationship to the land is reasserted. The revelation does not take place in the Promised Land. The people is led forth into a desert and there at Sinai the great covenant is proclaimed and ratified (Ex. 16, 19, 20; Jer. 2:2). The rabbis clearly understood the message: the Torah was given in the desert, an undefined place, open to all, to teach that it is not specific to a single land or framework (Medrash Rabbah). At the moment of peak affirmation comes the reminder that man's ultimate relationship is with God. Of course, the two bonds are not contradictory; they exist in dialectical relationship.

It is noteworthy that in the Exodus cycle the incident of the spies causes the Israelites to forfeit their chance to enter Canaan. Instead of trusting the Lord's promise, they judge the land by the outwardly imposing evidence of their enemies' power. In their lack of faith, they presume that they cannot conquer the Promised Land. It is this failure of nerve—of faith in the promise—and not their earlier sin of idolatry that condemns them to die in the desert (Ex. 32–34; Deut. 1:20ff.). Their children, and those of the parental generation like Caleb who have enough trust in God's promise to go forth and overcome, are the only ones deemed worthy to enter Canaan. Similarly, when Moses is denied the privilege of entering the Holy Land, lack of faith rather than lack of military, political, or moral fitness brings on this ultimate sanction. "And the Lord spoke to Moses and Aaron, 'Because you did not believe in Me, to sanctify Me in the eyes of the children of Israel, therefore you shall not bring this congregation into the land which I have given them'" (Num. 20:12).

Another lesson is to be learned here. The greatest of the prophets, the primary teacher, lived, taught, and died outside the Holy Land. These facts will exist in eternal tension with any tendency to make the land the exclusive place of revelation of God's presence. Thus the symbols and literary motifs heighten the extraordinary interaction and balance between possession of the land and rootedness in God.

IV. Theology of the Land

This dialectic of land, religion, and people is tightly interwoven in biblical history. From the articulation of this relationship throughout

Biblical literature, one can begin to formulate a theology of the land. This theology, in turn, explains why the event of the exile is so traumatic and had so powerful an impact on the people and its faith.

There are several underlying assumptions which comprise such a theology of the land.

A. God's Gift

Possession of the land is not taken by some arrogant exercise of power which could mislead people into believing and acting as if they were truly the absolute owners of the land. The land is God's gift to Israel (Ex. 6:8). Moreover, this gift is not related to any human claim (except perhaps to the unrighteousness of other nations) nor to any special merits of the people of Israel. It is given as a result of God's promise to the forefathers (Deut. 9:4–6). Deuteronomy is suffused with this theme of God's gift; it contains no less than eighteen references to this promise of the land to the fathers. To Israel of the post-Exodus generations, then, the grant of land is a measure of *Hessed,* of kindness and grace.[4] Nor does the land lose this giftlike quality when won by might. Even military conquest represents an act of God; the Lord overthrows the enemy and gives the land to Israel. We see this theological refrain throughout the books of Joshua and Judges which detail the conquest of the land. When Gideon prepares to go out with a large army, God exhorts him to take only a few, for "too many are the people that are with you that I should give Midian into their hands, lest Israel will glorify over Me saying 'my hand saved me'" (Judg. 7:2).

B. Sacred Space and How to Live in It

Because the land is God's gift, it becomes sacred space. The earth is the Lord's and all the land is held as conditional gift, or loan, from God.[5] To be worthy of this gift, to retain it, the people must live on the land in a special way. "These are the statutes and the judgments which you shall observe to do in the land, which the Lord God of your fathers gives you to possess it all the days that you live on the earth" (Deut. 12:1). "To possess it" is to make it into a homeland by living there, cultivating the land, building a society—all in a special way.

Thus there are special laws connected to the land. These are binding only when living in the Land of Israel. In the Holy Land, every seventh year is a sabbatical year and the land is not worked. The land and the people rest and regenerate to testify that the Lord is ultimate master of the land (Lev. 25:2–7, 23). The sabbatical year is also a year when existing debts are forgiven—a clear attempt to prevent the emergence (or soften the impact) of a permanent landless and poverty-stricken class. Eliminating poverty would be an expression of the blessing which God bestows in the land He has granted to Israel (Deut. 14:4–5).

Closely related is the jubilee year, which comes every fiftieth year. In the jubilee, the land was redistributed, real property reverts to its original owner, and the Hebrew bondservants go free. This testifies that the Lord is both master of the land and sole Lord of Israel (Lev. 25:5–17, 25–43, 50–55).

The first fruits were brought to the central sanctuary to be offered and eaten there. The prayer recited sounded the themes of thanksgiving for the produce and the land, remembrance of the past slavery and the exodus, and the culmination of redemption in the gift of the land flowing with milk and honey to Israel (Deut. 26:5–10).

The fruit of newly planted trees was restricted under the law of *orlah*. "When you come into the land and plant all kinds of trees for food, then you shall count their fruit as forbidden: three years it shall be forbidden to you, it must not be eaten. And in the fourth year, all their fruit shall be holy, a praise offering to the Lord. But in the fifth year you may eat of their fruit, that they may yield more richly for you. I am the Lord your God" (Lev. 19:23–25).

A cycle of tithes was given to the Levite, the widow and orphan, the poor and the stranger. Tithes were also taken to Jerusalem to be eaten there by the owners of the field (Num. 18:21ff.; Deut. 26:12–15, 14:22–29). Similarly, priests were given a special share of the crop (*terumah*), of the first-born animals, and of the sacrificial offerings (Num. 18). This was partly a "tax" to support the cultic officialdom, but it also underscored the message that the land belonged to God. Priests and Levites did not receive a share of the land, for "the Lord is their portion and inheritance" (Num. 18:20). Thus the tribes totally devoted to God's service concretize the biblical assertion that all Israel lives by God's grace and bounty, and not by physical possession of the land.

Laws of charity also had special application in the land. "When you reap the harvest of your land, you shall not totally remove the corners of your field nor gather the gleanings of your harvest—you shall leave them to the poor: I am the Lord your God" (Deut. 24:20). "When you reap your harvest in your field and have forgotten a sheaf in the field, you shall not go back to fetch it . . . when you beat your olive trees you shall not go over the boughs . . . when you gather the grapes in your vineyard, you shall not glean after you, for it shall be for the stranger, the fatherless and the widow."[6] (Here again the realization that God has given Israel the gift of security and possession of the land is expressed in sensitivity, especially in good times and moments of celebration, to the needs of those who have no share in the land; see esp. Deut. 12:11–19).

Justice and righteousness were also demands connected to the land—this was the kind of behavior that made Israel worthy of living in the holy land. "Judges and officers shall you make in all your gates, which the Lord Your God will give you . . . and they shall judge the people with righteous judgment. You shall not twist judgment; you shall not respect persons nor take a bribe . . . Justice shall you pursue that you may live and inherit the land which the Lord Your God gives you" (Deut. 16:18–20). Honesty in business dealings were also part of the relationship to the land. "You shall have a perfect and just weight, you shall have a perfect and just measure that your days be lengthened in the land which the Lord Your God gives you. All that do such things [unjust weights and measures], all that do injustice are an abomination to the Lord Your God" (Deut. 25:13–16). "You shall not remove your neighbor's landmark . . . which the ancients set in your inheritance which you shall inherit in the land which the Lord Your God gives you to possess it" (Deut. 19:14).

Good deeds were rewarded by longer life on the land. "You will do what is just and good in God's eyes; so that He will do good to you; and you will come and inherit the good land which God promised to your fathers" (Deut. 6:18). "Honor your father and mother that your days will be lengthened and it will go well with you on the land which the Lord gives you" (Deut. 5:16).

"And you shall do My statutes and keep My judgments and do them: and you shall dwell in the land in safety. And the land shall yield her fruit; and you shall eat your fill and dwell therein in safety" (Lev. 25:18–24). "If you walk in My statutes and keep My commandments, and do them: and the land shall yield its increase . . . and you shall eat your bread to the full, and dwell in your land safely. And I will give peace in the land, and you shall be down and none shall make you afraid: and I will remove evil beasts out of the land, neither shall sword go through your land" (Lev. 26:3–6).

Correspondingly, failure to keep the commandments will bring shorter life on the land—that is, exile. "If you do not listen to Me and do not do these commandments . . . I will bring them to the land of their enemies. Then their uncircumcised hearts will submit and they will pay for their sins" (Lev. 26:14, 41). Jeremiah proclaims destruction and exile as the punishment for failure to set the Hebrew servants free (Jer. 34:8ff.). Failure to observe the sabbatical year is particularly reprehensible and liable to bring exile (Lev. 26:34–35, 38–41, 43–44). Since the sabbatical year asserts that God is master of the land, nonobservance is an expression of human arrogance and claim of ownership. The punishment of exile is poetic justice and proof that the people lives on the holy land only by God's grace and sufferance. Thus the sacredness of the land does not bestow automatic immunity or distinction on the people of Israel.

Beyond the requirements for special holiness in way of life, there are stern warnings against "polluting" the land. Moral religious transgression is especially offensive because the land is sacred space and will not tolerate pollution.

The Israelites were to destroy all forms of existing idolatry when they entered the land. Magic, child sacrifice, and other abominable practices polluted the land; Israel was to reject all these practices or face expulsion just as did predecessor nations for such violations (Deut. 7:1–7, 7:17–26, 8:19–20, 9:1–7). Forbidden sexual practices also polluted the land—until it "vomited out the inhabitants." The land would do the same to the children of Israel if they violated the Torah's sexual norms (Lev. 18:21–28).

It is not just violation of a cultic category that causes pollution. Murder pollutes the land, as does the shedding of innocent blood—or failure to punish such acts. The Jews were required to build cities of refuge to which an unintentional slayer could flee from the revenge of relatives so that "innocent blood not be shed in your land which the Lord your God gives you for an inheritance" (Deut. 19:10, 21:1–9). Similarly, the body of a hanged person must not be exposed. "If a man commits a crime punishable by death and is put to death, and you hang him on a tree, his body shall not be left overnight on the tree. You shall bury him the same day, for a hanged man is a curse of God, and you shall not defile your land which the Lord your God gives you for an inheritance" (Deut. 21:22–23).

C. The Land as Instrument of Divine Will

The culmination of this theology of the land is that the land is an instrument of God's will. It is the vehicle of reward and punishment; thus its state is a barometer of the moral-religious condition of Israel. "If you hearkened diligently to My commandments to love the Lord your God and to serve Him with all your heart and all your soul, then I will give you the rain for your land in its due season . . . that you may eat and be full" (Deut. 11:13–15). " . . . if you hearken to these judgments and keep and do them then the Lord your God will keep the covenant and the grace which He promised to your fathers; He will love you, bless you, multiply you and will bless the fruit of your womb and the fruit of your land, your corn, your wine and your oil, the increase of your cattle and the flocks of your sheep in the land which he swore to your fathers to give you" (Deut. 7:12–13). On the other hand, if Israel sins, the land turns hard and dry: "the land beneath you will be as iron" (Deut. 28:23). "He will shut up the heavens, there will be no rain, the land will yield no fruit, and you will perish quickly from off the good earth which the Lord gives you" (Deut. 11:17).

In the book of Judges, Kings, and Chronicles, rule of the land by outside conquerors is perceived as punishment for disobedience. The classical prophets focus on exile as punishment for Israel's perfidy. Later biblical and rabbinic thought moved beyond the simplistic interpretation of prosperity and focused on independence and oppression as reciprocals of obedience and sin.

What all these interpretations have in common is the insistence that the ultimate rootedness of Israel is in God. Thus tendencies to rely excessively on the land as talisman for defense or on power and wealth for security are constantly rebuked by God's actions in nature or history. The longer Israel is on the land, the greater the danger of absolutizing the material prosperity or political power. The sense of the holiness of land runs the risk of glorifying its possession or of devaluing the moral-religious criteria for its retention. Therefore, the prophets constantly attack such idolatries of place. They hold up exile as the fruit of such a wrong transvaluation of space and as a way that God will detach Israel from this idolatry. Hosea holds up expulsion from the land as the way God will take Israel back into the desert to restore the pristine love of the initial covenant days—before the people entered the land (Hos. 2:16ff.).

Here is where the dialectic proved most powerful and crucial. As long as the people was in the land of Israel, the balance of the dialectic was turned toward excessive reliance on the land; still, classical prophecy was able to maintain the primacy of the reliance on God. This polemic, which runs through the prophetic period, enabled Israel to survive the shock of exile—without losing its relationship and yearning for the land.

> Once exile occurred, there was also a corresponding risk that losing the land (Exile) would be so shattering that the community would believe its God to be defeated or its covenant broken. To this the prophets responded with consolation. Rootedness in God and covenantal relationship could not be ended by exile. On the contrary, the religous moral demands carried over into the lands of the exile. They proved capable of abstraction from the Holy Land (and, in Christianity, of separation from the community of Israel itself). On the other hand, restoration of the land would be the best proof of the unbrokenness of the covenant. It would also restore the days of old where closeness to God was matched by economic and political well being. This explains why the longing for reestablishment in the land did not dissipate despite the long separation. The prophetic promise that restoration to the land would follow Israel's repentance and/or God's revelation confirmed the indissoluble links among land, people, and God.

V. From Land to Exile: The Crisis and Response of Faith

In the Five Books of Moses, the centrality of the land in the life and faith of the people is exquisitely balanced with rootedness in God; the dynamic tension between the two never weakens. However, a dialectical situation means that with certain people, or at certain moments or events, the balance may be pushed toward one pole or the other. This is a natural occurrence in the life of a people moving from the reality of the present to an ultimately redeemed future. Events and people's responses along the

71

way are bound to affect the perception, insight, and centrality of themes and symbols. Thus in Joshua, in the early days of conquest, the land's centrality becomes overwhelming. The Israelite victories testify that God is Lord of all (Hos. 2:16ff.); the crossing of the Jordan is a symbolic parallel to the crossing of the Red Sea (Josh. 2); the conquest shows God's presence in the midst of Israel (Josh. 3). In Joshua's final speech, movement from the region beyond the river into the land is by implication identified with the movement from idolatry to the worship of God (Josh. 3, and passim). This view is reflected in simplistic form (Josh. 24:2–15) in the anxiety and fear of the two-and-a-half tribes whose land is in Transjordan that they will be excluded from God's worship.[7] A similar sentiment echoes in David's complaint when he is driven away by Saul's persecution: "They drove me out today from my portion in the inheritance of the Lord, saying, go worship alien gods" (Sam. 26:19). Subtler versions of this view appear in Jonah; that Jonah arose to flee from before the Lord to Tarshish (Jon. 1:3) appears to indicate that prophecy and direct visitation can occur only in Israel. In Jeremiah and in Deuteronomy (Deut. 28:26) we find the theme, "and there [in exile] you will worship other gods of wood and stone."

The decadent form of this polarization is reflected in the belief that since the Holy Land (and the Temple) is God's own dwelling place, it cannot be conquered. Victory and security are guaranteed by the sheer *mana* (divine force) of the Holy Land and of God's presence in it. The polemic with this view was central to the messages of the prophets. The prophets railed against the people many times over for their excessive formal evaluation of Temple worship, their neglect of the simple laws of truth, justice, morality, and compassion. The prophets warned of exile and destruction to come, an experience that would utterly disprove the Israelites' idolatrous complacency.

Hosea carries the theme even further, questioning the very permanence of the covenant,[8] and the symbol of this "invalidation" is the exile! This is the dialectic in reverse; the land is not a talisman, but rather its loss is so grievous a wound that it implies a challenge to the validity of the covenant.[9] Since the land is so closely linked to the covenant, even without the imbalance in the people's grasp of its centrality, exile was bound to throw the whole future of the faith into question. Ultimately Amos, Hosea, and Ezekiel conclude that the covenant will not be broken; Israel will be purified and restored to the land (cf. Hos. 2:16–25).

The peak of the crisis and resolution is found in Isaiah and Jeremiah (Jer. 2, 3, 7, 9, 11, 14, 16 [esp. vv. 14–15], 23, 25, 27, 31). Here (as in Ezekiel) the crisis of destruction and exile leads to the possibility that the covenant itself is over or superseded (Ez. 1–30 and passim; Jer. 2–3 and passim; Is. 1:1–17, 36:13–27; Deut. 12:11–19). Drawing upon the reassurance that the people is rooted in God and that His promises are beyond destruction, the prophets conclude that Israel will be purified, not destroyed, by the exile. The exile will be followed by the restoration of a purified people to the land. In the second part of Isaiah that very act of restoration becomes the proof of the universal rule of God and of his role in history. Israel will reach its most potent level as witness to God, at the moment that it is restored to its patrimony. At that point, the land, the people, and the faith will all be renewed and vindicated (Is. 40–66).

This insight is dramatized in Jeremiah using the actual symbolism of possession of the land (chapter 32). At the moment when the enemy is at the door and Jeremiah's prophecies of doom are about to be realized, he is instructed to redeem his uncle's field by purchase. Jeremiah is stunned at the incredibility of the suggestion (Jer. 32:16–25). The answer he receives is clear and unequivocal. The purchase—the high valuation of the land— is the fitting symbol of the unbroken covenant, of the restoration to come, of the purification of the people. "Again, they will be My people and I will be their God" (Jer. 32:38).

The ultimate impact of the destruction and exile, then, was to bind the people more tightly to the truth of the covenant. Why did not the rupture from sacred space destroy a people who had become attached to the Promised Land as an existential reality for many centuries? Why did the relationship survive so well, despite the loss of the crucial center? It was precisely because of the dialectic that the relationship of land, people, and religion remained intact, even as it took on different emphases. To be sure, without the land, the law and mitzvot became more central. The enactment of holy deeds in holy time filled the vacuum. Ezekiel, Ezra, and Nehemiah all testify to the fact that the Babylonian exiles placed greater emphasis on observance of Shabbat and holidays than did the Palestinian communities. It is not that Israel has left the land and therefore has left God behind; rather, the theme that surges through the prophetic litera- ture is that Israel's exile is punishment for its sins, but God stays with Israel and with the people in exile (Ez. 11:14–20). This emphasis restores the balance that is lost when the holiness of the land is so exaggerated that it is perceived as guarantee against destruction and as the only place where God can be served. Yehezkel Kaufmann's thesis is that it was precisely the exile that dealt the death blow to idolatry and made monotheism irreversible.[10]

Later Christian theology focused on Jeremiah's vision of a new covenant (Jer. 31:31–34, 32–40), with the polemic goal of validating the New Testament and Christianity as the fulfillment of Jeremiah's prophecy. For the same reason, such theology spiritualized Isaiah's focus on restoration to the land (Is. 11:10–16, 14:1–2, 27:12–13, 52:7–72, and passim). Of course, once Christians assumed that Christ was the sole interpretive key to Hebrew Scriptures, such interpretation followed naturally. However, an indigenous hermeneutic would suggest that the renewed covenant is none other than that referred to twice by Jeremiah (Jer. 16:14–15, 23:7–8). It is the covenant to be lived by the light of God's restoration of Israel to its land even as the original covenant was lived by the light of the Exodus. The restoration-redemption will be so overwhelming and revelatory that it will be the benchmark of God's presence in the world, just as God's saving acts in the Exodus were unique symbols.

> Behold the days are coming, says the Lord, when the people will no longer swear: 'the Lord lives Who brought up the children of Israel from the land of Egypt'—but rather: 'the Lord lives Who brought up [to Israel] the children of Israel from the North and from all the lands He drove them to.' And I will set them on this land which I gave to their fathers (Jer. 23:7–8).

In both the old and the renewed covenants, the presence of God is marked by acts saving and freeing God's people and restoring them to the land.

This remarkable synthesis of God, land, and people was so powerful that it could sustain not only a seventy-year exile, but an indefinite one, one that in effect lasted nineteen hundred years. The void created by loss of the land was filled as Jews made their lives spiritual with holiness of time. The people of Israel developed new channels leading to God's presence. At times in the long night of exile, the land appeared so remote that a spiritualization of God's promises of the land took place in certain kabbalistic and hasidic circles. (The shift paralleled Christianity's treatment of this theme.) Despite all of these substitutions, transformations, and sublimations, the land as symbol and cement of an unbroken covenant maintained its magnetic pull. As long as the imagery and credibility of covenant remained, the built-in association of the Holy Land meant that no other land could take the place of Zion entirely. The dream and hope of fulfillment, the longing for Zion, the desire for return to the place of the earliest relationship with God, to the place of sacred history remained strong. This sentiment was true for the first exile, which approximates the end of the biblical period. It was refined in a thousand ways by the rabbis during the 1900 years' exile from which Israel has miraculously returned.[11]

When the Lord made possible the return of Israel's captivity to Zion, the living balance was restored. The promise was not for once; the promise was for all eternity.

VI. Epilogue

There has been great new awareness of the land since the beginning of the modern return to Zionism. However, the Six-Day War and the reuniting of Jerusalem raised the theological consciousness of Jews and non-Jews alike to this dimension. Charles Long has called the rediscovery of the land a new sense of cosmic orientation for the Jews. Richard Rubenstein has said that the earth and its fruitfulness and vicissitudes and power will once again become the central spiritual realities in a Jew's life. But for a Jew grounded in the theology of Hebrew scriptures and in rabbinic tradition, this is not something new, nor is it a rediscovery of the nuances and claims of sacred space. Rather it is a heightening of the long memory of a Jew, a quickening of the heart.

So powerful has been the upsurge of land consciousness that many have charged that a new idolatry of land is being created in the teachings of Rev Zvi Yehudah Kook and in the work of Gush Emunim. The old anti-Zionism of nineteenth-century Reform has been beyond resuscitation. However, rabbis and thinkers like Eugene Borowitz and Arnold Jacob Wolf who grow out of the deep spiritual tradition of modern Reform have repeatedly argued that the focus on the state and/or the land threatens to undermine covenantal fidelity to God and the dignity of Diaspora living.

Of course there are no guarantees that the rediscovered land may not be idolatrously absolutized. But we believe that even the excesses of Zionism should be seen as a phenomenon of the first stage of the recovery of the dialectic of land, faith, and people. The covenantal model gives the land centrality but also enters into polemic with all who would absolutize it. The self-correcting tendency in the dialectic will come into play even as the Jewish people learns to juggle better the claims of land and faith. The biblical vision affirms the dignity of rooted, landed living—including its errors and compromises—even as it points beyond to rootedness in God and the relativization of Israel. One need not choose between the dignity of Diaspora and the affirmation of Zion today, any more than one must choose between spirituality and incarnate existence in biblical values.

In our view, the secularity of many modern-day Israelis or the secular interpretation of the significance of Israel on the part of many American Jews does not represent a repudiation of the covenantal expectation that Jews living on the land must hold themselves to a higher standard. It does suggest that as God is no longer the One who guarantees possession for the Jews by overtly intervening when Jews live up to the covenant, so the threat of exile as direct punishment for failing to live at a higher standard is not an appropriate theological application today. Exile and rootedness will be earned by Jewish behavior in the real world and morality is part—but not all—of it.

The restoration of Zion gives Jews the chance again to balance and relate rootedness in God and land. The essential nature of state, army, society is affirmed, but so is the capacity to live by promises and the word of God, for millennia if necessary. Israel's rebirth, now in the making, is a paradigm for ethical rootedness and self-critical nationalism for all humanity. And the thought that once again the covenant has been fulfilled

75

has given Jews everywhere a firmer hope for the ultimate redemption of all mankind. Indeed, as Isaiah suggested, the restored Zion is paradigm of the once and future Eden which all human beings, in their dignity, deserve.

Notes

This article is offered in tribute to Herman Schaalman. He liberated us to become better (Orthodox) Jews by freeing us from our shallow conceptions about Reform Rabbis and their communities and their spiritual lives—even as he led Reform Jews to a deeper understanding of their capacity for observance, spirituality, Zionism, and peoplehood.

1. Bernard W. Anderson, *The Living World of the Old Testament* (London, 1967), p. 10. Gerhard von Rad in "The Problem of the Hexateuch and Other Essays" calls this passage "the Hexateuch in miniature" (quoted in Anderson, ibid.).
2. In "The Covenant of Grant in the Old Testament and the Ancient Near East," *Journal of the American Oriental Society* 90 (1970): 184–203, Moses Weinfeld suggests that this covenant is modeled on the royal grant of the ancient Near East. In it the master binds himself to bestow a gift on the servant in consideration of the latter's having faithfully served his master (cf. Gen. 26:4–5). See on all this Dennis J. McCarthy, *Old Testament Covenant: A Survey of Current Opinions* (Oxford: Basil Blackwell, 1973).
3. The Exodus and its commemoration are central to Jewish celebration and law.
4. This is what Patrick Miller calls "the central theological affirmation about the land." See Patrick Miller, "Gift of God: Deuteronomic Theology of the Land," *Interpretation* 23 (October 1968): 451–65.
5. Therefore land cannot be sold permanently (Lev. 25:23).
6. Deut. 24:21–22. "Remember you were a slave in the land of Egypt; therefore I command you to do this" (ibid.).
7. Josh. 22:21–24. By contrast, see Moses objections in Numbers 32, 6ff. and 20ff.
8. Cp. Hos. 1:6–7, 8–9 with 2:1–3; Hos. 2:5–6, 11–14 with 16–17, 20–22, 23–25. Cp. also Amos 5.
9. The same theme is evident in Amos 2. The relationship to God is in question when the land is lost.
10. Yehezkel Kaufmann, *The Religion of Israel*, epilogue.
11. We wish to call attention to Jon Levenson's book, *Sinai and Zion: An Entry into the Jewish Bible* (Winston Press, 1985), which brilliantly portrays Sinai and Zion, covenant and land as the fundamental beams on which the biblical construction of the world and of existence are built.

Gerard W. Kaye is the director of Camping and Youth Activities for the Great Lakes Region of the Union of American Hebrew Congregations. He serves also as a coordinator of all education of the Division of Youth Activities for the Union of American Hebrew Congregations. Jerry's education comes from De Paul and Roosevelt universities, as well as the Chicago Medical School, where he became an accredited psychotherapist. He has served as director of Olin-Sang-Ruby Union Institute for sixteen years, and has worked closely with Herman Schaalman, who was one of the founding rabbis of this camp. He brings a keen insight of Jewish education and youth awareness to his role with Herman Schaalman.

Jerry Kaye brings to us the issues of personal relationships and the symbols that identify those relationships. His keen insight into the psychological dimensions of life, added to his deep commitment to the Jewish people and tradition, provide a unique tension. It is from within that creative tension that Jerry Kaye points to covenant as a dynamic within the community. His essay represents a model for what is meant by a Jewish community, if only for a little while during the summer.

The Epoch Continues

Gerard W. Kaye

It is in the nature of humankind to seek the re-creation of those experiences which have imprinted themselves upon the soul. Legend and myth combine with fact and moment to weave a fabric capable of continuity. This impulse persists in such force that every nation, every people, from the most primitive to the most advanced, dedicate both personal and national events to the repetition of the calendar.

A substance of cohesion in personal relationships clearly relates to regular reminders of times which have carved a notch on the benchmark of memory. Anniversaries of births, deaths, marriages, and matriculations are among the most obvious and common symbols in the life of a family. Many families have assigned chronologists whose task is the organization of such events. Some family folk systems include regular correspondence to keep the far-flung connections as up to date as those who live down the block from one another. In these days of geographic distance, there appears a yearning to take advantage of whatever technology will allow the connectedness of kinship to increase. People are regularly attracted to each other at times of celebration and commemoration. Such opportunities allow for structured contact and even a kind of disciplined "intimacy" for which personal resources may not have provided.

National historicity commemorates the life of a community in like fashion. No matter where the land or what its politics, days of independence and celebrations of victory are on the calendar. In lands where theology is interwoven with the life of the society, ceremony marks the sacred as well as the social. Dignitaries, both elected and appointed, seek

79

to assume a larger-than-human role when invoking the inheritance of the nation. Many societies encourage the moral leadership of the clergy as repositories of the revealed belief responsible for its official transmittal to the community.

Literature speaks of the family of man as if there were a kind of bond that exceeds the simple understanding of genotype. The prophets and dreamers of the world, both ecclesiastical and lay, call upon our brotherhood for every cause ranging from nuclear annihilation to nuclear energy. Epictetus proclaims the "universe is but one great city, full of beloved ones, divine and human, by nature endeared to each other." This theme repeats itself throughout philosophies and theologies. Embroidered as it may become, the relationship between people and their deities is integral to a sense of well-being. This sense may be a pleasant notion of awareness or a highly personal devoted relationship. Martin Buber sought to explain these variations through his essential theme of human and divine interaction. No matter what facet this association may take, however, it remains a dominant and recurrent theme as a universal of culture.

Carl Gustav Jung approaches the nature of this relationship from the psychological perspective of the collective unconscious. Jung, himself a derived theologian, identifies the problem of human archetypes which recur throughout civilizations. No matter what the locale or variety, certain preeminent themes represent themselves in the Maori tribesman as well as the Madison Avenue wordsmith. Jung identifies a variety of such archetypical characters, including both heroic and extrahuman personalities. More important here, though, than the identification of qualities is the mere existence of the notion. If it remains true in the scientific borders of psychology as well as the world of theology and the soul that a kind of connectedness recurs, then, perhaps, clearer definition needs to be placed upon these circumstances. Such exposition begins to rise above mere ethnocentric pride and intrude upon essential blocks of relational matter when it offers insight into elemental levels of all humanity.

Covenant speaks to the idea presented above. Covenant seeks to provide a way of understanding both human relationship and commitment as well as that compact between mortal and the divine. The history of covenant is a record of continuous reinforcement of these relationships. And the history of covenant, particularly early statements of this bond, are unique to the Jewish people and their God. While exposition of the covenantal process in theological terms is best left to others who have devoted their lives to such work, this author seeks another level of this tie. As much as the experience of public *hakhel* commands the attention of the participant toward the impact of the deity, so, too, this common event must bind the participants in a unique and dedicatory fashion. Just as there is clear evidence of the tying together of those who have participated in every societal occasion, how could such a patently overwhelming experience leave its earthly participants without a sense of unification? Whether it be the revelation at Sinai or the witnessing of the prophets, those whose lives were personally touched must have themselves touched each other.

Legend promises that all of the people of Israel participated together at Sinai. Since that time, Jews everywhere have continually sought a reenactment of this extraordinary epoch. This longing may even account for the subsequent interminable meetings in which a thousand generations of Jews have participated on a variety of concerns so vast that the gap between heaven and earth could have been bridged a thousand times. All of them *b'shem shamayim*. Assume, however, that this historically unique event must have embedded itself in the collective unconscious of all of the Jewish world. This covenant seeks new manifestations in every generation of believing Jews as they confront their relationship with the rest of their Jewish world. Until modern times Jews depended on the covenant to rescue them from the frosty imposition of the outside world. Now Jews need to respond to the divisions amongst themselves at least as much as to the corners of enmity from the outside.

Covenant today may require a regathering of those who were once at Sinai with the emphasis on preparation to bear witness. It took a period of preparation for the authors to make ready for insight to the divine. In modern times, such preparation is foreign in a world that exists in a constant state of pursuit.

Heschel called for the world to understand the sanctification of time. He understood this to be one of Judaism's great contributions. This cannot be done easily or well in places subjected to the tyranny of the clock. Society today emphasizes the personal need to excise familiar pressures by seeking places devoted to personal pampering. The terms of covenant today call upon the personal need to expose the collective unconscious of the Jew to collective spiritual refreshment. As noted above, the time for such renewal calls first for the delineation of relationship. Biblical terms for the covenant have been couched in the language of suzerain and vassal. But the need existed, then as now, to understand that while there may have been only one suzerain there were many vassals. Those recipients of "monarchy" understood the need for a kingdom of subjects. This generation only begins to perceive the notion of comradeship in relation to deity.

Abraham was to receive the land and to David was committed the house. These were "places" which God set aside in order that kinship might become manifest. Today the land is extant but not always available. While the house has become a small sanctuary, the land remains distant. So it is that the need arose to establish a cognate for the inheritance of Abraham. So it is that the creation of a place for the implementation of the human level of the covenant increases in importance as the desire to forge the bonds between today's Jews increases in intensity. In this fashion do we set aside places like the Olin-Sang-Ruby Union Institute in pursuit of such goals. The work undertaken by the founders of this place provides a unique setting for those who would seek the exposure of the soul which exists when the clock is set to the days of creation rather than the inexorable counting of atoms.

While the testimony of Sinai reposes in the written Law, today's accounting lies in the lives which touch each other through the experiences which are continually repeated in Oconomowoc. Wisconsin is hardly the land which God promised to Abraham. It is not a biblical site flowing with milk and honey—perhaps a bit of beer and cheese. It does provide an antechamber for those who are willing to be surrounded by the *bindel* of community. It offers a kind of perpetuity through the tales which are told and retold by father and daughter, mother and son as they remember all that they found that was good when they were free among other Jews in the pursuit of excellence that is the teaching of Torah. History has already begun to make its mark on families whose children walk paths earlier dug by rabbis and teachers who now turn the mantle of leadership over to the next generation. This camp today assumes new trappings that its founders barely conceived. But the great bonds which were forced nearly four decades ago contribute mightily to the sense of pervasive covenant which touches every Jewish *neshamah* that finds a moment's respite as the words of Torah become the measure of time.

André LaCocque is professor of Old Testament at the Chicago Theological Seminary and director of the Center for Jewish-Christian Studies. He has served as visiting professor at Spertus College of Judaica. He has studied in Paris, Jerusalem, and Strasbourg. He has been one of the leading biblical scholars in the field of interfaith dialogue. He has written several books and scholarly articles. He has lectured widely, especially at Emanuel Congregation. His close relationship with Herman Schaalman spans more than two decades, and their dialogue is an essential part of forming Herman Schaalman's future vision for work in Jewish-Christian relations. Herman currently sits on the Executive Board for the Center of Jewish-Christian Studies at Chicago Theological Seminary.

André LaCocque brings to the task of biblical theology the keen and provocative mind of a Christian committed to interfaith dialogue. He forces us to ask difficult scholarly questions about Torah in its relation with covenant. LaCocque's commitment to his own Christianity is partly based upon his conviction of the distinction to be made between Judaism and the religion of Torah. There emerges from Torah a sense of "law," which Christianity understood as a necessarily different revelation. LaCocque's scholarship brings us inside the process of the dialogue, so that each faith community is sustained and yet a stronger bridge between the two is built. André LaCocque is an example of a Christian for whom the covenant is neither old or new, only living.

Torah—Nomos

André LaCocque

The occasion of this *Festschrift* provides me with the welcome opportunity to prolong lines that have been only sketched in conversations with Rabbi Herman Schaalman, especially when I have repeatedly lectured at Emanuel Congregation as a scholar in residence.

The object of my contribution is to again look into one of the greatest obstacles on the road to our dialogue, namely, the problem of "the Law." More specifically, my task will be to provide the backdrop against which the Pauline (and the Christian) critique of the Law took the shape of such an astonishing radicalism.

As a preliminary but crucial point, it must be stressed that Paul's approach to the question of the Law, as different as it is from the one which prevailed in normative Judaism, is not his invention; it is well within the very diversified Judaism of the Second Temple period. Our historical perspective, which contains the filter of the triumph of rabbinism, tends to distort by antedating a situation that prevailed only later. Too often we retrospectively consider the time between 538 B.C.E. and 100 C.E. as the period of Judaism's formation. This, however, does not imply that there was then a recognized orthodoxy surrounded by more or less far-fetched sects, which were condemned from the start to fall in disrepute and deserved oblivion. Taking into consideration the major modern contributions to the history and understanding of that period,[1] this point need not be labored. It will be good however to keep it in mind for the sake of the argument defended here.

I. Law in the Prime Testament

As is well known, according to G. von Rad, followed by C. Wester-mann among others, the Sinai traditions had originally an independent existence. They have been more or less successfully inserted into the Exodus narratives where they constitute a foreign body. More recently, Norman Gottwald has defended the thesis that the apodictic law "resists being cast into the form of a narrative" because its nature is purely cultic.[2] The later narrativity of the law is the upshot of a developmental objectification of the praxis, for the community had consciousness that YHWH was in covenant with them and instructed them.[3] The casuistic laws were introduced into the basic theme of the revelation at Sinai well into monarchic times. Probably this first occurred in the ninth-century Northern Kingdom in response to socioeconomic deterioration, especially under the policies of the Omrides.[4]

"The Law" is first cultic (the so-called apodictic laws), and what will become the casuistic laws are originally the jurisprudence of the community. Through their narrativization, however, they both accede to the category of the prescriptive. And the intertextual relation of the narrative framework with the prescriptive content shores up the covenantal nature of the whole. Thus, for example, the Decalogue's "introduction" is its indispensable characterization: "I am the Lord your God who took you out of Egypt . . . " *Within* the consciousness of herself as being in intimate relationship with God,[5] Israel integrates the prescriptive. It is second to a primordial situation that creates the raison d'être and the conditions for the law, namely, the *berit*. The import of this is immeasurable.

When during the Second Temple period the terms' sequence is reversed, the prescriptive becoming the enclosing and all other elements of Israel's consciousness the enclosure, the situation is radically altered. The narrative is now seen as more or less episodic to the extent of becoming more or less ornamental at the service of the core of revelation, "the Law." Such a situation is reflected in the traditional precedence of the "halakhah" over the "aggadah." It is also why "historiography . . . played at best an ancillary role among the [postbiblical] Jews, and often no role at all . . . the collective memory [was] transmitted more actively through ritual than through chronicle."[6]

At the dawn of the revolution we find the Deuteronomic school equating *Sefer Ha Berit (Book of Covenant)* with *Sefer Ha-Torah* and making the covenant an objective reality in need of being acknowledged and adhered to as a *code,* a character that Torah had not before. Thus, King Josiah, accompanied by all the people as one man, takes solemnly upon himself "to walk after the Lord and to keep his commandments and his testimonies and his statutes . . . and to perform the words of his covenant

. . . " (2 Kings 23:1–3). As Delbert R. Hillers writes, "the Covenant has become an affirmation of loyalty to a code of conduct."[7]

During the Exile in Babylon, it was of course impossible to celebrate the Covenant in its natural cultic setting. It is thus understandable that its prescriptive aspect was pushed to the fore as the only way left to the people to affirm their identity in response to the then greatest historical challenge to their self-consciousness. Especially the commandments regarding circumcision, *kasherut,* and sabbath were singled out as particularly important tokens of "belonging." This had an eminently far-reaching effect on Judaism and, by way of consequence, on Christian anti-Judaic polemics, as we shall see below. It remains true that, as writes M. Noth, "only by observing those laws could they demonstrate their mutual solidarity and communal differentiation in relation to the world around them." Nothing of this lost any of its actuality after the return from Exile as "the 'Gentiles' . . . now shared with them the political unity of the Persian Empire."[8]

The conception of the Torah reached an important turning point in the fifth century, when Ezra and Nehemiah were sent by the Persian government to Jerusalem to ensure the respect of the Torah as *state law.* This was the first time in history that the Torah had this function.[9] It shifted to the level of a legal code recognized by the powers and applied to an entire local population by designated magistrates. It is legitimate to wonder whether the Persian conception of the Law was indeed shared by the Jewish leaders and the Jewish people in the fifth century. It is possible that some Judeans saw in this a fiction useful to regain a degree of independence from the occupying forces.

With time, however, this "fiction" undoubtedly became less and less sustainable. In the fourth century, Judea passed from Persian jurisdiction to the Alexandrian empire. The Torah became *Nomos,* that is, the fundamental principle in the cosmic structure as it was practiced in Jerusalem.[10]

In 200 B.C.E., Antiochus III conquered Palestine from the Ptolemies and granted the Jews a charter, or "letter of emancipation," which recognized the Law of Moses as the legal code of the *ethnos* of Judea. This accorded an intrinsic value to the Law and detached it completely in its application, if not in its origin, from the divine legislator. If there ever had been any question of a fiction fostered by the inhabitants of Jerusalem concerning the double nature of the Torah as viewed either from the exterior or the interior, this fiction had now dissolved and the Torah had become a state constitution.

In this manner, during the period of the Second Temple, the Torah underwent a progressive secularization due, paradoxically, to the fact that it was becoming more absolute. This process put increased emphasis on the intrinsic value of the Law, whereas originally its authority was mediated and guaranteed by the authority of God, who had given it. This means that it became possible, at least in theory, to obey the Torah without believing in YHWH; in any event without necessarily making the connection between the Law and the Legislator. The guarantor of the Torah was no longer God but the sovereign.[11] The Torah was *one* possible law in a Hellenized world; it was *one* expression of the cosmic law, standing beside other expressions specific to the various peoples, each of which had its own character.

If certain Jews persisted in recognizing a divine origin to their Law, then they were not necessarily in the wrong in the eyes of the Jewish Hellenizers; for cosmic law was so transcendent as to be divine in its essence. However, these "orthodox" Jews were thought of as confusing one manifestation of the Law with the Idea of the Law. To the extent that their particularism made them intransigent, it was "barbarian" and comported dangers for all concerned. Even the High Priest of the Jews, Menelaus, was in agreement on this point: his desire was for measure in all things. Moreover, when the Oniad faction in Jerusalem, for political reasons but probably also through religious conviction, rebelled against Antiochus IV and placed the survival of the Jewish *ethnos* in danger in 168 B.C.E., Menelaus obtained the "privilege" of a change in the city constitution and its promotion to the status of a Hellenistic "Polis."

With the backing of such a guarantor, Antiochus IV razed the walls of Jerusalem and built the citadel-polis of Acra. To be sure, he was not at first aware that he was attacking the "Word of God" when he overturned the previous Judaic constitution. Quite simply, what Antiochus III had recognized in 198 B.C.E. as the legal code of Judea was reduced to the status of popular custom and, as such, was susceptible to replacement by an authentically Hellenistic constitution. A Jerusalem elite was established, called *politeuma* or *demos,* with the guardian of the constitution, the High Priest Menelaus, at its head.

It is conceivable that in the terms of the new constitution there was no actual prohibition of the ancestral Jewish customs. The alimentary regulations, for example, probably could be followed in the name of a tradition without religious significance. One might even find reasons a posteriori to follow them for dietetic reasons and to praise the physiological wisdom of the ancient legislator.[12]

The opposition in Jerusalem to that state of affairs was extremely vigorous in popular milieux. It did not prevent, however, the Alexandrian Jews from rendering *Torah* of the Hebrew Scriptures by *Nomos* in Greek, that is, Law. This far-reaching philological reduction is furthermore aggravated as the Torah's elements are now *entolai* (prescriptions), thus leading to an understanding of Torah marked by what has been called "the Performance Principle."[13] True, the gift of Torah continues to be celebrated as a sign of God's grace, but divine grace and human performance tend to part company. As writes M. Noth:

> Whereas it was originally the relationship of God and man depicted as a "covenant" . . . and whereas it had been the presence of this institution which had provided the necessary prerequisite for the validation of the old laws, it was now the acknowledgment and observance of the law by the individuals which constituted the Community—for whoever undertook to keep the law joined the community. . . . It was the law, as the unprecedented primary entity, which fashioned this community, which was nothing but the union of those people who submitted to the law on all points.[14]

As said earlier on, the Jewish reaction to the "legalistic" understanding of the Torah was profound and vigorous. It crystallized in a subversive literature during the centuries that precede the Christian era, and especially in Apocalypses. No wonder those books were rejected and repressed by rabbinic Judaism and were conserved only in Christian churches. It is clear that space here does not allow for a development of the ideologies of that vast literature. Suffice it to emphasize a few points.

One is struck by the fact that in the "intertestamental" books, the Torah is not fragmented into *entolai* (prescriptions) as in the LXX. 1 En. 5:4 speaks of "the commandments of the Lord," and 99:2 of "the eternal Law [Torah]." 2 Bar. 41:3 mentions "Your covenants . . . the yoke of your Torah," and lets God say, "My Torah . . . wisdom . . . intelligence" (51:4). This last text is particularly important as Torah is clearly no code of commandments, any more than wisdom is a collection of wise things to do. (See also 2 Bar. 84:7–9; 2 Esd. 7:20, 24; etc.) In brief, the divine gift that constitutes Torah is here more emphasized than its parts, for it is a sign of election. (See 2 Esd. 5:27: "Out of all the countless nations, you have adopted one for your own, and to this chosen people you have given the law which all have approved.")

We have hardly scratched the surface of things, and I must apologize to the reader. It is clear that in all Judaism, from right to left of the whole spectrum of Jewish movements, the Law is at the center of all theological reflection. It is the very basis for any understanding of covenant, election, justice. . . . Even for the Apocalyptic thinking, to sin means to go astray from "the Law" (cf. 1 En. 99:2, 10; 5:4; 2 Bar. 67:6; 44:3; 54:5; 4 Esd. 7:24, 79). An interesting case is provided by 2 Esdras, where Torah both leads Israel to glory and declares her guilty (3:21; 7:68, 118). But there is here a remarkable absence of halakhic development or exegesis, a situation that is again conspicuous in the Pauline corpus in the New Testament.[15]

II. Paul

In the background of Saint Paul's assessment of the Law, there are three points recognized in Part I:

1. Under the pressure of circumstances, the theologically far-reaching sequential order of Covenant—Torah has been for all practical purposes reversed to Torah—Covenant in the fifth century B.C.E., thus making conditional the entry into the people of God.
2. The Alexandrian Jewish version of Scriptures has rendered the Hebrew term *Torah* (instruction, orientation, way of life) as *Nomos* (law) with the apologetic design of asserting that *Torat Moshe* is the cosmic law that makes the universe an *oikoumene*. On the one hand, *Nomos* universalizes the bearing of Torah; on the other hand, it accentuates the performance principle.
3. This understanding of Torah did not remain unchallenged. In the subversive literature of the Second Temple period, and particularly in the Apocalypses of the time, the Law is seen as an entity, indivisible in its parts, commandments, and prohibitions. It is the Word (Will, Wisdom) of God. As such, it is eternal, heavenly, divine, and therefore inalterable. Its earthly points of impact, however (i.e., its discrete commandments), are susceptible to change and even omission. Along that line of thinking, Jesus sums up the conception by saying, "For your hardness of heart Moses allowed you to divorce your wives, but from the beginning it was not so" (Matt. 19:8).

One will notice in this logion the argument of antiquity; it recurs time and again in Paul's writings about the Law. Paul, we recall, in his letters to both Galatians and Romans draws important conclusions from the anteriority of Abraham's faith over Moses' Law. Clearly, it is not merely a matter of chronology. For Jesus, there is a pragmatic aspect to the Law in its present form that is marked by empiricism and relativity. For Paul, the sequence Abraham→Moses demonstrates that the law is inserted in a prerequired context, namely, the context of faith that supersedes performance (Gal. 3, Rom. 4).

Paul's treatment of the law must be studied *in perspective*. His statements about *Nomos* are contextual and aspectual. He rages against what a disciple of his encapsulated so well in Eph. 2:15, "the law of commandments and ordinances." No Jew in the world, not even Paul, would dare pit God's will against God's will. But, when Torah is envisaged as Nomos, Paul can cite the Law against itself. He calls on Scripture to demonstrate that circumcision is not required (Rom. 4:9–12). He even manages to show that the Law condemns those who are under it (Gal. 3:10, quoting Deut. 27:26). In Rom. 14:1–6 Paul dismisses the laws on food and days as optional. In summary, the Apostle has thus sapped three essential distinguishing commandments of Judaism: circumcision, *kasherut*, sabbath.

Before we raise the question of Paul's motivation for doing so, let us not leave the issue of the distinction I have suggested between Torah and Nomos. In his book *Paul, the Law, and the Jewish People*, E. P. Sanders writes, "Though I wince at the possible anachronism of the phrase, I think that Paul had found a canon within the canon." And, Sanders adds with regret, "[Paul] did not formulate it."[16] I suggest that the terms of the problem are somewhat different. What Sanders calls the "canon within the canon" is in fact the Torah as the opponents to the legalistic and theocratic party understood it. No one ever rejected the Torah as Word/Will of God, but the conflict of interpretations ran very deep during the pre-Christian centuries and came to its highest pitch with the Apostle Paul.

Paul criticizes the Law to the extent that it is law-as-utility, Law as way of salvation through the works of the Law. For the Law does not save anyone; only God saves, graciously. In this affirmation lies the "coherence" of Paul's unsystematic statements about the Law.[17] Even within the most "tortured" formulations of his critiques, this remains firm: the Law is no prerequisite for entering the body of the saints. Not the Law but Christ is the head of that body. This does not mean that Christ is antilaw. Indeed, Paul speaks of the "law of Christ," that is, the Law as incarnate in and accomplished by Christ (1 Cor. 9:21). But, while Nomos insists upon human obedience, upon the human compliance to the terms of the treaty with God, Christ reveals that such human part is never fulfilled, so that salvation—as revealed in Christ—is purely, totally, unequivocally, the upshot of God's grace (Rom. 8:3).

Is this an economy without foundation in Scriptures? Is this a new move of God contradicting former moves? Was there ever, in other words, an economy of human performance with the divine expectation of human fulfillment leading to salvation? There never was. Putting one's hope in such a human performance was and is for Paul delusion and, more gravely yet, motive for pride and exclusivism ("boasting," cf. Rom. 3:27). To that very extent, the Law is utterly negative. It provokes one to sin (Rom. 5:20; 7), or at least, sin uses the Law to incite transgression, as the weakness of the flesh renders its injunctions inoperative (Rom. 7:25; 8:3). The Law's utility is in its demonstration of human sinfulness, thus putting us in captivity (Gal. 3:22ff.) and enslaving us (Gal. 4:1ff.) until God has mercy upon us and frees us by grace. "Law came in, to increase the trespass; but where sin increased, grace abounded all the more" (Gal. 3:22-24; Rom. 5:20-21).

If hypothetically we substitute here "Torah" for "Law" ("Torah came in to increase the trespass"), it becomes evident how self-contradictory and self-defeating the proposition now sounds. God's will and promise in the

Torah is not the increase of sin but its eradication. Paul's point is precisely that "the law of commandments and ordinances" runs contrary to the spirit of Torah. The Apostle reaffirms and restores a situation well grounded in Scriptures, viz., before Torah is Covenant (Rom. 3:27–4:12). In other words—those of Karl Barth—"Gnade" precedes "Gesetz"; or again, the unconditionality of God's grace precedes the conditionality of the Law. True, the divine initiative from beginning to end demands, also for Paul, a human response. That is *faith* (trust, love) and the relinquishing of all pride, privilege, and works of the Law as means to salvation.

We can follow E. P. Sanders when he considers Phil. 3:4–11 as particularly enlightening of Paul's attitude vis-à-vis the Law. The Law which used to occupy the center stage in Paul's pharisaic theology has been replaced by Christ, and the glory of the latter is such that the former, in comparison, is to be considered as "loss" or even "refuse"! For while formerly the Law's fulfillment provided self-righteousness, now Christ's gift is God's righteousness granted to Paul. While the Law segregated the Benjaminite Pharisee Paul from the rest of humankind, Christ is granting righteousness to all equally, to Gentiles as well as to Jews, thus canceling all segregation and all ground for "boasting" (Rom. 3:27, etc.).

So that what the translation by Nomos attempted to do in the first place, namely, to demonstrate that the Mosaic Law is the very foundation of the cosmos and hence the principle by which an *oikoumene* is made possible (provided that all nations convert and abide by that divine law) Paul now sees it achieved in the proclamation of a purely gracious divine initiative. The grace of God, not the human universal compliance with the Law, puts all people, Jews and non-Jews, at the benefit of righteousness that they do not deserve or merit (so that they cannot boast about it) but receive equally. Jews and non-Jews must respond by *faith,* without performance, without "the works of the Law." So is it exemplified by Abraham, the first one on the line of believers, the father of the faith, "430 years" before the gift of the Law at Sinai. He was archetype of the "Covenant of Grant," whose unconditionality transcends—in its absoluteness, steadfastness, and perenniality—the temporal, provisionary, and transient conditionality of human responses.

Torah is not exhausted by its *Nomoi* (commandments and ordinances). Any initiatory role of the Law and all performance principle with its accompanying illusion of deserving one's salvation or of establishing a Jewish privilege over the Gentiles, must be dispelled. Only then can the Torah be fully reaffirmed as the expression of the will of God for those who are in covenant with Him. Such a reaffirmation by Paul is found, for example, in Rom. 13:8–10. As writes E. P. Sanders, "When Paul discusses correct behavior, he quotes Lev. 19:18 in both letters (Gal. 5:14; Rom. 13:8–10). In the latter passage Paul also cites four of the ten commandments."[18] The ethos of fulfillment has meanwhile completely changed.

The "in order that" has become "in response to." The fulfillment of Torah is now "for naught" as it does not save nor add anything to one's being graced by God. Obedience is now purely gratuitous, a work of love. Some 1700 years later, Hasidic masters taught the same thing. A Dow Baer of Miedziborz rejoices that he has lost his share in the world to come because now he is able to serve God without expectation of being rewarded.

The works of love—or the "works of faith" as Paul puts it in 1 Thess. 1:3; cf. Rom. 12:8; Gal. 5:6—are as diverse and multiform as human creative imagination is boundless. They conceivably take the form of circumcision or uncircumcision; of *kasherut* or rejection of all distinction between categories of food for the glorification of the Creator; of respect of Sabbath or of "the day of the Lord." It is not that a stamp of indifference be put upon human behavior before God, for there is uncircumcision (as an option) *because* there is circumcision (as an option). One choice is not presence while the other choice is absence; for, if not the "law of Moses," then "the law of Christ" (Gal. 6:2; cf. Rom. 8:2; 1 Cor. 9:21; see also James 1:25). To be uncircumcised in the Church is a decision comparable to being circumcised in the Synagogue. Circumcision, *kasherut*, sabbath, are revealed by the Law. Whether the one in faith chooses or not to fulfill those commandments, the referents of those rites remain intact. The signified reality subsists (1 Cor. 7:19; Gal. 5:6, 6:15). By their nature, the rites are useful but insufficient to justify anyone (i.e., to transform him/her into the image and resemblance of God). Signifier and signified cannot be confused. The circumcision is a promise in the flesh of a fulfillment to come in spirit (Jer. 31:31; Ezek. 36:26). Now, as Paul Ricoeur aptly says about "symbol," the literal is indispensable for carrying the metaphorical: "the first, literal, patent meaning analogically intends *a second meaning which is not given otherwise than in the first.*"[19] Jesus reminds the Pharisees of the "beyondness" that transcends the letter of the law. Says he, "Woe to you, Pharisees! for you tithe mint and rue and every herb, and neglect justice and the love of God; these you ought to have done, without leaving the others undone" (Luke 11:42).

Paul's coherence is thus emphasized when he addresses the community of the saints and reaffirms Deut. 25:24 (1 Cor. 9:8f., 14); prohibits divorce (7:10), and ranges circumcision, *kasherut*, and the respect of sabbath among the optional choices of the Christian. Whatever may be the option it is proper provided that it be a fuller expression of one's love of God and of fellow human beings.

III. Conclusion

The role of the law is dialectical. It reveals a normative human behavior within the framework of covenantal relationships with God. It is no initiatory rite for entering the community of God, for such an entry is purely gracious, gratuitous, and universal. Nor does it either lead to self-righteousness, for righteousness also is the initiative of God. The behavior prompted by the law is therefore a model of response; it is indeed the paradigm after which all human responses in faith are either conformations or transformations. Keeping Sabbath is a work of sanctification, not in and of itself, but in faith (in love, in hope); not keeping Sabbath is also a work of faith when it is a sign of liberation from all performance principle and from the understanding of the Law as a condition to fulfill. Be it through keeping Sabbath or through not keeping Sabbath, the sign's referent is affirmed through a behavior pointing to the signified.

Paul's conviction is that all distinction between Jews and Gentiles is over (Rom. 2:10f.; 3:22, 29; 10:12 . . .). The bedrock under such a stance is a belief that both groups are equally in need of God's salvation and justification. Paul's radicalism must be tempered however with the simple remark that a *Jew* is speaking. Coming from a Gentile, the very same conclusions would immediately become suspicious. Only the "normative" can uplift the non-normative to its own level. The Gentile is put at the benefit of God's universal love *because* the Jew is, not the other way around (Rom. 2:10; etc.). The nonaccomplishment of the "commandments and ordinances" is significant and signifying, *because* they were given to the Jews for being fulfilled. The question is not, as Paul showed, for the non-Jew to become a Jew, but the root being what it is and the branches what they are, the non-Jew shall forever be supported by the root and find a self-definition in relation to the Jew. As far as he is concerned, at any rate, the Christian André LaCocque wants to situate himself in relation to the Jew Herman Schaalman.

Notes

1. I think of the works of S. Baron, M. Hengel, E. P. Sanders, G. Vermes, M. Black, F. Millar, et al.
2. *The Tribes of Yhwh* (Maryknoll: Orbis Books, 1979), p. 114.
3. Ibid., p. 91.
4. Ibid., p. 114.
5. See Ex. 19:5; Deut. 7:6; 14:2; 26:18; Ps. 26:18; 135:5; Mal. 3:17, among others.
6. Joseph H. Yerushalmi, *Zakhor: Jewish History and Jewish Memory* (Seattle: University of Washington Press, Delbert R. Hillers, 1982), pp. xiv, 15.
7. *Covenant: The History of a Biblical Idea* (Baltimore, 1969), p. 149. That we find the same situation later prevailing in an opposition party such as Qumran shows how influential this new understanding of Covenant upon the whole spectrum of Judaism has been. Cf. D. R. Hillers, At Qumran,

"Covenant is understood as an oath of loyalty to an established set of precepts, as interpreted by a clearly defined authority, the Zadokite priests" (p. 178).

8. M. Noth, *The Laws in the Pentateuch and Other Studies*, trans. D. R. Apt-Thomas (Philadelphia: Fortress Press, 1967), pp. 74, 78.

9. Ibid., pp. 18–19, etc.

10. Thus the *Nomos* can be universal in its essence and still be applied by and to a given, particular population. This explains why Jewish thinkers interested in apologetics found it necessary to prove the universality of the Torah, which they found even more "universal" than any Greek philosophy of law.

11. In 161 B.C.E. Judas Maccabaeus had to confront a royal Jewish army led by Nicanor. These men, according to 2 Macc. 15. 1f., were loyal to the king and to the Torah.

12. We can find even in Dan. 1, with all of its apologetical character, an echo of this secularizing interpretation. After ten days of severely restricted diet, Daniel and his companions are in better physical form than their counterparts, for the sole reason that they have faithfully followed the dietary laws.

13. For an illustration of this, cf. Richard Rubenstein, *My Brother Paul* (New York, Harper & Bros., 1972).

14. *The Laws in the Pentateuch*, pp. 80, 87.

15. One will find a wealth of material in D. Rössler, *Gesetz und Geschichte: Untersuchungen zur Theologie der jüd. Apokalyptik und der pharisäischen Orthodoxie* (Neukirchen, 1960).

16. E. P. Sanders, *Paul, The Law, and the Jewish People* (Philadelphia: Fortress Press, 1983), p. 162.

17. Ibid., pp. 147–48.

18. Ibid., p. 149.

19. Paul Ricoeur, *The Conflict of Interpretations* (Evanston, Ill.: Northwestern University Press, 1974), p. 290. It is so unless, as in the case of Christ according to Paul, the "second meaning," or the signified itself, is given through the rending of the "veil" that the literal had become by filling the horizon of sense. In that latter situation, the Law instead of pointing beyond itself, points to itself; the "institution" substitutes itself to the "event."

Eugene J. Lipman is rabbi emeritus of Temple Sinai in Washington, D.C., where he served for more than a quarter of a century. He is one of the leading rabbis in America, currently serving as vice-president of the Central Conference of American Rabbis, the president-elect as of 1987. He is widely known for his critical and seminal views in the area of social action as it pertains to Jewish tradition. His relationship with Herman Schaalman goes back during an entire rabbinate. They have been friends and colleagues, and have served one another in an ongoing dialectic of teacher and student.

Eugene Lipman helps us to understand better the process of rabbinic thought and interpretation; all too often, idioms get swept up into overused meanings. Lipman brings to our attention some of the finer details of one idiom, "Mipne Tikkun Olam." Lipman's essay clarifies the rabbinic idiom and offers a careful comparative study which opens up the process of rabbinic thought, which is a model itself. The covenant is a contemporary context within Jewish thought and is rooted within thinking in such a process. Lipman's essay is therefore a model for contemporary Jewish thought in a life of covenant.

Mipne Tikkun Ha'Olam in the Talmud: A Preliminary Exploration

Eugene J. Lipman

For more than forty-five years, I have known Herman Schaalman as friend, teacher, model rabbi. His soaring spirituality, his profound understanding of the realities of Judaism, his unending compassion and caring, his pixy humor—all have warmed me and have raised the *ramah* of my life. My gratitude to him and to Lotte is touched only lightly by the dedication of this paper to them.

I

On the bulletin board of a nearby synagogue hangs a poster. On it is emblazoned, in large print:

TIKKUN OLAM

To Build a Better World

Equally prominent uses of the phrase are to be found in many publications of the Reform and Conservative movements in Judaism in our time. Certainly, to participate in the shaping of society is a major *mitzvah* in contemporary liberal Judaism. The Orthodox community gives it less prominence, though it continues to appear in the *Siddur* in aspirational form in the *Alenu: l'taken olam b'malkhut Shaddai*.

This concept has had a long and convoluted evolution in Judaism. It is the purpose of this paper to trace its talmudic origins.

II

The verb *taken* derives from the Assyrian root *takanu,* "to set straight."[1] In the Hebrew Bible, it appears only in the book of Kohelet, Ecclesiastes. In two verses (1:15, 7:13) it is declared that individuals cannot *set straight* the fundamental futility of human life. In 12:9, we read *v'izen v'hiker tiken m'shalim harbeh.*

The new Jewish Publication Society Bible translates: "And he listened to and tested the soundness of many maxims." The old (1917) translation was more literal: "He pondered and sought out and set in order many proverbs."[2]

The verb appears once in the Apocrypha, in Ben Sirach (47:9), speaking of King David, *n'ginot shir lifnei mizbe'ah v'kol nevel b'shirim tiken* ("Music of stringed instruments he *ordained* before the altar. . . . ").[3]

The whole complex of uses of the verb *taken,* which set the phrase *mipne tikkun ha'olam* along the road to its present significance in Jewish thought, began after the completion of the written Torah in the fifth century B.C.E.

Aggadic tradition does not agree. It describes a sequence of legal developments—called *Takkanot*—which it traces back to Moses. The list is extensive, but two examples should suffice.

"R. Nachman said: Moses instituted [*tikken*] for Israel the benediction [*hazan et hakol*] 'Who feeds' [the first blessing in *Birkat Ha'mazon*] at the time when manna descended for them."[4] (B. Ber. 486).

"Our Rabbis taught: Moses laid down [*tikken*] a rule for the Israelites that they should enquire and give expositions concerning the subject of the day—the laws of Passover on Passover, the laws of Pentecost on Pentecost, and the laws of Tabernacles on Tabernacles" (B. Meg. 32a). That is to say, Moses instituted the practice of reading Torah portions relevant to the festivals (*Shalosh Regalim*) on those days rather than pursuing the routine annual cycle of Torah readings.

In the Talmud, *Takkanot* are attributed to Joshua, Boaz, King David, King Solomon, the early prophets, the later prophets—both before and after the destruction of the Temple in 587/6 B.C.E.—Ezra, and the men of the Great Assembly (*Otzar Yisrael* 10:297ff.).

These regulations, pre-Talmudic only in their attribution, are in a unique category. They do not have a Torah proof-text. They are not called "halakhah l'Moshe mi'Sinai." They are *Takkanot.* But none of them is described in the Talmud text as having been instituted *mipne tikkun ha'olam.* For the rabbis, Tannaim and Amoraim alike, the phrase's use was not justified in connection with them. The ancients, they apparently felt, had special rights to divine the divine will before the processes of *torah she-be-al peh* were instituted.

We must inquire briefly into the uses of *taken* in *Pirke Avot,* the non-halakhic sayings of the Tannaim which were collected and appended to the fourth section of the Mishnah. Do these ethical maxims give us any clues regarding the origins of *mipne tikkun ha'olam?*

The word *taken* appears three times in *Pirke Avot.*

v'hatken azm'cha hlmod torah she-einah yerusha lach.

"Rabbi Yossi says: "Make thyself *fit* for the study of Torah, for it will not be thine [automatically] by inheritance.""[4]

In the posttalmudic eras, the *Tikkun* of the individual person became a major preoccupation of Jewish scholars and writers.

Rabbi Ya'akov omer ha-olam hazeh domeh lifrozdor bifne ha-olam haba; hatken azm'cha bifrozdor k'dei she-tikanes litraklin.

"Rabbi Yaakov says: "This world is like an ante-room before the world-to-come. Prepare yourself in the ante-room so that you may enter the banquet-hall" (*Pir. Av.* 4:21).

Rabbi Akiva said: *ve-hadin din emet ve-hakol metukan lis'udah.*

". . . the judgment is a judgment of truth; and everything is prepared for the banquet" (*Pir. Av.* 3:20).

In *Pirke Avot,* we see, the Tannaim did not use the word *taken* to theorize about the role of the Jew and of *Mitzvot* in changing or improving the world.

One other concept which appears with some frequency in talmudic literature must be explored. Certain regulations are called *halakha le-Moshe mi-Sinai* ("a law given to Moses at Sinai"). The number is limited, although authorities differ on the specific count (*Otzer Yisrael 4:148ff.*). (The largest number suggested is fifty-two; most authorities place it between thirty and forty.) These appear to have been early post-Torah rules for which no Torah sanction could be found. They do not change Torah law and certainly do not uproot it.[5] They were accepted as part of oral Torah earlier than other Tannaitic *Takkanot.* (The phrase is also used aggadically.)[6] There is disagreement between Maimonides and Nachmanides regarding these rules. Maimonides considered them rabbinic in origin (*d'rabbanan*) and consequently of lesser authority than Torah law. Nachmanides called them *mid'Oraita,* Torah law (*Otzar Yisrael* 4:148ff.).

III

The Tannaim, the creators of rabbinic Judaism, whose thoughts and decisions are recorded in the Mishnah and in the Tosefta, were the historical instituters of the *Takkanah* and of the *G'zerah.*[7] It was also during the period of their work (fourth century B.C.E. to the end of the second century C.E.) that the phrase *mipne tikkun ha'olam* came into the vocabulary of Judaism.

There is substantial agreement among scholars of the period that the Takkanot of the Tannaim were responses to *Zorekh hasha'ah* ("the immediate need of the hour").[8] In fact, some are designated as *hora'at sha'ah* ("an order of the hour"), a specific case decision which might or might not be precedential.[9]

The Mishnah states (Chagigah 1:8): *heter nedarim porhin ba-avir ve-ein lahem al mah she-yismekhu* ("Permissions to dissolve vows hover in the air and have nothing to rest on"). The Gemara brings several disagreements and refutations of these *Takkanot*. Weiss designates them as *hora'at sha'ah*.[10]

Takkanot were not theoretical constructs. They were responses to communal necessity.

The functions of oral Torah in general were three, according to Weiss:[11] (1) new sources and bases were found for old regulations; (2) new and necessary regulations were worked out; (3) old regulations no longer feasible were uprooted. Most of the time, the hermeneutic rules of Hillel, as augmented by Rabbi Ishmael and others, served as the techniques for accomplishing these tasks. When it was not possible to use them, the *Takkanah* or the *G'zerah* was resorted to.

Though the schools of Hillel and Shammai disagreed on many matters, including fundamental ones like the extension of the process of Midrash—Torah text interpretation—both schools issued *Takkanot*. There is no indication in the Talmud that either school opposed the *Takkanot* of the other.[12]

The range of *Takkanot* in the hundreds of uses of the word in the Talmud is broad indeed. Rules requiring repairs to public utilities—watercourses, roads, and such—are called *Takkanot*. From matters of ritual acceptability (*taharah*), to *B'rachot* and when to say them, to civil litigation, rabbinic changes are called *Takkanot*.

Because the distinction between *mid'Oraita*, a regulation traceable directly or by indirection to the Torah, and *d'Rabbanan*, a direct rabbinic regulation, is such a sharp one in terms of relative authority, the status of the *Takkanah* in this regard is discussed often in the Talmud. The discussions are both general and specific. I shall be noting some of the specific Torah citations for specific *Takkanot*. But to the extent that a general Torah proof-text for *Takkanot* is indicated by the talmudic sages, it is found in Deut. 6:18: *ve-asita hayashar vehatov be-einei adonai*, "Do what is right and good in the sight of God . . . "

But the use of the Deuteronomy proof-text did not satisfy all the scholars, from the Talmud to our time. Zeitlin declared categorically of each *Takkanah:* "It must be supported by a Biblical verse."[13] The same scholar, however, also described the *Takkanah* as "an amendment of an earlier law, either Pentateuchal or old halaka" (emphasis mine).[14]

One example should indicate that, though many *Takkanot* had biblical verses connected with them, this was not always true.

In *Ketubot* 10a we read: "Rab Nachman said that Samuel said in the name of Rabbi Shimon ben El'azar: The scholars ordained (*tiknu*) for the daughters of Israel (as the *mohar* [bride's equity] in the *Ketubah,* which is clearly rabbinic in origin but which sometimes is given Torah-law status): for a virgin, two hundred *zuz* and for a widow a *maneh* (one hundred *zuz*) ... What have the sages accomplished with *their ordinance (b'takkanatam)*?" The statement that the *Ketubah* itself was instituted by the sages is repeated a sentence later in connection with the quality of land with which the *Ketubah's* requirement could be paid off. Because the poorest quality land could be utilized, the ordinance had to be rabbinic in origin, not Torah law. (In the Tosefta, a *Takkanah* regarding the *Ketubah* is validated *mipne tikkun ha'olam,* with no Torah verse indicated [Tos. Ket. 12:2].)

Two talmudic passages are of interest in connection with the concern about the rabbinic or Torah authority of *Takkanot.* In Gittin (64b–65a) there is a complex sequence, not relevant here. But it leads to the following passage:[15]

> Rabbi Hisda said: Waradan was reduced to silence. What could he have answered? [He could have said that] the Rabbis gave to their regulations the force of rules of the Torah. What could the other say to this? That the Rabbis gave to their regulations the force of rules of the Torah in matters which have some basis in the Torah, but not in a matter which has no basis in the Torah.

This qualification is not present in another passage (B. Avod. Zar. 349, Soncino trans., 165.)

> And should you say that leaven [on Passover] is forbidden by the Torah, whereas the wine of idolators is merely a Rabbinic prohibition, [surely it is an established principle] that *tikkun rabanan k'em d'oraita,* whatever is instituted by the Rabbis is [treated] as [that which is ordained] by the Torah!

It would appear that the sages were determined to give their Takkanot maximum power. The best way to do so, obviously, was to invest them with Torah (i.e., Divine) authority. That they could not always do so is clear in the Talmud. After all, some *Takkanot* openly repudiated and uprooted Torah law, as we shall see, and a Torah passage was not always available to justify this.

Though no traditionalist would necessarily agree, the words of Chaim Tchernowitz (1:178) must be given serious consideration: "In truth, one cannot support these matters (*Takkanot*) on the basis of law but only on the basis of the proper and moral, which the Sages called *mipne tikkun ha'olam*.[16]

IV

The phrase *mipne tikkun ha'olam* appears about thirty-five times in the Babylonian Talmud. Twenty-four of these are in tractate *Gittin* (divorces); this concentration is not without significance. The phrase appears often in the Jerusalem Talmud and in the Tosefta as well. There are no significant variations in meaning among these sources in the use or meaning of the phrase.

We must differentiate between *mipne tikkun ha'olam* and several other phrases whose usage is possibly similar to the meaning of our phrase in the talmudic literature.

The phrase *mipne tikkun hamizbe'ah* is used several times in the Talmud. One Mishnah reads (Gitten 5:5, Gittin 55a–b): *al hatat hagezulah shelo nod'ah larabim she-hi mekhaperet mipne tikkun hamizbe'ah.* ("A sin offering which has been stolen, so long as this is not known publicly, makes expiation, in order to *prevent loss* to the altar.") The Gemara accepts the reason in its exposition.

The preventive use of *mipne tikkun* is found in another connection in the same Mishnah: *ve-al hamareish nagazul she-b'na'o bavirah she-yitol et damav mipne takkanot hashavim.* " . . . if a beam which has been wrongfully appropriated is built into a palace [or any other building, say the commentators], restitution for it may be made in money so as not to put obstacles in the way of penitents." (That is, the actual beam need not be ripped out of the structure and returned to its rightful owner.)

During a long sequence about captives and related matters, we read (B. Gittin 45a): *ein mavrinin et hashvuyim mipne tikkun ha'olam. Rabban Shimon ben Gamliel omer, mipne takanat hashevuyin.*

"Captives should not be helped to escape, to *prevent abuses.* Rabban Shimon ben Gamliel says that [the reason is] to *prevent the ill treatment* of fellow captives (*mipne takkanot hashevayim*)."

Two different considerations are present in the general discussion of captives in our text. The *Takkanot* are offered (a) to prevent the abuse of existing captives and the expansion of banditry and piracy and/or (b) to prevent increased financial burden on the Jewish community, which considered the ransom of captives to be a major *Mitzvah*.

Of great interest is the phrase *mipne darkhe shalom*, which appears at least seventeen times in the Babylonian Talmud, and in the Jerusalem Talmud and the Tosefta as well. A glimpse of a few of them may help in differentiating between this phrase and *mipne tikkun ha'olam*.

Ir she-yeish bah yisrael vegoyim, haparnasim govin min Yisrael umin hagoyim mipne darkhe shalom mefarnesin aniyei goyim mipne darkhe shalom.

"In a city inhabited both by Israelites and by non-Jews, the local authorities collect both from Israelites and non-Jews *mipne darkhe shalom* and they support the poor both among the Israelites and non-Jews *mipne darkhe shalom*" (Tos. Gitt. 5:4) (Zuckermandel, p. 328).

The Tosefta goes on to rule: *Maspidin meitei goyim umenahmin avle goyim ukovrin meitei goyim mipne darkhe shalom.* "We eulogize non-Jewish dead and comfort their mourners and bury their dead (*mipne darkhe shalom*)."

Joseph Schechter differentiates between the two phrases as follows: "*Mipne darkhe shalom* is a *Takkanah* whose purpose it is to establish peace among peoples, to cut down on disputes and arguments. *Mipne tikkun ha'olam* is a *Takkanah* of Rabbinic origins [established] in order that a matter not bring on dismay or trouble."[17]

Though Schechter's verbiage is indefinite, it appears that the first phrase deals primarily if not totally with relations between Jews and non-Jews and the latter, our concern, is applicable within the Jewish community. As we shall see, this is not totally correct.

In the comprehensive encyclopedia, *Otzar Yisrael,* edited by J. D. Eisenstein, the same distinction is made. *Mipne darkhe shalom* is defined as a *Takkanah* "for the sake of the human community and to decrease the evil of non-Jews against Jews." A number of examples of each is cited (Otzar Yisrael 10:299ff.).

But there is a major exception in his list of examples from the Talmud text. In the Mishnah (Gittin 5:8) there is a listing of six *Takkanot* enacted *mipne darkhe shalom* in the interest of promoting peace. The first two have nothing to do with non-Jews: *Kohen kore rishon ve-aharav levi ve-aharav yisrael mipne darkhe shalom. Mo'orvin babayit yashan mipne darkhe shalom.* "A priest is called up first to read the Torah and after him a Levite and then a lay Israelite *in the interests of peace.* An Eruv is placed in the room where it has always been placed *in the interests of peace.*"

The distinction between *mipne tikkun ha'olam* and *mipne darkhe shalom* is not, then, precise and sharp. We are reminded of Tchernowitz's statement (p. 000) about the essentially moral quality of *mipne tikkun ha'olam,* which would certainly apply to *mipne darkhe shalom.* We shall continue to test that conjecture.

It might be well to do so by citing a number of specific *Takkanot* in connection with which the phrase *mipne tikkun ha'olam* is utilized as the reason for the decision.

1. The Tosefta collects a number of Takkanot which are enacted *mipne tikkun ha'olam.* Here we get a glimpse of the sweep of issues and problems to which the concept was applied.[18]

> At first they used to say that one who caused a consecrated thing to become unfit or consecrated and unconsecrated things, to which they later added even one who causes damage to another's wine (either through using it for a libation to a heathen idol or by mixing

acceptable wine with heathen wine), if it was done inadvertently he is not liable and if it was done deliberately, he is liable *mipne tikkun ha'olam*. If priests cause something in the sanctuary to become unfit through improper intention, if it was done inadvertently they are not liable, but if deliberately they are liable *mipne tikkun ha'olam*. If a person authorized by a court to administer a flogging inadvertently caused physical damage, he is not liable (for the various categories of compensation described in the Mishnah [Mishnah Bava Kama 8:1]), but if it was done deliberately he is liable *mipne tikkun ha'olam*. If a trained physician healing by the authority of the court causes harm to the patient inadvertently, he is not liable (as above), but if deliberately he is liable *mipne tikkun ha'olam*. If one conducts a therapeutic abortion with the permission of the court and harms the mother, if inadvertently there is no liability, and if deliberately there is liability *mipne tikkun ha'olam*."

2. Rabban Gamliel the Elder instituted a *Takkanah* that *ha-edim hotmin al haget*. "Witnesses sign their names to a Get, *mipne tikkun ha'olam* (B. Gittin 34b–35a)." In the Gemara it is asked, Is this rule only *mipne tikkun ha'olam*? The implication: Consequently it is of rabbinic origins only. The idea that *mipne tikkun ha'olam* is only rabbinic is disputed in the Talmud, as we shall see. A biblical proof-text is cited (Jer. 32:44): *vekhatov basefer vehatom* ("and write the deeds and seal them"). (The use of a prophetic text instead of a Torah text does not enter into the Gemara discussion.)

Rabba, in the name of Rabbi Eleazar, agreed since it was the delivery of the *Get* which made it effective, not its signing by witnesses at all. Nevertheless, it was instituted that witnesses must sign, since the witnesses to the delivery of the *Get* could die or leave the community, and ongoing evidence of validity was needed.

3. The Mishnah discusses the cancellation of a *Get* after it has been delivered to the woman (Mishnah Gittin 4:2; B. Gemara 33a). "In former times," we learn, "a man could bring together a Bet Din [of three] wherever he was to cancel the *Get*. Rabban Gamliel the Elder laid down a *Takkanah* that this should not be done, *mipne tikkun ha'olam*.

In the Gemara two different reasons are given to explain why the change was *mipne tikkun ha'olam*: to prevent *mamzerut* (if she married again and had a child, not knowing that the *Get* had been canceled), and to prevent wife-desertion.

Nevertheless, the new ruling was challenged. In this case, *mipne tikkun ha'olam* did not prevail!

4. Whether or not to adduce *mipne tikkun ha'olam* as the basis for a ruling can come under dispute in the Talmud (B. Gittin 45b, 46b). The Mishnah lays down several rulings regarding the right of men to remarry after divorces for causes which have proven groundless,

including vows made by the woman. Then a case is brought in which the man has vowed to divorce his wife, does so, and thereafter decides to remarry her, which is permitted. The sequence ends *mipne tikkun ha'olam.*

The Gemara asks, What *Tikkun Olam* is here? Rabbi Sheshet said that it referred to the earlier clauses in the Mishnah, but not to the last one. Ravina insisted that it did refer to the last clause, but negatively: there was no ground for forbidding the remarriage on the grounds of *mipne tikkun ha'olam.*

5. The propriety of utilizing *mipne tikkun ha'olam* as the grounds for a decision arose in another situation. In the Tosefta we read:[19] *ein osin ketuvat ishah min hametaltelin mipne tikkun ha'olam.* ("One does not set up a woman's *Ketubah* on movables [*M'talt'lin* are materials other than real estate] *mipne tikkun ha'olam.*) Rabbi Yossi said, "Why is this a matter of *mipne tikkun ha'olam*? Such an arrangement has no specific definitions." (That is, there can be no indications of possible variations in quality, as in real estate, and the woman could be cheated.)

6. There can be disagreement between two sages regarding the meaning of a *Takkanah*, though both agree that it is being enacted *mipne tikkun ha'olam.* The Mishnah reads (B. Gittin 40b–41a): *eved she-asa'o rabo apotiki la-aherim reshihraro, shurat hadin ein ha-eved hayav klum; ela mipne tikkun ha'olam kofin et-rabo ve-oseh oto ben horin ve-khotev shtar al damav.* ("If a [Hebrew] indentured servant is made security by the master for a debt to another person and he emancipates him, legally the servant is not liable for anything, but his master is compelled to emancipate him and the servant gives a bond for the purchase price.") Rav and Ulla disagree on who has done the emancipating and who gets the money, who in fact is "the master" referred to. But the basis for the *Takkanah* remains *tikkun ha'olam,* lest the master come up to the emancipated one in the marketplace and address him as "my servant," a humiliation.

7. Probably the most famous *Takkanah* known to us is Hillel's *prosbul.* The Gemara describes the matter (B. Gittin 34b, 36a–37b): "A *prosbul* prevents the remission of debts [in the Seventh Year, as required by Torah law in Deut. 15:1–3]. This is one of the *Takkanot* made by Hillel the Elder. For he saw that people were unwilling to lend money to one another, and disregarded the precept laid down in the Torah [Deut. 15:9], 'Beware lest you harbor the base thought,' the seventh year, the year of remission, is approaching, so that you are mean to your needy kinsman and give him nothing. He [Hillel] therefore decided to institute the *prosbul.*" The text of the document, given next in the Talmud text, transfers to the court the responsibility for collecting the debt, no matter what.

There is no pattern in the situations which utilize *mipne tikkun ha'olam.* Though issues of human relationships dominate my selection, it is not limited to them, and other purely ritual issues are found in the Talmud.

V

The *prosbul* was the occasion for discussion among the sages regarding the duration of a *Takkanah*—for the generation of its instituter only, or for future generations as well? The generalization appeared to be: it could be abolished only by a court greater in wisdom and in numbers than the instituting authority (B. Avodah Zarah 36a). The following dialogue between Samuel and Rabbi Nachman is instructive (B. Gittin 36b): "Samuel said: this prosbul is an *ulbana* on the part of the judges; if I am ever in a position, I will abolish it." [He implied that Hillel instituted it for his generation only. The word *ulbana* is discussed in some detail. It is translated by various authorities as "unwarranted assumption," "mere convenience," "arrogance." In sum, not everyone was happy with it.] But Rabbi Nachman said: "I would confirm it." Confirm it? Is it not already firmly established? What he meant was: I will add a rule that even if the *prosbul* is not actually written, it shall be regarded as written" (B. Gittin 36b).

It must be noted that, in the Jerusalem Talmud, there is a full discussion of the *prosbul* with no mention of *Tikkun Olam* at all (Jerusalem Sh'vi'it 10:1–2).

Hillel's *prosbul*, enacted *mipne tikkun ha'olam*, had a Torah source. What about other such Takkanot? There is much disagreement among authorities on this question, both within the Talmud and over the centuries down to our own time.

Two passages in the Talmud may or may not give us contradictory views. The first may suggest that an enactment *mipne tikkun ha'olam* is not Torah law (B. Gittin 47a–b).

The Mishnah: "If a man sells his field to a heathen, he has to buy annually the first fruits from him and bring them to Jerusalem, *mipne tikkun ha'olam.*" The purpose of the *Takkanah* is to try and prevent the sale of land to heathen, within the Land of Israel, and to make such a sale sufficiently expensive that the Jew might repurchase it. Torah law does not require the bringing of first fruits or tithes from the produce of the Land of Israel which is not owned by Jews.

The Gemara: "That is to say, the reason is *mipne tikkun ha'olam*, but the Torah itself does not require this." Is this a question or a statement? If the former, the Gemara's response is certainly inconclusive. If it is a statement, it stands.

The second passage, too, depends on the way it is read (B. Gittin

48b). There is a series of enactments in the Mishnah having to do with various payments which must be made from land of the highest quality, of medium quality, or of poor quality. At the end of the passage, the phrase *mipne tikkun ha'olam* appears. (There is one further enactment, not relevant here; it, too, ends with *mipne tikkun ha'olam*.) It is decided that the phrase refers, not to the last of the enactments in the series, but to all of them. Therefore, continues the Gemara: *mipne tikkun ha'olam de-oraita hi dikhtiv metav sadehu umetav karmo yeshalem*. There are two readings and, inevitably, two contradictory translations. "This *mipne tikkun ha'olam* is of Torah origins," is a possible one. Or: *mipne tikkun ha'olam?* "Of course not, it is of Torah origin." And Exodus is quoted. The translator, Rabbi E. Epstein, believed the first. But Solomon Freehof wrote: "I think that the translation in the Soncino of 48b is a mistaken translation. The translation indicates that the decision of estimating (from the best qualities of the land) is both of Torah and of Tikkun Olam. However, the correct translation is evident to me as follows: In 48b: You say it is because of Tikkun Olam? No, it is from the Torah, as it is written. . . . "[20]

Freehof evidently concludes that *mipne tikkun ha'olam* must, at least in this case, be considered purely rabbinic enactment. Schechter goes even further. He calls our phrase a "Takkanah of Rabbinic origins," with no qualifications.[21]

VI

It is as impossible to designate the legal status of *tikkun olam* in the Talmud as it is to define the phrase in a way which will cover all its uses in talmudic literature. Most of the classical medieval commentators appear to have taken it for granted as an idiom which is used periodically to serve as basis for one form of *Takkanah* or another. But there are exceptions. Nachmanides, in his *Sefer Ha'Zchut,* a detailed critique of Abraham ibn Daud's critique of Alfasi's halakhic commentary on the Talmud, indulges in a long excursus on *Tikkun Olam* in connection with the need, or lack of it, of an oath from a person restoring a lost article. He appears to distinguish three categories of *halachot* Torah, rabbinic, and Tikkun Olam.[22] Isaac Di Trani (the Elder), thirteenth-century Italian scholar, in his misnamed *Tosefot Rid,* appears to agree with Nachmanides and gives to decisions *mipne tikkun ha'olam* almost the status of natural law. When no other technique or method is applicable, this can be virtually assumed.

No decisive conclusion is possible, it seems to me.

Before I attempt to undertake some tentative suggestions, one more question must be looked at. I have not yet tried to define *mipne tikkun ha'olam*. Both operative words, *tikkun* and *olam*, present complexities.

Olam literally means "world"—the whole world. That certainly is the way the phrase is used in our time as a major mitzvah for contemporary Jews and for the Jewish community: to move the entire world toward our messianic goals. It is universalistic.

It was not so in the Talmud. None of the material which has been adduced here could serve to bring me to the conclusion that the talmudic sages were speaking of all humanity in their enactments.

Rashi was totally on target, it seems to me, in his comment on a passage in B. Shabbat.[23] The Gemara says:

"Whoever can forbid his household [to commit a sin] but does not, is seized [i.e., punished] for [the sins of] his household; [if he can forbid] his fellow citizens, he is seized for [the sins of] his fellow citizens; if the whole world, he is seized for [the sins of] the whole world."

Rashi's comment on "the whole world": *bekhol yisrael kagon melekh o nasi she-efshar limhot she-yar'in mipanav umekayemim devaran.*

("All *of Israel,* as a king or a president [of the Sanhedrin or of a local Jewish community] for whom it is possible to forbid because they are afraid of him and will fulfill his demands.")

Many translations appear for the word *Tikkun.* Some of them:

"precaution for the general good"	(Danby)
"to prevent abuses"	(Soncino ed. Babylonian Talmud)
"for good order"	(Strack)
"amendment"	(Zeitlin)

"Reformation," as in the biblical reformations of Josiah and of Hezekiah. I cannot find the source of this usage. But Tchernowitz specifically denies it. He calls it an inaccurate product of historicocritical thinkers.[24]

It seems to me that, in the Talmud, *tikkun olam* means "for the proper order of the Jewish community." (The relative concentration of its uses in tractate Gittin is now easier to understand. Marriage and the family were the matrix of Jewish communal life.)

It is a long way from that definition to "build a better world." The evolution was a tortuous one over many centuries. It needs tracing.

VII

What has been learned in this exploration to begin to build a structure of meanings for the phrase *mipne tikkun ha'olam* which can move across the centuries to our day?

1. It was well established in the Tannaitic period. It always appears in the same wording, distinctively.
2. It is clear that it was not a full-blown legal concept to be applied always when technically appropriate. It has some of that aura, but the cautious student will hesitate before assigning such a status definitely in the Talmud.
3. But on the other hand, the sages themselves were sufficiently acquainted with the implications of the phrase that they could use it with some frequency and with a degree of consistency while covering a rather wide range of subjects. It was certainly not limited to the "moral," as suggested by Tchernowitz.
4. It is difficult to argue from the negative, but I am struck by the degree to which the medieval commentators followed the talmudic sages in not discussing the phrase or making an issue of it. This phenomenon is still true. The indices of books about talmudic ideas and methods and about rabbinic tradition conspicuously do not list *Tikkun Olam* as a subject for exploration.

I look forward to further digging into the uses of *Tikkun Olam* over the centuries: in the Geonic literature, in later medieval writings, in *Kabbalah,* and among Reform and Conservative thinkers over the past two centuries.

Notes

1. Brown et al., *Hebrew and English Lexicon of the Old Testament,* p. 1075.
2. Jewish Publication Society, *The Writings* (1981), p. 401;
   Jewish Publication Society, *The Holy Scriptures* (1917), p. 996.
3. Box and Oesterley, trans., in Charles ed., p. 496.
4. *Pirke Avot* 2:17, Goldin trans. Others: "prepare yourself . . . " Subsequent references will be abbreviated in the text.
5. Chaim Tchernowitz, *Toldot Ha'Halachah,* 1:29.
6. Cf. Menachot 29b, the most famous Aggadah about Halachah l'Moshe Mi'Sinai.
7. A *G'zerah* is a rabbinic enactment, without necessary Torah sanction, whose purpose it was to prevent evil or sin within the Jewish community.
8. Tchernowitz, 1:175f.
9. A full discussion can be found of *Hora'a and Hora'at Sha'ah* in *Otzar Yisrael,* 4:120ff.
10. I. H. Weiss, *Dor Dor V'Dorshav,* 1:86.
11. Ibid., 2:42.
12. Ibid., 1:174.
13. In *Jewish Quarterly Review,* N.S., 39 (no. 1): 26.
14. Ibid., N.S., 54 (no. 4): 288.
15. Soncino trans., p. 306.

16. In the Soncino trans. of Ketubot 49, the phrase "moral duty" is used to translate *mitzvah*.
17. Joseph Schecter, *Otzar Ha'Talmud* (Tel Aviv, 1973), 239ff.
18. Tosefta Gittin 4:5–7; Zuckermandel, 327f.
19. Tosefta Ketubot 12:2; Zuckermandel, p. 274.
20. Personal letter to me dated December 15, 1978.
21. Schechter, p. 240. This view is buttressed by the sharp distinction made between a Torah law and *mipne tikkun ha'olam* in B. Gittin 53a.
22. In B. Gittin, see *Sefer Ha'Zchut*, 25b–26a of Alfasi, and commentaries in Vilna ed.
23. Rashi on B. Shabbat 54b, headed mipne *ha-olam tikkun*.
24. Tchernowitz, 2:198.

John T. Pawlikowski is professor of social ethics at the Catholic Theological Union. He has written six books and contributed to several others, especially those which deal with interfaith issues related to the Shoah. *He served on the United States Holocaust Memorial Council, as well as on several committees and commissions on Jewish-Christian relations. He is the former chairperson of the Catholic-Jewish Commission sponsored by the Archdiocese of Chicago and the Chicago Board of Rabbis. The Reverend Pawlikowski has been in several Jewish-Christian dialogues with Herman Schaalman and lectured at Emanuel Congregation several times. He currently serves with Herman on the advisory committee for the Center for Christian-Jewish Studies at the Chicago Theological Seminary.*

John Pawlikowski adds to the growing scholarship in the area of Jewish-Christian dialogue. He offers a critique of Christian thought through the focus of the covenant. How does Christianity integrate the Jewish value of the covenant as a category of Jewish identity? Pawlikowski continues to force Christians to draw away from their use of triumphalism and exclusivity. Christian thinkers cannot be honest to their own Christian faith and not respond to Pawlikowski's challenge of a Jewish covenant that continues to live, without diminishing Christianity.

The Jewish Covenant: Its Continuing Challenge for Christian Faith

John T. Pawlikowski

In recent years we have witnessed a marked increase in Christian acknowledgment of the ongoing validity of the Jewish covenant as well as an enhanced awareness of the church's intimate connection with this covenant. This link was clearly established by Pope John Paul II in a remark originally made to an international catechetical meeting in Rome in 1982, and repeated in the 1985 Vatican-issued *Notes on the Correct Way to Present Jews and Judaism in Preaching and Catechesis in the Roman Catholic Church*:

> Because of the unique relations that exist between Christianity and Judaism—"Linked together at the very level of their identity" (John Paul II, March 6, 1982)—relations "founded on the design of the God of the covenant" (*ibid.*), the Jews and Judaism should not occupy an occasional and marginal place in catechesis: Their presence there is essential and should be organically integrated.[1]

A similar theme is sounded by Cardinal Carlo Martini of Milan, in a 1984 address to the International Council of Christians and Jews. He argues that deepened relations between Christians and Jews are vital to the future health of the church itself:

> What is here at stake is not simply the more or less lively continuation of a dialogue. It is the awareness of Christians of their bond with Abraham's stock and of the consequences of this fact, not only for doctrine, discipline, liturgy and spiritual life of the Church, but also for its mission in the world of today.[2]

113

Cardinal Martini makes another crucial point in this same address: the original split between Judaism and Christianity must be viewed as a schism, not a permanent rupture. As with all schisms in history, Catholicism was impoverished by loss of living contact with its Judaic roots. He puts it this way:

> Every schism and division in the history of Christianity entails the deprivation of the body of the Church from contributions which could be very important for its health and vitality, and produces a certain lack of balance in the living equilibrium of the Christian community. If this is true of every great division in Church history, it was especially true of the first great schism which was perpetrated in the first two centuries of Christianity.[3]

Following the lead set for us by the Vatican *Notes* and major Catholic leaders such as Cardinal Martini, we need to probe Jewish covenantal understandings for their potential contribution to Christian faith expression today. Such probing, let it be said clearly, can never stop with biblical Judaism. It must encompass the reinterpretations of the covenantal tradition by rabbinic, medieval, and modern Judaism as well—a point clearly emphasized in the recent *Notes*.[4] To restrict our examination of the Jewish covenantal tradition to the Hebrew Scriptures, as positive as our interpretation may prove, would involve implicit stereotyping. For we would be falling back into the classical pattern—Judaism's creative contribution ended with the Christ Event and whatever valuable religious insights are to be found in pre-Christian Judaism have been subsumed by Christianity.

Turning to the Jewish biblical tradition, we find several dominant themes which, while generally present in Christianity to some degree, have lost the centrality given them in Judaism. The absence of these themes has frequently impoverished and even distorted the church's self-understanding.

The first of these Jewish biblical themes is the sense of peoplehood, of community. There is a strong sense in Judaism that individual salvation must take second place to the salvation of humankind. Only when the whole human family has attained its salvific completeness can the individual human person be considered fully saved in a personal sense. This sense of peoplehood is an integral part of the covenantal tradition of Sinai in which the revelation of God's presence was given to Moses for the well-being and mission of the whole people rather than simply for the good of the individual.

As we examine Christian history, we see that so very often Christian faith degenerated into an almost exclusively individualistic sense of the divine-human encounter. Personal salvation assumed a primacy that it never had in biblical Judaism and which it never had for Jesus (or even for

Paul, contrary to later interpretations of his thought). This individualistic approach to Christian faith often was accompanied by an other-worldly/ahistorical (even at times antihistorical) interpretation of spirituality. The world for Christians frequently became a place they longed to escape from rather than one they were called to transform as a people along with their Jewish partners.

The individualistic tendency even infiltrated the most central of religious acts for many Christians—the Eucharist. The origins of this primal sacrament are directly rooted in the pharisaic communal meals which formed a crucial part of Jesus' constructive appropriation of Second Temple Judaism. The Eucharist tended to become in later Christianity an occasion when the individual Christian believer offered personal prayers to God while the priest performed sacred mysteries on the altar. Such a tendency mitigated any communal consciousness among the individual believers assembled for worship.

It was only with the liturgical reforms of the Second Vatican Council that this began to change. Picking up on its definition of the church as the people of God, a notion that was absolutely central to the reformation produced by the Council, Vatican II restored Christianity's historical and communal orientation which had been lost in the original schism with Judaism. This is clearly seen in its attempts to reform Eucharistic practice. And a check of bibliography for this Eucharistic reform will clearly show that many of the key liturgical scholars who shaped this reform were significantly influenced by new contacts with the Jewish liturgical tradition beginning with the Hebrew Scriptures and the sacred meals which formed a core element in Second Temple Judaism. This is but one example of how the enhanced Christian-Jewish dialogue not only has benefited intergroup understanding but also has positively influenced the general renewal of Christian faith expression widespread in our time.

Liberation theology, controversial in many ecclesiastical leadership circles in the church but popular with significant numbers of Christians at the local and regional levels in the Third World, is another example of some constructive appropriation of Judaism's communal/historical sense. Several of the leading theologians in this movement have turned to the Exodus covenantal tradition as the inescapable starting point for the ongoing process of human liberation from all forms of oppression. One cannot fully understand the liberating mission of Jews, according to Gustavo Gutierrez and Jose Miguez Bonino, without seeing how it flows from the liberation of the people Israel recorded in the Hebrew Scriptures. Without this positive connection with the Exodus tradition of liberation, interpretations of Jesus' preaching frequently become overly individualistic ("Jesus as my personal Savior") and ahistorical.

To be totally honest, it has to be said, there are also disturbing trends in liberation theology regarding Judaism. Not all of the theologians related to this movement view the Exodus covenantal tradition as positively as Gutierrez and Bonino. Examples of this are Leonardo Boff and Jon Sobrino. They not only are silent about any link between the liberating spirit of Jesus' proclamation and the liberating spirit of Exodus, but they reintroduce the notion of Jewish responsibility for his death that seems to return us to the unfortunate days prior to the II Vatican Council and its clear repudiation of the deicide charge. And even Gutierrez and Bonino are not free of legitimate criticism for their inadequate understanding of the role of Torah in biblical Judaism, for the unsatisfactory way in which they tie the Exodus tradition of liberation to the Christ Event, and for their silence on Jewish liberation in our time.[5] But given the history of Christian neglect of the Hebrew Scriptures as a resource for contemporary articulation of the Christian faith, the positive use of the Exodus covenantal tradition by Gutierrez and Bonino, though in need of substantial reformulation, represents a step forward in the "re-Judaization of Christian theology," as Robert Gordis has termed the process.

Before leaving the discussion of liberation theology, mention should be made of another way in which the Jewish biblical and rabbinic traditions can correct distortions often present in Christian theology. The issue I have in mind here is that of the meaning of authentic freedom. This has been a major focal point in liberation theology. Historically it has also been a central concern for European theology, especially in its Protestant manifestations, and the basis for the disastrous contrast between Judaism and Christianity as religions of law and freedom, respectively.

The overwhelming majority of Christian theologians have failed to appreciate the richness of the term *Torah* and its constructive place in any comprehensive understanding of human political liberation. Far too often the liberation seen by Christians as integral to Jesus' message is spoken of in very generalist terms. In reality, liberation will not be fully realized in a society until it has been transformed from political/religious ideals into concrete sociocultural structures. This is what the Torah process tried to do. Jesus himself, given his close relationship with the Pharisaic movement, was certainly aware of the need for this. The notion of "oral Torah" that became pivotal for the reforms in Jewish society introduced by the Pharisees and picked up by Jesus and the early church certainly expanded the understanding of Torah Second Temple Judaism inherited from the biblical period. But it did not totally replace the earlier Torah tradition.

Unlike Jesus and apostolic Christianity, later church theology often lost touch with this Torah tradition, much to its own harm. The Christian-Jewish dialogue, by enabling Christians to understand better the function of Torah, can help direct the Church away from mere generalized statements about the freedom it believes was made present through the Christ Event to actions that create concrete liberating structures in human society. Far too often Christians naively express preference for the unspecified statements about freedom in Christ in the New Testament over the lists of legal requirements found in the Hebrew Scriptures, without recognizing that a notion of freedom that does not move us into the realm of the concrete, as the Torah process does, will prove terribly ineffective in terms of the actual realization of freedom on a long-term basis.

Another important dimension of the Jewish covenantal tradition that can positively influence Christian faith is its sense of the human person as co-creator, as responsible for history and for the world God created. This notion of co-creatorship emerges both from the biblical tradition and from the later Jewish mystical tradition. In light of the *Shoah,* it has taken on a new importance. The American Catholic Bishops' statement on energy released in 1981 highlighted the enhanced co-creational role of humanity. And this emphasis has been repeated by Pope John Paul II in his encyclical letter *Laborem Exercens* ("On Human Work") as well as by the American Catholic bishops in their letters on peace and economic justice.

Critical for the recovery of this Jewish co-creationship concept by Christians is the reacceptance of the notion that the salvation of human-kind is a task yet to be accomplished. The premature claim of Christianity for so long a time that the messianic kingdom had arrived fully in Christ seriously undercut a sense of responsibility for the destiny of the world. Now that the theological discussions among Christian scholars connected with the dialogue have resulted in the discarding of simplistic assertions about total fulfillment in Christ,[6] Christians are faced with the need to recover a religious basis for continuing social involvement in human affairs. Nothing will serve as a better bedrock for such a theology of justice than this biblically based theme of shared co-creational responsibilities between God and humankind.

There is yet another way in which renewed exposure to the Jewish covenantal tradition will constructively affect Christianity's vision of the human person. By and large Judaism has always had a more positive image of the human person than Christianity. Catholicism has been somewhat better in this regard than Protestantism. But both have tended to stress sinfulness rather than goodness in their theologizing about human nature. Judaism is not ignorant, of course, of a sinful drive in the human person. But it does not stress this as dominant in the way Christianity generally has.

Lack of contact with the Jewish biblical and rabbinic viewpoint on human goodness by Christian theology for many centuries has resulted in a distorted emphasis on certain statements in the Pauline writings without counterbalancing them with other parts of the Hebrew Scriptures and the New Testament. Some scholars such as Krister Stendahl,[7] now bishop of Stockholm, would even argue that later Protestant theologians projected

117

back into Paul guilt feelings arising from their own introspection which would have been foreign to Paul the pharisaic Jew. As a result, there has been an exaggerated emphasis on the sinfulness of the human person in Christianity that can be modified through contact with Judaism. While Judaism may also need to do some rethinking about the innate power of evil in light of the *Shoah* experience, Christianity's approach stands in even greater need of correction. Since so much of Christianity's approach to human sinfulness, especially in Catholicism, has been related to sexuality, increased interchange with the Jewish tradition may help restore the far more positive outlook on sexuality as an avenue for experiencing the divine presence found in both the Hebrew Scriptures and the later Jewish mystical tradition.

A connected issue that can be raised here is that of the Christian understanding of forgiveness of sin and, for sacramentally based Christian denominations, the sacrament of Penance. For centuries the understanding and liturgical celebration of forgiveness has focused on the cleansing of the individual sinner from the stain of sin. This rather distorted interpretation of forgiveness and the sacrament of Penance was due in large part to the teachings of the Irish monks in the pre-medieval period. Unfortunately they took the church's understanding of forgiveness far afield, cutting it from its roots in the Jewish tradition where it involved reconciliation with the person or persons affected by one's sinful action rather than inner cleansing. The New Testament in its story of the return of the Prodigal Son and its injunction not to dare offer gifts at the altar until one has made amends with the person against whom the sinful act has been directed carries on this authentic Jewish spirit. We can hope that Christians will rediscover this understanding of forgiveness and Penance through the modern encounter with Judaism.

The final issue I would raise in relation to the biblical part of the Jewish covenantal tradition is the potential impact of the Jewish land tradition on Christian faith expression. Christian scholars such as Walter Brueggemann and W. D. Davies have completed recent important studies on this question in the past several years.[8] It is not possible here to go into the details of their analysis. Both assert, however, that failure to grasp the insights of this land tradition not only leaves Christians with a falsified picture of Judaism but also deprives Christianity of a vital rootedness in history and of a full appreciation of the role of nonhuman creation in the emergence of the eschatological kingdom. While I would maintain that there are some fundamental differences between Christianity and Judaism regarding the present meaning of the land tradition,[9] the church's *faith* expression must always be firmly rooted in the earth. Far too often concentration on the "heavenly Jerusalem" as a supposed replacement for the Jewish "earthly Jerusalem" has led to an excessively ethereal spirituality in the churches.

Brueggemann writes partially in reaction to the school of New Testament exegesis associated with the German scholar Rudolf Bultmann, whom he holds responsible for much of the loss of the land tradition in recent Christian theology. This Bultmannian approach to the New Testament mistakenly tried to free the New Testament from the biblical land tradition in favor of personal, existential meaning for the individual believer acquired through instantaneous and radical decisions of obedience. The central problem for Christians, as Brueggemann sees it, "is not emancipation but *rootage,* not meaning but *belonging,* not separation from community but *location* with it, not isolation from others but *placement* deliberately between the generation of promise and fulfillment."[10] Both the Hebrew Scriptures and the New Testament, Brueggemann maintains, present homelessness as the central human problem. They seek to respond to it in terms of promise and gift. No truly believing Christian can avoid making land a principal category in his or her belief system. On this point Brueggemann is unbending. "Landed" faith is as much an imperative for Christians as it is for Jews.

W. D. Davies nuances the required Christian appropriation of the biblical land tradition much more than Brueggemann. Davies feels that after all is said and done the New Testament must be described as ambivalent regarding the land promises found in the Hebrew Scriptures. Strata exist within the New Testament that take a critical view of these promises, and one passage (Acts 7) rejects it outright. But other passages are to be found where the land, the Temple, and Jerusalem in a clearly geographical sense are looked upon quite positively in terms of their continued meaning for the Christian gospel.

The New Testament, Davies concludes, leaves us with a twofold witness with respect to the land tradition. On one hand, there is a sense in which faith in Christ takes the believer beyond the land, Jerusalem, and the Temple. Yet its history and theology cannot escape concern about these realities. In the New Testament, holy space exists wherever Christ is or has been. The Christ Event has "universalized" the land tradition in a significant way, but it has not eliminated its centrality. Davies would no doubt concur with Brueggemann that the Bultmannian approach is very misguided in this regard. Davies summarizes the impact of the Christ Event on the land tradition in this way:

> It (i.e., the New Testament) personalizes "holy space" in Christ, who, as a figure of history, is rooted in the land; he cleansed the Temple and died in Jerusalem, and lends his glory to these and to the places where he was, but, as Living Lord, he is also free to move wherever he wills. To do justice to the personalism of the New Testament, that is, to its Christocentricity, is to find the clue to the various strata of tradition that we have traced and to the attitudes they reveal: to their freedom from space and their attachment to spaces.[11]

There is yet one other way in which contact with the land dimension of the Jewish covenantal tradition can enhance Christian faith expression today. In much of Christian liturgy we have lost almost all consciousness of the need to proclaim the glory of creation. Our liturgical cycle is virtually bereft of any festivals which highlight God's continuing presence in nonhuman creation. Such sensitivity must be resurrected by Christians if the churches are to assume a leadership role in protecting our ecological heritage.

Before ending this consideration of the biblical dimensions of the Jewish covenantal tradition and its potentially positive impact on contemporary Christian faith, several cautionary points are in order. First of all, it must be stressed that the approach taken above in no way implies that Judaism exists merely for Christian faith completion. As Cardinal Joseph Bernardin of Chicago declared in a November 1984 address to the American Jewish Committee, Judaism carries ongoing theological meaning in its own right apart from any significance it continues to have for Christian faith. Jews do not need Christian affirmation for their own faith integrity.

We must also be careful how we use the term "people of God" in Christian theology. Though this term is important in returning Christian faith to the communal context, after the schism with Judaism we frequently lost sight of the fact that it must be used in a way that clearly affirms that the Jewish people also remain "people of God." This crucial Vatican II image of the church must not be allowed to become an occasion for Christian theological imperialism vis-à-vis the People Israel. The noted ecumenical biblical scholar Gerard S. Sloyan makes this point forcefully and quite correctly in an essay written several years ago:

> The very eagerness of the Christian bodies to employ the term "people of God" to describe themselves only is an indication of how little alerted they are to their own coming to birth from a Jewish mother who continues in good health. The problem is therefore as much one of an understanding in depth of Christian origins as it is of ecumenical relations with the Jews.[12]

Finally, the aspects of the Jewish biblical tradition outlined above must not be viewed simply as important ancillary themes for the Christian faith. Combined under the more general theme of the Sinai Covenant they need to be seen as standing on equal footing with the Incarnational revelation of the Christ Event in terms of the totality of Christian Faith. A. Roy Eckardt, the pioneer scholar in Christian-Jewish relations, put it well in one of his earliest writings: "If there is a true sense in which God has manifested himself uniquely in Jesus of Nazareth, it must be said that the mystery of this divine act is in principle no greater than the sacred acts through which Israel was originally elected."[13]

This essay has concentrated its attention on the biblical dimensions of the Jewish covenantal tradition. Before ending, however, it would be important to lift up at least two areas where postbiblical Jewish reinterpretations of the covenantal tradition will prove most important for Christian theologizing in our day: the problem of God after the *Shoah* and the link between spirituality and the quest for justice. Space will permit only a brief mention of each. In other works I have written far more extensively on these two subjects.[14]

The God question has become a central issue for Jewish theology after the *Shoah*. I concur with David Tracy that it must become so for Christianity as well.[15] The discussion will be a complex one because of the growing controversy and polarization about this issue in Jewish scholarship. Most Orthodox Jewish writers, such as Michael Wyschogrod and David Hartman, have argued for the understanding of the *Shoah* as a monstrous example of the recurring problem of evil. While we must continue to mourn the victims, our appreciation of the God–human community relationship must have the same starting point it has always had: the Sinai covenant. Some Christian theologians involved in the dialogue with Jews, such as Paul Van Buren, support this orientation.

On the other end of the spectrum stand people like Richard Rubenstein, Irving Greenberg, Emil Fackenheim, and Arthur Cohen. While major differences exist among them, they are agreed that the description of the God–human community relationship needs fundamental restatement after the *Shoah*. I generally stand on their side of the fence, though I am not entirely happy with any of their present formulations. All of them, I believe, leave us with an overly impotent God. I feel we must discard any simplistic notions of a "commanding" God after the experience of the Holocaust. But we still need to understand the continued direct influence of a "compelling" God. However we come out on this issue, we must as Christian theologians take very seriously these contemporary Jewish reflections on the meaning of the covenantal tradition.

As for the question of the spirituality/social justice link, it has become apparent to me that both the rabbinic tradition and the Jewish mystical tradition can prove of significant help to current Christian discussions of this vital issue. A better grasp of the Mitzvah system developed by rabbinic Judaism will show Christians a model for integrating the experience of God and the performance of the just deed. As Max Kadushin has put it, for the rabbis a particular mitzvah was always a communication by God here and now.[16] The same can be said for the Jewish mystical tradition. Rabbi Herbert Weiner, following the lead of the great Rabbi Nachman, says that for Judaism the real problem in the mystical experience was not the *r'tzo,* the going out, but the *shuv,* the return. How to transmute the lofty mystical illumination into this-worldly terms was the problem that concerned Jewish mysticism in the view of Weiner.[17]

121

Christianity has often experienced deep polarization within its ranks between those who would give priority to justice concerns and those who have chosen to emphasize the path of mystical union with God. Hence it is possible for the church to learn a great deal about unifying these concerns from an examination of the Jewish mystical tradition. This is likewise true with regard to the writings of modern exponents of the Jewish mystical traditions such as the first chief rabbi of Israel, Rav Kook, or the legendary giant of our time, Abraham Heschel.

The above examination, though skeletal, tries to make the basic points that a Christian faith which has not incorporated the major themes of the ongoing Jewish covenantal tradition is an incomplete and impoverished faith. It must be stressed over and over again that a Christian who takes only the New Testament as the basis for contemporary faith has in fact selected a truncated version of Jesus' message. I believe Christianity will not even approach spiritual wholeness, spiritual *Shalom,* until it reestablishes an ongoing link with the Jewish covenantal tradition. How Jews might understand such a link from their side is also a vital question. But it is something that Jewish leaders will have to take a lead in examining.

Notes

1. See *Origins* 15 (July 4, 1985): 103.
2. "The Relation of the Church to the Jewish People," *From the Martin Buber House* 6 (September 1984): 9.
3. Ibid., p. 13.
4. See *Origins,* p. 107.
5. On problems in liberation theology's approach to Judaism, see my volume, *Christ in the Light of the Christian-Jewish Dialogue* (New York/Ramsey: Paulist Press, 1982), pp. 59–73.
6. See *Christ in the Light,* pp. 8–75; also see Franz Mussner, *Tractate on the Jews* (Philadelphia: Fortress Press, 1984), and Paul Van Buren, *A Christian Theology of the People Israel* (New York: Seabury Press, 1983).
7. Krister Stendahl, "The Apostle Paul and the Introspective Conscience of the West," *Harvard Theological Review* 56 (July 1963): 199–216.
8. Walter Brueggemann, *The Land* (Philadelphia: Fortress Press, 1977); W. D. Davies, *The Gospel and the Land* (Berkeley: University of California Press, 1974), and *The Territorial Dimension of Judaism* (Berkeley: University of California Press, 1982).
9. See *Christ in the Light,* pp. 127–33.
10. *The Land,* p. 187.
11. *The Gospel,* p. 367.
12. "Who are the People of God?" in *Standing before God,* ed. Asher Finkel and Lawrence Frizzell (New York: Ktav, 1981), p. 113.

13. *Elder & Younger Brothers* (New York: Schocken Books, 1973), p. 142.
14. See my essay "Christian Ethics and the Holocaust—a Dialogue with Post-Auschwitz Judaism," in the forthcoming volume, *The Future of Holocaust Studies: a Search for Directions,* F. Burton Nelson, and my essay, "Spirituality and the Quest for Justice," in *Liturgical Foundations of Social Policy in the Catholic and Jewish Traditions,* ed. Daniel F. Polish and Eugene J. Fisher (Notre Dame: University of Notre Dame Press, 1983), pp. 79–97.
15. "Religious Values after the Holocaust: A Catholic View," in *Jews and Christians after the Holocaust,* ed. Abraham J. Peck (Philadelphia: Fortress Press, 1982).
16. *Worship and Ethics: A Study in Rabbinic Judaism* (Evanston, Ill.: Northwestern University Press, 1964), p. 225.
17. Herbert Weiner, *9½ Mystics: The Kabbala Today* (New York: Holt, Rinehart & Winston, 1969), pp. 304–5.

Jakob J. Petuchowski is Sol and Arlene Bronstein Professor of Judeo-Christian Studies and Research Professor of Jewish Theology and Liturgy at the Hebrew Union College–Jewish Institute of Religion in Cincinnati. He has written or edited more than thirty books, contributed to several encyclopedias, and published more than five hundred articles in various languages. He has lectured at several universities, including Oxford, Harvard, and several West German universities. He has been awarded the Order of Merit First Class by the president of the Federal Republic of Germany. Like Herman Schaalman, Jakob Petuchowski fled Nazi Germany. Herman Schaalman brought Petuchowski together with a group of covenantal theologians in the early sixties, and their friendship has flourished over the last three decades. Professor Petuchowski has lectured at Emanuel Congregation several times.

Jakob Petuchowski gives us another gem of rabbinic thought, in both process and content. Petuchowski, the consummate teacher of texts, asks several taxing questions about the seriousness with which we use language. The scholarship is a model for how the covenant is itself a way of thinking about Jewish thinking. Rabbinic thinking is a contemporary model for Judaism, because as Petuchowski shows once again, covenantal thinking emphasizes thinking as a process, rather than a content. Petuchowski helps us to realize how important the question is to Jewish thought.

The Beauty of God

Jakob J. Petuchowski

The God who, to the accompaniment of thunders, once proclaimed at Mount Sinai: "You shall not make for yourself a sculptured image!" (Ex. 20:4), is supposed to be beautiful? The God who said of Himself: "You cannot see My face, for man may not see Me and live," (Ex. 33:20), is supposed to be apprehended in aesthetic categories? Jewish monotheistic sensitivity must surely shrink back from such a thought.

Or must it? There is love in the world, and we regard God as the Source of Love. There is the search after righteousness in the world, and we see God as the Fountain of Righteousness. We human beings, even (or is it particularly?) in this technocratic world, want to be regarded as persons, and not as statistical numbers. However, if we claim personhood for ourselves, then it would follow that the Creator, to whom we owe our existence and our personhood, must have at least as much personhood as His creatures. And, then, there is beauty in our world. Does it, therefore, not make sense to assert that beauty, too, has its origin in God, so that whatever we perceive as beautiful, and call "beautiful," goes back to something which is also an attribute of God?

Yet we should be careful. It is not that easy to make assertions about God. Moreover, there is no unanimity in the evaluation of the beauty which we experience. What I consider to be beautiful—in music, in sculpture, in the graphic arts, in literature—might be considered "ugly" by others. And what others regard as "beautiful" might be something which I simply cannot stand. We human beings are, after all, very subjective in our evaluation of the beautiful. Is it possible to reduce the

125

most diverse concepts of beauty to a single common denominator? Philosophers and aestheticians have tried to do that ever since the days of the ancient Greeks. But they have not yet succeeded—unless one sees a manifestation of beauty in harmony and in the right proportions, as the ancient Greeks already did.

That God "creates harmony in His heights" is stated in Scripture (Job 25:2). But what happens in His heights is by and large unknown to us. We only know our way around on earth; and here we encounter not only harmony, but also disturbances of harmony. Here we find a verification of the words which Deutero-Isaiah spoke in the name of God: "I am the Lord, there is none else. I form light and create darkness, I make weal and create woe" (Is. 45:6–7). Some of us, in spite of the woe and the darkness, find enough light and weal in the world to put our trust in a God, who, one day in the future, will remove the darkness from before the light and the woe from before the weal. For the word which we have here translated as "weal" is the same Hebrew word, *shalom,* which, when quoting Job 25:2, we have translated as "harmony." This harmony may indeed not yet exist on earth today, but there are hints, intimations that, one day, it will be established here, too—when Messiah comes, as we Jews say, or when Christ returns, as the Christians say. On the other hand, there are those who find that, in spite of the few rays of light and the intimations of salvation, there is too much darkness and woe in the world to enable us to conclude that there will be a future salvation. This, after all, is the point at which opinions divide. From the perspective of strict logic, neither the one perception nor the other can be proved.

But let us assume for a moment that God is indeed the Creator of Harmony, the *'oseh shalom.* From this it would follow that God creates something beautiful; and if one creates something beautiful, one might oneself be described as "beautiful." All the while, however, we remain conscious of the fact that the expression "beautiful" is a component of *human* language. Can human language be used in speaking of *God*? Of course! For what other language is available to us? We have to use our human language when we talk about our daily bread, about factory and office, about the planets, about science, about the soul—and about God. And if human language mirrors human experiences and human relationships, then those experiences and relationships in the human sphere also serve as metaphors for what we want to say about God. "As a father pities his children," we read in Psalm 103:13, "so the Lord has pity on all those who fear Him." And the Prophet spoke in the name of the Lord: "As a mother comforts her son, so do I comfort you" (Is. 66:13). The love which husband and wife feel for each other, too, is used by the Prophets Hosea and Jeremiah as a parable for the love of God and His people. The use of that parable even went so far that, in the Synagogue and in the Church, the love poetry collected in the Song of Songs was understood as depicting the love of God and Israel, or of Christ and the Church.

However, what the lover and the beloved in the Song of Songs say to each other also includes remarks about physical beauty. For example, the girl describes her lover in the following manner:

> My beloved is clear-skinned and ruddy,
> Preeminent among ten thousand.
> His head is finest gold,
> His locks are curled
> And black as a raven.

> (Song 5:10–11)

But the lover in the Song of Songs is supposed to be God Himself! In that case, one assumes, God will simply have to tolerate being described in this way. Of course, there are difficulties involved in this, because we know that God has no skin color and that He has no locks of hair. But in what other way can we express His "beauty" in our human language?

The verses from the Song of Songs which we have quoted here are utilized in a synagogal hymn, the "Song of the Glory," which is still sung in many synagogues today. It was written by Rabbi Judah the Pious of Regensburg (ca. 1150–1217). But even before Rabbi Judah makes use of the quoted and similar verses, he explicitly states in his hymn:

> Your glory I shall tell, though I have never seen You.
> I know not what You are, but image can describe You.

> Through Your prophets and in Your servants' mystic speech
> You let us a mere likeness of Your glory reach.

> Your greatness and Your power, too, they named
> But after Your works for which You are famed.

> They visioned You not in Your absolute.
> Your deeds alone vouchsafed them Your similitude.

Covered by this introduction, Rabbi Judah the Pious could permit himself to describe God as "beautiful," and to utilize the terminology of the Song of Songs. Armed with similar reservations about the limits of human language, I, too, can permit myself to speak about the beauty of God, when I want to point to the origin of the beauty which I experience and apprehend in the world.

> Our Masters taught: When one sees beautiful creatures and beautiful trees, one says: "Praised be He, who has the likes of this in His world!"
> (B. *Berakhoth* 58b.)

It is written in 1 Sam. 2:2: "There is no rock like our God." But the Hebrew word *tsur*, which has here been translated as "rock," can, with the minor change of a consonant, also be read as *tsayyar* (= "artist"); and thus

127

it was understood by one of the ancient Rabbis: "There is no artist like our God." (B. *Berakhoth* 10a.) There is beauty in the world, because the Creator of the world is the fountain and origin of beauty. Saying this does not even have to mean that *everything* in the world is beautiful. Perhaps the beautiful stands out precisely because we can always compare it with what is not beautiful. Not every sunrise and sunset is as enchantingly beautiful as those we have experienced last year at the shore of the sea. Obviously, this too is a purely subjective statement. But my personal experiences are of necessity subjective. And if, in prayer, I turn to God, *I* turn to Him—*I*, and not humankind in general, making an objective statement. "Praised be He, who has the likes of this in His world!" Quite conceivably, He also has others.

> "He is my God, and I will glorify Him," we read in Exodus 15:2. But the Hebrew word for "I will glorify Him" *(we-anwehu)* can also be understood as "I will beautify Him."
>
> That is why Rabbi Ishmael said: "But is it possible for a mere creature of flesh and blood to beautify his Creator? That verse can, therefore, only mean that, in the observance of the commandments, I shall do beautiful things for Him. On the Feast of Tabernacles, I shall make up a beautiful festival bouquet *(lulabh)* for Him, and erect a beautiful tabernacle *(sukkah)*. I shall make beautiful ritual fringes, and don beautiful phylacteries.
>
> (But the Hebrew word *we-anwehu* can also be read as a combination of the words *ani wehu* = "I and he.")
>
> That is why Abba Saul said: This means: "I shall endeavor to be like Him." Just as He is merciful and gracious, so you should be merciful and gracious!
>
> (*Mekhilta, Shirah*, chap. 3, ed. Horovitz-Rabin, p. 127.)

This early rabbinic pericope summarizes in a few words what is regarded as "beauty" in the Jewish tradition. The view of Rabbi Ishmael and Abba Saul do not exclude each other. Rabbi Ishmael adopts a purely aesthetic position. God is the supreme Source of Beauty. Human beings cannot make Him more beautiful than He already is. But when we have the choice of fulfilling God's will in either an aesthetic or in a nonaesthetic way, we should choose the aesthetic way, the beautiful manner. The letter of the Law can be fulfilled even by erecting an ugly tabernacle or by putting together a festival bouquet which does not look pretty. But, according to Rabbi Ishmael, the letter of the Law is not the point here. Rather, it is a matter of serving the Source of Beauty in an aesthetic way.

Abba Saul goes further than this. Without denying the importance of aesthetic beauty, he insists that, in addition to it, there is also another kind of beauty, the *ethical* kind. It is our duty to imitate God's attributes as much as that is possible for us. Beautiful is the person who is merciful to others, and who is gracious to them, as God Himself is merciful and gracious to His human children. *Imitatio Dei,* imitating God under human conditions, is taught by Abba Saul (and by other rabbis) as the highest form of art. Thus it is that, until this day, in Jewish popular parlance someone is called a *schöner Jud,* a "beautiful Jew," who, irrespective of his exterior, and irrespective even of the degree of his ritual practice, translates the ethical teachings of Judaism into the concrete terms of his or her daily life.

Can the God who once proclaimed at Mount Sinai, "You shall not make for yourself a sculptured image," can this God really be described as "beautiful"? Yes, indeed, He can—if His human children, through the kind of life they live, manage to invest the world with His beauty.

Notes

This is the author's own English translation of his German essay, "Der Schöne," originally published in Rudolf Walter, ed., *Die hundert Namen Gottes. Tore zum letzten Geheimnis* (Freiburg i. Br.: Verlag Herder, 1985). It is offered here to Rabbi Herman E. Schaalman as a token of friendship and felicitation with the gracious permission of the German editor and publisher.

Rabbi W. Gunther Plaut is the Senior Scholar of Holy Blossom Temple in Toronto. He has served with distinction in the North American rabbinate since he came from Germany where he was a schoolmate of Herman Schaalman's at the Hochschule. *Rabbi Plaut is an internationally known scholar and lecturer. His most important of many published works is the so-called Plaut Torah Commentary published by the Union of American Hebrew Congregations. He is the immediate past president of the Central Conference of American Rabbis. He has served with distinction in several different national and international Jewish organizations. His relationship with Herman Schaalman spans more than forty-five years, and they are the closest of friends.*

Rabbi W. Gunther Plaut provides us with a critical analysis of the Star of David as a symbol of the covenanted people. This is more than a historical reflection; it is a statement of faith. Plaut has a personal connection with the star, as a symbol of Jewish redemption. This essay adds another important dimension to the growing genre of testimony—in the face of radical evil—to the life of the covenant. A life of faith is the ultimate response to evil as rabbis Gunther Plaut and Herman Schaalman have lived it.

Badge of Shame—
Badge of Pride

W. Gunther Plaut

When in September 1935, five of us—Herman Schaalman, Wollie Kaelter, Leo Lichtenberg, Alfred Wolf, and I—left Berlin to become students at the Hebrew Union College in Cincinnati, we had one overriding experience in common: we had lived for two and a half years in the Third Reich, with all that this entailed. Anti-Semitism was now state policy. We had become second-class humans and would soon be without any legal protection whatever.

To be sure, anti-Semitism was nothing new to us; we had grown up with it. Long before the Nazis had come to power they had vilified the Jews at public gatherings and, with unremitting intensity, in their publications. Among these, Julius Streicher's *Der Stürmer* easily outdid the rest. Lurid tales of alleged Jewish depravity, especially in matters sexual, titillated the readers, and vicious cartoons fixed in their minds the image of the Jew as seen by Streicher and his cohorts: hooked nose, bulging eyes, thick lips dripping with lascivious saliva, money bags tucked under his arms, and a pure Aryan girl about to be violated by the monster. And almost always a *Magen David* would be added to complete the pictorial masterpiece.

The *Judenstern,* as it was known in Germany, was by now familiar to the Jews. During the last hundred years synagogues and ritual items had increasingly been decorated with it, and the Zionist flag had assured the acceptance of the symbol by Jews everywhere. But Gentiles in Germany and elsewhere had not yet come to see the *Magen David* in this light. Here, as in many other countries, it was also seen as a neutral, geometric configuration and was found in places which had nothing to do with Jews, like

131

churches and public buildings. The Nazis changed this once and for all. Their powerful propaganda machine made sure that the *Magen David* would henceforth be recognized by everyone as the *Judenstern*, the Jewish Star.

On April 1, 1933, the Nazis organized a nationwide boycott of Jewish businesses. They scrawled "Jew" or painted the Star, or both, on every store owned by Jews. On that day, the *Magen David* was transferred from the pages of *Stürmer, Angriff,* and *Völkischer Beobachter* to the public realm. The Jewish Badge of unlamented medieval memory had not yet been resuscitated—that was to come later—but figuratively it was already affixed to every Jewish breast.

Robert Weltsch, editor of Berlin's *Jüdische Rundschau,* addressed his readers in a memorable editorial: "Wear the Yellow Badge with Pride."[1] The Jews, he wrote, were singled out for contempt and contumely. No matter, as long as Jews knew their own worth and had a proper measure of self-esteem, the ignominy heaped on them by the outside world could not touch them. It might restrict their physical existence but not their soul. The Jewish spirit was beyond the reach of the enemy.

German Jews were deeply moved by the message. It could not gauge the full sweep of evil that was to engulf our people, but it helped us to salvage our humanity and our pride.

In time the yellow badge was introduced wherever the Nazi tide swept. The effect was profound. It isolated the Jews and marked them for the final solution. The systematic treatment of the Jewish question did in fact begin with the introduction of the badge.[2]

It was first tried out in Poland, shortly after the Germans had occupied the country. On October 24, 1939, the Jews of Wloclawek were instructed by Oberführer Cramer of the SA to wear a yellow triangle, and a month later Governor General Frank introduced a Jewish badge for all of Poland: a white cloth, ten centimeters square, with the *Magen David.* Later on, when the badge became more or less standardized in the lands of Nazi domination, the background color was to be yellow (following medieval precedent) and the star black. Sometimes the badge was simply a yellow star. To heap insult on injury, Jews had to supply their own badges, which had to be sewn on tightly, usually on the breast and on the back.

But the authorities hesitated to introduce the order in Germany proper or in the occupied West. Almost two years passed before the atmosphere was deemed propitious.[3] The general *ukase* which made it official was issued on September 1, 1941, when the Ministry of the Interior published it in the *Reichsgesetzblatt:*

> Beginning with the 15th of September 1941 Jews who have reached the age of six are forbidden to appear in public without a Jewish Star (*Judenstern*). They are also forbidden to leave their community

without written permission by the police, or to wear orders, medals or other insignia.

This does not apply to the Jewish partner of a mixed marriage if there are offspring who are not considered to be Jews, or if their only son was killed in the war, or to a Jewish wife in a childless mixed marriage, as long as she is married.[4]

Sometimes the letter "J" or the word "Jew" was inscribed in its center, in the language of the land: *Juif, Jood, Jude.*

Issuing the decree was one thing; having it accepted, quite another: In Berlin, some Gentiles wore the badge in order to show their sympathy for the Jews, and Provost Lichtenberg, a Christian cleric, publicly declared that he would identify with the Jews. He wore the badge and went to concentration camp, where he perished. Except for these few, however, there was no resistance from Germans.

It was different in Denmark, where King Christian X was quoted as saying that, were the badge to be introduced, he would be the first to wear it. The Nazis did not put him to the test; they abandoned the plan.

There was resistance in Holland as well, but Nazi control was stricter there than in Denmark. A German official reported that Jews failing to wear the star were arrested at once and shipped to the notorious Mauthausen camp in Austria. Non-Jews wearing the star in sympathy were incarcerated for six weeks and given vigorous indoctrination.[5]

The best documented record comes from France[6] where, it is interesting to note, the popular *Paris-Midi* still called the hexagram the "Seal of Solomon" *(Sceau de Solomon),* while it characterized the pentagram as Islamic, Pythagorean, and (without further explanation) anti-Semitic. It spoke of harmony and art, of life as opposed to the death message of the hexagram which, the erudite writer proclaimed, was found in snow crystals and other inanimate matter.[7]

Thomas Keneally, in his novel *Schindler's List,* has a German observe the reaction of the Jews in Cracow during the occupation in World War II. The Star, he says, was "*their* national insigne, the insigne of a state that had been destroyed by the Romans, and that now existed only in the minds of Zionists. So perhaps people were proud to wear the star."[8]

Having to wear the *Magen David* was in a way comparable to being forced to live in a Jewish ghetto. Keneally makes a Cracow Jew explain this feeling to a sympathetic German when he writes, "We'll be inside, the enemy will be outside. We can run our own affairs. No one will envy us, no one stone us in the streets. The walls of the ghetto will be fixed."[9]

In the fourteenth century, the Jews of Prague had been issued a flag with the *Magen David.* It was the first time the symbol had served in an official capacity. Five hundred years later the Jews of that old imperial capital, like Jews everywhere in the German realm, were issued the same

133

symbol as a mark of fateful identity. They wore it inside and outside the ghettos, and on the trains that took them to Auschwitz.

> The yellow Jewish star, as a sign of exclusion and ultimately of annihilation, has accompanied the Jews on their path of humiliation and horror, of battle and heroic resistance. Under this sign they were murdered; under this sign they came to Israel. If there is a fertile soil of historical experience from which symbols draw their meaning, it would seem to be given here. Some have been of the opinion that the sign which marked the way to annihilation and to the gas chambers should be replaced by a sign of life. But it is possible to think quite the opposite: the sign which in our own days has been sanctified by suffering and dread has become worthy of illuminating the path to life and reconstruction. Before ascending, the path led down into the abyss; there the symbol received its ultimate humiliation and there it won its greatness.[10]

Three years after the Nazi nightmare came to end, the State of Israel was proclaimed. The *Magen David* now flew over a Jewish nation. It had made its way in uncharted waters; it had been used for noble as well as dubious and even evil purposes. It had emerged alone among the other symbols, a star of hope that had survived the night. All Jews now put it on their shields, as David the King was thought to have done in days of yore. The badge of shame had become a badge of pride, and at last all Jews recognized it as their own.

Notes

1. April 1, 1933; Weltsch died in England, in 1982.
2. This point is made by Gerald Reitlinger, *The Final Solution* (New York, 1953), p. 53.
3. After Poland, the badge was introduced in the Baltic states (July 8, 1941), but nowhere else.
4. I 547; see also *Das Sonderrecht für die Juden im NS-Staat*, ed. Joseph Wolk (Heidelberg/Karlsruhe: F. Müller, 1981), p. 347.
   The German text is as follows:
   > Ab 15.9.41 ist es Juden, die das sechste Lebensjahr vollendet haben, verboten, sich in der Öffentlichkeit ohne einen Judenstern zu zeigen. Juden ist es verboten, ohne schriftliche, polizeiliche Erlaubnis ihre Wohngemeinde zu verlassen und Orden, Ehrenzeichen oder sonstige Abzeichen zu tragen.
   > Dies gilt nicht für den in Mischehe lebenden jüdischen Ehegatten, sofern Abkömmlinge aus der Ehe vorhanden sind, die nicht als Juden gelten oder der einzige Sohn im Krieg gefallen ist, ferner nicht für die jüdische Ehefrau bei kinderloser Mischehe während der Dauer der Ehe *(Polizeiverordnung über die Kennzeichnung der Juden).*
5. Leon Poliakov, *L'Étoile Jaune* (Paris, 1949), p. 70.
6. See Poliakov's study, and M. R. Marrus and R. O. Paxton, *Vichy France and the Jews* (New York: Basic Books, 1981).

7. June 8, 1942.
8. Thomas Keneally, *Schindler's List* (New York: Simon & Schuster, 1982), p. 66.
9. Ibid., p. 84.
10. Gershom Scholem, *The Messianic Idea in Judaism* (New York: Schocken Books), p. 281.

David Polish is the Founding Rabbi of Beth Emet, the Free Synagogue in Evanston, Illinois. He has written five books and numerous scholarly essays. His rabbinate has had a strong focus in the synthesis of Zionism and religion. He is the vice-president of, and active in, ARZA. He is the past president of the Central Conference of American Rabbis. It was during his presidency that Herman Schaalman served as the chairman of the Select Committee on Mixed Marriage. David Polish is the visiting lecturer at the Hebrew Union College— Jewish Institute of Religion in Los Angeles, and he teaches a senior seminar at Northwestern University. David and Herman have been rabbinic neighbors for more than three decades in Chicago. Both have served together on various rabbinic boards, regional and national. These two close friends are considered among the "G'deloay Ha' Dor," the great of their rabbinic generation in Chicago.

David Polish brings his noted scholarly mind to the creative polarity of universalism and particularism. The creative tension between the poles is the covenant. For some, universalism and particularism are theological categories which have little meaning in today's discussion, yet Polish's approach adds new zest to a classic argument. His depth of historical and textual analysis provides the process of thinking *within* a covenantal tension, not simply thinking about the tension of the covenant. Polish's historic commitment to Jewish peoplehood and Zionism adds an important backdrop for this discussion of a serious challenge within contemporary Jewish life.

Covenant: Jewish Universalism and Particularism

David Polish

The *brit milah* is usually understood as an exclusive relationship between God and Israel, as particularistic, separating Israel from others. There is warrant for perceiving it in that light. During a *brit milah* among Sephardic Jews, the father of the newborn son recites, *Im eshkhahekh Yerushalayim* ("If I forget You, Jerusalem"), thereby embracing the highest worldly aspirations of the Jewish people and dedicating his son to them. The *v'shamru* prayer for *shaharit* on Shabbat declares: "The uncircumcised may not share in its [Sabbath's] rest."

There is also reference to circumcision as a requirement for attaining the world to come: "The world is reserved for the righteous, that is, Israel" (*Yoroh Deah, Hilkhot Gerim* 268b).

This is based on the assumption that a precondition for the afterlife is circumcision, thus qualifying nearly all Jews, except the most evil, and including infants who died and were circumcised before burial. Non-Jewish *arelim* can be a deterrent to personal Jewish redemption. As Jacob lies dying, he adjures his sons not to allow an *arel* to touch his coffin lest the *Shekhinah* depart from him, presumably lest his entrance to the next world *(olam ha-ba)* be thwarted (Gen. *Rabbah* 118b). This would refute the conventional belief that righteous gentiles may enter *olam ha-ba,* and is closer to the Christian idea of "no salvation outside the church."

Yet there is also warrant for viewing the *brit* as transcending the bounds of particularity. Nothing could make this clearer than God's promise to Abraham: "All the families of the earth shall be blessed through you." The *brit* with Abraham thus is not self-contained, and, in

137

fact, it requires the world for its fullest consummation. In addition, there is another *brit* which, while moving in its own orbit, also intersects the *brit* of Abraham and Israel, each exerting a centripetal pull upon the other. This is the *brit* of Noah. Yet, as a prelude to examining it, we must search for covenantal clues in the creation of Adam who is, at times, explicitly perceived as a precursor to Noah's *brit*. In the Genesis account, an overture to this is the implicit covenant with humanity in which God blesses newly created man, places the divine "image" upon him, gives him the earth to possess, and hallows the seventh day (as a sign) on which He ceases His labors. Even after the expulsion from Eden, none of these divine enactments is annulled.

Hosea equates the sinful nation with Adam, both of whom "transgressed the *brit*" (Hos. 6:7). (Rashi differentiates the prophet's Adam from "mankind" by identifying him as *"Adam Ha-rishon."*) This is not the only extra-Genesis reference in Scripture to Adam, about whom Job asks, "Did I hide my transgressions like Adam?" (Job 31:33). The theme of Adam's breach of God's command is, as in Hosea, expanded into a protocovenant in Midrash and Talmud. While the technical term *brit* is not used, the dialectic of a cosmic call to human responsibility and response is employed. There is even an explicit indication that Adam was a predecessor of Noah in receiving a universal law. "Seven commandments were ordained for Bnai Noah. . . . R. Judah says that Adam was commanded only concerning idolatry.—R. Judah ben Beteira says, 'also blasphemy'" (*Sanhedrin* 56b).

In this context, Adam becomes the potential guarantor of the world's well-being. God shows Adam all of the trees in Eden and says to him, *"Everything* I have created, I have created for you. See to it that you do not spoil or ruin my world, for should you spoil it there will be no one after you to repair it" (Kohelet *Rabbah* 7). Here is a "scandalous" concept, that *all* of the trees in the garden were under Adam's stewardship. In addition, there is the intimation and the warning of what is to occur if Adam and his kin defy that warning. It is the intimation of the Flood, except that Noah did, indeed, repair the world. The theme of universal law is stated most extravagantly in *"Adam Ha-rishon* was worthy of receiving the Torah" (Gen. *Rabbah* 7). This is of a piece with the theme of Israel's Sinaitic contemporaries, who were deemed eligible for receiving the Torah but rejected it. In Adam's case, however, the concept is even more daring.

Thus, as he evolves primarily in rabbinic literature, Adam appears as primordial covenantal man. He is no longer solely the one who, in the language of both God and the serpent, might be like God. He becomes subject to a pre-Toranic law, applicable to all his descendants, a law that is moral, that but for his rebellion might have been the Torah itself, and upon which, even in its attenuated form, the existence of creation depends. From Genesis Man, a potential threat to God, he emerges as

Covenant Man, admonished to be a moral guardian of the world. He is transformed into Noah's moral ancestor.

Brit as Universal

The major thesis of this presentation is that, in its fullest sense, the *brit* is universal as well as ethnic. Subsumed under this and deriving from it are five other propositions which attest to the ethnic side of the *brit*. First, the *brit* is both pluralistic and unitary. Second, the *brit* is manifested in theophany and also in anthropophany. Third, whatever the ways in which it is perceived, it is redemptive, with the Land as the locus of final redemption. Fourth, it is ethically grounded. Fifth, all of these components bear heavily on Jewish life today. All of these are subsumed under the God who manifests Himself in history and to Israel.

We stress the *brit* with Noah because, unlike that with Adam, it is explicit in the biblical account. Through the primal universal encounter with Noah, God prepares us for the covenantal encounter with Abraham and then with Moses, and then with all Israel. In addition, before entering into the *brit* with the fathers of the People and then with the People itself, God chooses to forge a *brit* with humanity. This *brit* is more than a recognition that God is concerned with humanity, and that as an overture to the appearance of Israel on the cosmic scene, He pays due heed to all of His creatures. It also suggests, both textually and even more in rabbinic and apocryphal literature, that Israel is inseparably bound up with humanity, in fate and in destiny. Israel's rescue from a reign of evil in water is related to the rescue of the new humanity as embodied in Noah and his family. "They [the Egyptians] said: We cannot subjugate them by means of water, since God declared that He would not [again] bring a flood upon the world. God said: Fools, I declared that I would not [again] *bring* a flood upon the world, but you will descend into the [existing] flood. Hence, He drowned them in the sea" (Midrash *Vayoshah*). Noah's significance and relationship to the patriarchal covenants are evoked in a most awesome part of Jewish liturgy, in the *Zikhronot* for *Rosh Ha-Shanah*. "You remember Noah in love. . . . His memory comes before You so that his seed might increase like the dust of the earth. . . . (You have said in Lev. 26:42) I shall remember My covenant with Jacob; My covenant with Isaac; I shall remember My covenant with Abraham; and the earth *[aretz]* I shall remember." The biblical reference clearly applies to the Land of Israel. In the Noah context, is *eretz* also an allusion to the earth? And "dust of the earth" evokes the promise to Abraham.

Following the miraculous delivery from Egypt, Moses transmitted God's law to the people amidst awesome circumstances. Following the abatement of the waters, God transmitted universal laws to Noah under the marvelous sign of the rainbow. The origin of those laws is disputed in Jewish literature. One position asserts that the Noahides took the laws upon themselves, *kibblu aleyhem* (*Babba Kama* 38a). Rambam contends *she'niztavu*, they were commanded by God (*Mishneh Torah, Hilkhot Melakhim* 8:11). The presentation of laws, however incomplete, to the family of Noah becomes a universal prefiguration of *Matan Torah*, the transmission of Torah. Those laws are not isolated from Jewish concerns, not only because they are related in content to Jewish law itself, and especially to the Ten Commandments, but because Judaism is concerned with their observance by Noah's descendants. We are mindful that the laws of Noah may have been promulgated for non-Jews living under Jewish jurisdiction in the Land of Israel. Under those circumstances which assume the concept of submission to Jewish government—*kibblu aleyhem*—provision is made for the enforcement of those laws by Jewish courts. But if we follow Rambam—*she'niztavu*—who, in turn, follows the biblical text, we draw a different conclusion, that even though the Bnai Noah may be beyond Jewish law's enforcing power, they are still bound to their original covenant with God. Yet this distinction is not consequential, since rabbinic tradition is similarly divided on whether the Torah was accepted by Israel or imposed upon it by God. Willing or not, Noah's descendants and Israel alike came forever under both the promise and the demands of their covenant.

The consciousness of Israel's connection to all of this manifests itself again and again in Scripture. When Isaiah wishes to convey God's ultimate commitment to Israel's unending endurance, he cites "the waters of Noah" and analogizes them to a *brit shalom* for Israel (Is. 54:9). (This does not mean a different *brit*, any more than does Jeremiah's *brit hadashah*, but, rather, the confirmation, once and for all, of Israel's original *brit*.) Equally striking is Ezekiel's linkage of Noah and Job to Daniel (or, as others would have it, to Danel, another non-Jew), as members of a saintly pantheon who would not be able to save a sinful Israel (Ez. 14:19). For Ezekiel, that archetypal Judeocentric prophet, to invoke Noah as the prototype of saintliness is to confirm the connection of biblical Judaism with its transparticularist world, however attenuated that connection did, at times, become. The connection to the non-Jewish world is also evident in God's promise, first to Abraham, then to Sarah, that kings would spring from their loins. Hosea evokes Noah's covenant as the paradigm of the ultimate redemption of all of life. Sanhedrin 56 states: "Every *mitzvah* enjoined upon Bnai Noah and repeated at Sinai, was addressed to both [them and to Israel]." Also, "The burning of the Temple was foreseen from the days of Noah" (Midrash *Tad'sheh* 9).

In rabbinic literature, "Noah is listed among the five who saw a new world along with Joseph, Moses, Job and Mordecai" (Gen. *Rabbah* 30:8; Es. *Rabbah* 6:3). Urbach cites Talmud and Midrash where Noah is depicted as an intercessor between man and God, and whose birth, proclaimed in advance, was accompanied by remarkable circumstances. He had exceptional spiritual and moral faculties, and all marveled at him when he was an infant and a child. His knowledge came directly from God, he divined mysteries, foresaw the future, had mastery over nature. He was a redeemer of people, also saving them from the wrath of God and nature, a helper of the poor and the suffering.[1]

The Book of Tobit refers to "Noah, Abraham, Isaac and Jacob as 'fathers of old'" (Tob. 4:12). In Jubilees, included in a lengthy account of the Flood, we find the following: "Of the children of Israel it has been written and ordained: if they turn to Him in righteousness He will forgive all their transgressions" (Jub. 5:17). The celebration of Shavuot is attributed to Noah (Jub. 6:18, 19), although note is made of its rejection by his sons. Shavuot is also identified with the covenant with Abraham. The biblical Noah who receives the law becomes the transmitter of law and a teacher of morality (Jub. 7:28). In the blessing by Jacob, the following is included: "May He give you all the blessings, wherewith He blessed Adam and Enoch, and Noah and Shem" (Jub. 29:27).

In Tobit and Ben Sirach, "Noah is discussed in terms which indicate that he was considered in his age to be an equal of the Hebrew patriarchs."[2] Most compellingly, Judaism has never rejected the laws of Noah as irrelevant. Unlike Christianity, it saw an important place for those laws without suggesting that it had come to do away with the old dispensation. It added to the laws; it did not abolish them. Nor is Noah demoted and even rejected, as is Moses by Christianity. Judaism is a linkage of law from law, whereas Christianity is a discontinuity from the Law.

Thus, Israel has an unbreakable relationship with Noahides, even if it is often violent. They were first given ethical *mitzvot,* and these were revealed. The Noahides were the first to be explicitly covenanted. Noah became a prototype of the recipient of the law, and a prototype of righteousness in our literature. He became a paradigm of "the righteous among the nations," from Jethro to the groves of the righteous in Yad Va-Shem. He and his family were the first survivors of a massive catastrophe. So there is a relationship of spirit as well as an interrelationship of fate. There are duties *of* the Noahides; there are moral duties *to* them, "for the sake of peace." The family of Noah were the first witnesses to *hamas* (lawlessness) on a worldwide scale. The Noah account is, therefore, an *ur*-prophetic text. Altruistically and selfishly, Israel has had an interest in the sons of Noah adhering to their *brit.* Jews also have an interest in God adhering to His *brit.*

There is also an implicit recognition that Israel's well-being is bound up with the sons of Noah. There is, first, the curse of *hamas,* which brought on the universal catastrophe and which the chastisement of the flood was intended to bring under control. Second, there is the dread of another catastrophe which could befall all of humanity, Israel as well, because as one component of Rabbinic consciousness recognized, the world could next be engulfed by fire (*Tosefta, Taanit* 2).

If nothing else, Jewish tradition recognized that the first *brit* served not only to lead toward the introduction of the People of Israel, but to link Judaism to humanity irrevocably. In addition, this linkage is weighted with moral imperatives. The first echoes of communal justice, of the prophetic cause and effect of social violence and retribution, are imprinted deep in the narrative. (It could be argued that this already appears in the Cain and Abel account, but that event does not yet bear on social and communal evil.)

To be sure, there are invidious as well as laudatory references to Noah. "Should any of the Bnei Noah observe Shabbat, they would not only receive no reward but even deserve death" (*Vayikra Rabbah* 25, 15). This confirms that here, as in other areas of Jewish thought, there are conflicting opinions, but that does not diminish the weight of the positive position.

Daniel Polish has called attention to the perception, by some, of rabbinic approval of Noah and his laws as patronizing. This approval is analogous to that aspect of Christian theology which views Judaism as a forerunner to Christianity but little else. But he also points out that the rabbinic view can be perceived as recognizing the symbiosis of Judaism and the universal mandate of Noahism. Patronizing or not, the rabbis understood the universal nature of the moral law which preceded Sinai and with which they identified. We take note of Rambam's recognition of Christianity and Islam bearing Judaism's spirit throughout the world. We can also credit Noahism with bringing humanity under the law of the same God whom Judaism called YHWH.

The Pluralism of the *Brit*

Kabbalistic and rabbinic literature understood that there were varieties of covenantal experience. There were *brit milah* (circumcision), *brit keshet* (rainbow), *brit melah* (salt), *brit yesurin* (suffering), *brit kehunah* (priesthood) (*Zohar Hadash, Bereshit* 4). Also, "God made three covenants when Israel went out of Egypt" (*Tanhuma, Nizavim* 3). This may refer to the covenants at Moab, Horeb, and the second set of commandments (Ex. 34:10). Finally, "seven ancestors made a covenant—Abraham, Isaac, Jacob, Moshe, Aaron, Phineas, David" (*Derekh Erez Zuta* 1).

These passages do not intend to suggest the existence of various different and unrelated covenants, but they do stress two other factors: first, they represent varying elements of the same covenant; second, in the case of the seven ancestors, the same covenant asserted and reconfirmed itself in a succession of generations, confirming our earlier thesis. All of the other covenants impinge directly on Israel's responsibilities to God. The *brit melah* is related to the heave-offering as "an everlasting law before God for you and your descendants" (Num. 18:19). The *brit yesurin* is proclaimed after the terrifying admonitions of *Ki Tavo*—"these are the words of the covenant which God commanded Moses to make with the children of Israel in the Land of Moab in addition to the covenant He made with them at Horeb" (Deut. 28:69). The *brit kehunah*, referred to in Nehemiah 13:29, may refer to Ex. 29:9 where the statute of the priesthood is referred to as "everlasting." None of the covenants referred to in the Zohar are actually covenants but covenantal referrents. The *brit yesurin* summarizes the consequences of violating the *brit*. The *britot* of *milah*, *keshet*, and *melah* are external "signs" of the *brit*. The *brit kehunah* identifies the priest as an instrument of the *brit*.

The Unitary *Brit*

The congruence between *brit Avraham* and the *brit* at Sinai is striking. They are two covenants, yet one. It is not coincidental that the first declares, "I am YHWH Who brought you out of Ur-Kasdim," and the second opens with "I am YHWH Your God Who brought you out of the land of Egypt." God is the first and enduring constant in the *brit*. A second binding component of both *britot* and a common denominator for all the varieties of *brit* experience is redemption, physical and moral. The people is rescued in body and spirit, or both. A third component of both covenants is the promise of the land after a time of suffering. "They will enslave and torment them. . . . Then they (Israel) will go forth." The bridge uniting both *brit* events is Ex. 2:24, where God hears Israel's outcry and "remembers his *brit* with Abraham, Isaac and Jacob." As the people are prepared for the theophany, God declares to Moses, "You have seen what I did to Egypt . . . I bore you on eagles' wings" (Ex. 19:4). The covenant is invoked—"keep my covenant" (Ex. 19:5). A precondition for the inheritance of the land is allegiance to God which Abraham acknowledges—"He believed in God," and which the people affirm at Sinai saying together, "All that God has said, we will do" (Ex. 19:8). In the episode following the shattering of the tablets, the same components emerge. God announces, "I make a covenant." He declares that He will expel the nations before Israel. He warns against "a strange God." The covenant with Abraham and the People is enhanced by parallel references to God at work in human history and inflicting judgment upon the nations. All of this is recapitulated in *Nitzavim* "to enter into the covenant of the Lord your God . . . to the end that He may establish you . . . as His People and be

143

your God . . . And the Lord your God will bring you to the land" (Deut. 29:11, 12; 30:5).

The covenants are then sealed by numinous acts—the *brit* between the animal parts, and the sacrifice by the elders, with the blood of the covenant and the book of the covenant, following the Sinai theophany (Ex. 24:7, 8). Jeremiah refers to a parallel *brit* between the animal parts, but that *brit* involves the idolatrous act of the People in the Sinai wilderness.

Anthropophanic Covenants

Thus, a People is fashioned—a People chosen to be holy, a People redeemed from oppression, a People destined to have its land, a People whose God places moral demands upon it—born both of its suffering and His repugnance of idolatry. These unitary, nuclear factors, reiterated in varying events and by a progression of people in different periods and distinguished by God disclosing Himself to His People, constitute the paradigm for the covenantal process which informs Jewish life through the ages. That process is invoked as various men in biblical history reenact it in what may be called an anthropophanic manner, that is, it is transmitted by men by way of the Sinai model. David covenants with the people in Hebron (2 Sam. 5:3). He is represented as chosen by God to shepherd the people whom David had defended even in Saul's days. When Yehoash is sequestered from the tyrannical Ataliah, a *brit* is consummated "between God and the King and the people, to be the people of God." The People are liberated from internal tyranny, and as a consequence, the idols are destroyed. Both events involve *britot* in which the People, acting in God's behalf, covenant to place the monarchy into the hands of God's anointed. It could be argued that, in these events, the *brit* has been politicized and the gravity of the covenant has, consequently, been debased. This may partly have been the case, yet we should not overlook the implications of David's reign upon which both Jewish polity and messianism—the concept of the "King-Messiah"—is based. Nor should we overlook the religious reformation attendant upon Yehoash's reign.

Indeed, the reformationist motif accompanying the *brit* process as consummated within history by men is manifested in the Josianic episode (2 Kings 23:3). The reformation is introduced by the public reading of *Sefer ha-Brit*, thus identifying the event and the people with the primordial moment. Then, "he made the covenant before God." This is done in the presence of "all the people, small and great," not fortuitously evoking *atem nitzavim*. The purification of the faith, the demolition of the idols ensues. The reinstitution of Pesach, neglected from the days of the Judges, also ensues. The hope that, as in ancient days, the People will be delivered, proves, however, to be futile. This is made explicit in Hezekiah's reformation: "I desire to make a covenant with YHWH, the God of Israel, so that His wrath might depart from us" (2 Chron. 29:10).

The most striking reformationist note is sounded in Jeremiah's intervention in behalf of the Jewish slaves. Here there is a direct and unambiguous line to the *brit* of the wilderness which Jeremiah identifies as primarily theo-ethical. King Zedekiah had covenanted with "all the people" to liberate their Hebrew slaves. Following the manumissions, the People reenslaved them. Jeremiah's ensuing denunciation cites God's *brit* "on the day I brought them out of the land of Egypt, from the house of bondage." The quotation from the first pronouncement of the Ten Commandments, linking it unmistakably to the law of manumission, could not more emphatically assert the primacy of the moral law. In effect, Jeremiah virtually incorporates the law of manumission into the Ten Commandments. The word *brit* is recited six times, both as a reminder and as the knell of doom. The word *dror* (freedom) is repeated sardonically, inverting it from the promise of liberation—"You shall proclaim *dror* in the land"— to the terrible liberation of the avenging sword. The act of the people is equated with a demonic covenant with idolatry which the people, in a perverse imitation of the "covenant between the parts" and the sacrifice at Sinai, enacted *as a covenant* with the calf between whose severed parts they passed. Another inversion is proclaimed by Jeremiah—if the covenant is informed with the People's redemption, it follows that its violation means their destruction as in *Nitzavim*. The "everlasting covenant," reiterated frequently in Scripture, is challenged. "I will render desolate the cities of Judah, without any inhabitant." For Jeremiah, the reformationist-covenantal moment has been desecrated. It was a ruinous failure.

Nevertheless, Jeremiah transcends despair. Faith in redemption overcomes fear of annihilation. Chapters 31–34 are the despairing, exulting elegy of the *brit*. The Jeremiah who predicts "overthrow, destruction, disaster" (31–38) also proclaims, "He who scattered Israel will gather them" and, "I will make an everlasting covenant with them" (Jer. 31:10, 32:40).

The *brit* is recapitulated, invoking the attributes of God when He covenanted with Moses, recalling the enslavement and the Exodus of the People, retelling the inheritance of the Land, mourning the People's defections from God and His laws (Jer. 32:16ff.). Faith and despair, ruin and restoration interlock.

An additional comment about Jeremiah's "new covenant" *(brit hadashah)* (Jer. 31:31) is warranted. The prophet's statement that it will "not be like the covenant I made with their ancestors" superficially suggests a radical break with the original *brit*. The clear intent of the verse is, "The covenant which is the same covenant will be new in respect to the fact that Israel will not again reject it." The ensuing reference to God's implanting the Torah in the People's heart is equally clear. It will be the same Torah; there is no reference to a different Torah, but it will be internalized. This is congruent with *Nitzavim*, which declares, "You shall circumcise your hearts" (by being faithful to the Law). Significantly, Jeremiah twice employs a metaphor that is strikingly similar to the Noah covenant.

> Thus says YHWH who established the sun for light by day, the laws of moon and stars for light by night . . . If these laws should ever be annulled by Me . . . only then would the offspring of Israel cease to be a nation before Me for all time . . . If the heavens above could be measured, and the foundations of the earth below could be fathomed, only then would I reject all the offspring of Israel. [And] if you could break my covenant with the day and my covenant with the night . . . only then could my covenant with my servant David be broken (Jer. 31:35–37, 33:20).

The Renewal

In the context of our discussion, the pluralistic-unitary *brit* continues to be operative and renewable for the Jew. Although it is anthropophanic, it is far too early to plumb its implications to the full.

When leaders of the Yishuv, acting in behalf of the entire Jewish People, signed their names to the Declaration of Independence of the reconstituted State, Jews underwent yet another covenantal experience. Redemption, restoration, the commitment to a just society based on the vision of the Prophets, the invocation of *Zur Yisrael* (the deliberate ambiguity of the term notwithstanding), all converged at that moment. Many dimensions of the Exodus inform that moment. As Sinai began to possess the People only after a period of time, its continuing resonances only now begin to penetrate the thunder and clamor of temporal existence. Certain categories need to be addressed in this context.

A. The People

The ethnocentric illustrations alluded to at the outset compel us to confront two issues which are inherent in the *brit* idea. First, what should be the relationship of the Jew today to the outer world, a world which, we acknowledge, has not been peacefully disposed toward him even in the post-*Shoah* age? Second, what are the Jewishly defined limits of ethnicity? We should deal with each question in the context, not of Jewish politics, but of the *brit*.

If, as has been suggested, Judaism is involved from the beginning with the children of Noah, there is no theological basis for a radical separation from the nations of the world, as some anti-Noahide passages suggest. Jews are understandably tempted to shut themselves out from universal concerns because of well-known and well-founded *religious* distrust and disappointment. It can be summarized in the statement on the Jews, proclaimed in 1948 by the first assembly of the World Council of Churches meeting in Amsterdam:

> We cannot forget that we meet in a land from which 110,000 Jews were taken to be murdered . . . (and) that we meet only five years after the extermination of 6 million Jews. To the Jews our God has bound us in a special solidarity linking our destinies together in His design. . . . It was Israel to whom He promised the coming of His Messiah. We have, therefore, in humble conviction to proclaim to the Jews, "The Messiah for Whom you wait has come." . . . Only as we give convincing evidence to our Jewish neighbours that we seek for them the common rights and dignities which God wills for His children, can we come to such a meeting with them as would make it possible to share with them the best which God has given us in Christ. . . . The establishment of the state "Israel" adds a political dimension to the Christian approach to the Jews and threatens to complicate anti-Semitism with political fears and enmities. On the political aspects of the Palestine problem and the complex conflict on "rights" involved we do not undertake to express a judgment. . . . To the member churches of the World Council we recommend: that they seek to recover the universality of our Lord's commission by including the Jewish people in their evangelistic work.[3]

Having indicted the Christian world, the following may be added: Involvement with the covenant of Noah requires that the Jewish People be concerned with the moral well-being of the non-Jewish world, because both its own destiny and the destiny of humanity are involved. Concern for Bnai Noah does not imply a gullible disregard for the betrayals which Jews have experienced. It does imply that, as between the moral and worldly risk of engagement and the risk of isolation, isolation presents the greater peril. It is not an act of selfishness unworthy of theological discussion for Jews to warn, for our sake as well as others', that *M'ken derharget verren*. The Jewish bond with the covenant of Noah does not require theological partnership with other *faith systems*. It does, however, require a sharing with other systems in the struggle for world improvement *(Tikkun Olam)*. The methodology for achieving this end requires special attention, but Jews must first come to terms with the issue, which is, Can Jews live up to the full measure of covenantal responsibility and, at the same time, withdraw from major global issues that represent current extensions of the Noahide requirements? If Jewish law theoretically extends to the Noahide laws against murder and for just courts of law, does covenant responsibility permit Jews, often for the best strategic reasons, to separate themselves from issues impinging on those laws?

It is not suggested that the entire Jewish People has adopted this position. When vast numbers of Israelis filled *pushkes* for the relief of boat people, brought some of those refugees to Israel, and sent medical teams to Cambodia, they were acting in response to the *brit.* They were also responding, covenantally, to the ethically and politically prescient *aggadah* about the man boring a hole in his end of the boat. Yet large numbers of Jews, in the name of their own construction of the *brit,* pursue a course devoted to Jews alone. Conversely, for members of the Covenant People to seek to disappear out of exalted universalist considerations would be a violation of a cardinal convenant principle which affirms the redemption and restoration of Israel. But it is also a violation of the covenant to exclude the Bnai Noah from Jewish concerns for the world as well as the future world. The issues of global hunger, the maldistribution of the world's resources, the threat of nuclear annihilation, the struggle by despairing people for liberation, should challenge Jews. Considerations of covenant morality should weigh more heavily than do political tactics alone, which sometimes betray both the People's self-interest and its vocation. The growing peril of the return of the Flood requires that our millennial sensitivity to this kind of danger be employed more forcefully than Jewish pronouncements have thus far reflected. The Flood can come by fire, says our tradition. It can also come by the downfall of Western civilization. Israel has spoken prophetically to civilizations in peril of life and soul. Out of its millennial literature, Israel can address itself authentically to the social and economic issues of our time. It is not enough that this be confined to the State of Israel, as some like Ha-Rav Kook and Shimon Federbush have magnificently done. If there ever was a time for Judaism to speak globally in the canonized words of Judaism, it is now, especially when the proponents of liberation theology lean so heavily on the Torah and the prophets of Israel for the support which their system requires.

As we read liberation theology, in whose spirit parts of the world are awakening, we must be impressed that Judaism has, in fact, been a "light to the nations." Liberation theology, as developed by Christians, is primarily a systematic evocation of Jewish prophetic and legal positions on justice as well as the paradigm of the Exodus. This theology has been appropriated by an awakening mass of oppressed people, but many Jews have not known it. Should it not be the Jewish task to live and interpret what has always been the doctrine of Jewish liberation, to the Bnai Noah of our time? It should simultaneously be our task to reject the misapplication of liberation theology, which too often identifies the Jew as the adversary of liberation. Jews have not adequately conveyed to the West that, however some may individually conduct their struggle for survival, Jewish tradition is bound to no socioeconomic systems of the Left or the Right, but that the only authentic Jewish system is rooted in the Torah and the prophets.

B. Non-Jewish Residents of the Territories

Biblical treatment of the local inhabitants is mixed. Israel is instructed to love the stranger "as yourself." This is a general principle whose specific application in certain instances is instructive. Concerning the Seven Nations, there are the admonitions: "You must doom them to destruction . . . give them no quarter" (Deut. 7:1ff.), "You shall destroy all the Peoples that the Lord your God delivers to you, showing them no pity" (Deut. 7:16). Concerning a conquered city: "You shall put all its males to the sword. You may, however, take as your booty the women, the children, the livestock . . . and enjoy the use of the spoil" (Deut. 20:16, 17), "The Lord will be at war with Amalek throughout the ages" (Ex. 17:15).

It is not my intention to suggest even remotely that contemporary official Judaism or Israel is guided by these principles. The intent is to demonstrate how in this context, as in so many others, recourse to biblical authority, unmediated and uncontrolled by rabbinic transmutation, can result in dangerous moral consequences. It is enough to cite one "authority" who invoked Deut. 7:16, "You shall show them no pity," or others who have raised the intriguing possibility that the Arabs of the West Bank might be Amalekites. Jews cannot succumb to biblical fundamentalism which could subvert millennia of rabbinic moral metamorphosis, any more than we can succumb to the biblical territorialism by which a zealous chaplain in the IDF overwrote Beirut on a map as Israel's ancient B'erot.

Concerning the stranger living in the midst of Israel, Maimonides says that the resident stranger is to be treated as a Jew is to be treated. This includes even idolaters: "We should treat resident aliens with the consideration and kindness due to a Jew, for we are bidden to sustain them. . . . Even with respect to heathens, the Rabbis bid us visit their sick, bury their dead along with the dead of Israel, and maintain their poor with the poor of Israel, for the sake of peace" (*Hilkhot Melakhim* 10:12).

Referring to Deut. 23:16ff., the rules are applied as follows: If even a slave is to be given sanctuary and equal treatment and is not to be extradited when he finds shelter in Israel, how much more does this apply to any gentile who wishes to reside in the Land of Israel with the understanding that he will accept the laws of Noah? However, this does not apply ever since the Jubilee ceased in Israel (*Erakhin* 29a). Nevertheless, in the context of our concerns, the principle is of paramount importance. In addition, we are admonished that even when the Jubilee is not in effect, Jews must, nevertheless, deal kindly with the *ger toshav* at all times. This is reaffirmed in *Sotah* 37, which states that even members of the biblical Seven Nations who accept the laws of Noah are to be treated kindly ("If they repent, they are to be welcome").

Concerning Amalek, whom some extremists contemporaneously

identify with Arabs on the West Bank, we know the rabbinic dictum that "Sennacherib mixed up the entire world" and, therefore, Amalek really does not exist. In a remarkable interpretation, Naftali Zvi Judah Berlin comments that Ex. 17:15, declaring that God wages a war against Amalek, refers to everything for which it stood—war, violence, immorality, idolatry. Thus, God is not continuing a violent conflict with Amalek, since it does not exist, but, although it has perished, its evil ideology persists and it is against this that God carries on His conflict.

There is, of course, the passage in *Sefer Hamitzvot* of Maimonides in which he makes the startling statement that there are still Amalekites in the world and that they must be destroyed. This, however, is not reaffirmed in his later writings. As for those who want to make a case of this today, Aaron Soloveitchik says, "Any other opinion is grounded in ignorance." Obviously, there are also rigorous positions, such as Rashi's comments on Deut. 21:11—"They shall be tribute to you." On one hand, according to the Sifrei, even members of the seven nations may be kept alive if they surrender, but, on the other hand, their surrender may not be accepted unless they submit to taxation and servitude. Yet it is the task of religious Judaism to offset such positions with more compassionate but, for many, no less authentic stands by the same tradition.

C. The Limits of Ethnicity

Does the *brit* allow Jews to be ethnic alone? Clearly not. The Jewish People has undergone rescue after rescue, but never has the passage through the Sea of Reeds failed to bring it to Sinai. The *brit* demands both the outstretched rescuing arm and God's commanding voice. It has been difficult for even well-disposed non-Jews to understand Nation and Land as components of a covenant. But, in restoring them, it must be stressed that, *alone,* nationalism betrays the *brit.* This was not God's intent, as the Torah perceived it. It is possible, and for some desirable, to separate the ethnic from the spiritual-moral once and for all. It makes sense for many to create a nation "like all the nations," unencumbered by the moral restraints and the expectations which no other nation must bear. Why should Jews alone be possessed by a superego and live tormented lives as the superego of the world? But if that is the course that Jews choose to take, it becomes difficult to designate ourselves simultaneously as "like all the nations" and "a holy People." We must then abrogate the *brit* as we have done, in fact, in the past. Some have been prepared to do so, but they are only now beginning to face the consequences of such a choice in a raw nationalism which, on a global scale, certainly among older nationalisms, is becoming repugnant and discredited. We can also choose to shatter the synthesis of Jewish religion and nationalism, allowing each to pursue its own way (as in early Reform and anti-Zionist Orthodoxy, on one hand,

and early political Zionism on the other), with religion alone clinging to the *brit*. This dichotomy is alien to Jewish thought, absurd, and dishonest. It would be deceptive for Jews to claim the *brit* in our own religious lives and to disavow it in our national existence. This is only sacralized nationalism. Even more, it is a betrayal of the *brit* which is operational only when *umah* (nation) and *emunah* (faith) are joined in some significant manner.

I am not proposing to endow the state with the coercive power of religion. I prefer the proposal by Federbush that the *halakhah* and religious values, free of political power, permeate the nation and teach it how to apply, in law and practice, the far-ranging social implications of the legal corpus of Jewish tradition. The task of an authentic fusion of the national and the religious is exceedingly arduous. Taking precedence over that issue is the challenge: Do Jews want to strive for a covenant existence, or would we rather be free of it? Jews have already made one choice: we wish to be neither a de-ethnicized cult with an abstract belief in ethical monotheism, nor an eternally exiled community of faith which periodically undergoes *kiddush ha-Shem*. Martyrdom, too, is an incomplete *brit* experience. Can Jews now, as an act of collective will, choose to restore the *brit* to its religio-national fullness? This issue is joined to at least two elements of the paradigmatic *brit*.

Paradigmatic *Brit*

A. *Brit Yesurin*

Jews are bound to the sons of Noah by the ties of the Shoah which has added another Noahide law, against genocide. Jews have been its victims. Jews must be its warning witnesses to the world that, as long as humanity endures, no people is immune to the eruption of the demonic. As Judaism held the sons of Noah accountable for the seven laws, now that these laws have become (imperfectly) internalized by man, Jews hold them accountable by virtue of Israel's ordeal, by its stubborn presence, by its refusal to be silent, for this newest law, until it, too, becomes internalized. I am not among those who reject what they call the overexploitation of the Shoah. True, it has been vulgarized by some. But its essential demand that it be confronted continually by Jew and Christian is valid. It is the *Shoah*, the unmitigated disaster. It is not the "Holocaust" which could come to suggest vicarious atonements (an un-Jewish concept) by Jews for collective Christian sin. The Holocaust must be exorcised, but the *Shoah* must enter Jewish liturgy as a *zekher*, on a level with *maasei breshit* (creation) and *yeziat mitzrayim* (the Exodus).

The original *brit yesurin* describes the suffering consequent to the

People's violation of the covenant. In the post-*Shoah* world, it is heinous to perpetuate such a concept. What guilt of little children was so appalling as to incur such an affliction? But we can invert the concept and declare that, instead of a *brit* of terror, Jews embrace a *brit* that has survived terror; that, for all the agony endured by this People Israel, it has not only endured but has chosen to endure. Israel has remained a *brit* community despite all of the afflictions imposed upon it. We are told, "In reference to *brit yesurin,* affliction cleanses one's sins" (*Berakhot* 20). A Jew today may transmute this to suggest a prayer that the *brit* of terror might cleanse the Jewish People of its tryst with the lure of Jewish self-annihilation. Isaiah evoked Israel's torment when he said, "When you pass through water I will be with you. . . . When you go through fire you shall not be consumed."

Yet the nuance in this day's evocation of that passage is not God's protective care but the People's will to remain Jewish and to create a new world for its posterity despite the fact that the fire consumed its millions. The *brit* of suffering is reminiscent of the Jew in *Shevet Yehudah* who cries out, "Despite what You, God, have done to me, the death of my wife and two sons, a Jew I am and a Jew I shall remain," and having said that, he goes on in search of a Jewish settlement.[4]

An additional covenant is *brit ha-aretz,* the covenant of the Land. It is set forth in Gen. 15, where Abraham's commitment is the act of circumcision while God's is the bequeathing of the Land. Reference to this solemn, reciprocal pact has long been incorporated into the Jewish prayer book. In a Jewish Scripture where the dimensions of the Land are variously construed, its delineation in Genesis 15 need not be of primary concern. That is a political issue. But the primal relationship to the Land as Covenantal, as sacred, should be of enormous importance in an age when human loyalties can no longer be sustained by uninhibited political nationalism alone. Zionism in its deepest sense did not begin in the nineteenth century. Chaim Weizmann, the secularist, best understood this when, in response to a query by a British royal commission about the source of the Jewish People's claim to the Land, he replied, "Our Bible."

B. *The Brit of Ahavat Yisrael*

Tragically, the incident in *Shevet Yehudah* does not end with the Jew's settling among his people. Ibn Verga concludes, "and when he set forth, no one paid attention to his suffering, because everyone was steeped in his own trouble." Thus, the *brit* was flawed. Jeremiah's sense of pain over the injustice of Jew to Jew, and hence the breach of the *brit,* applies to this day. The paradox of a people united in confrontation with the world, but torn by internal conflict, challenges Jews ever more ominously. Voices, hands, and weapons are lifted by Jews against Jews. The politics of contempt and hatred is the obverse side of the struggle over Judea and Samaria. These are not only geographical areas; they represent the ancient rift that once tore the Jewish People irrevocably apart. Is there a malignant subterranean fault in the Jewish people, erupting periodically in dark outbursts of viciousness? Can Jews overcome outer menace if internal frenzy seizes us? This is the most intractable issue of all. Too often in the past, the seizures of hatred were brought under control only by the intervention of foreign powers. In mid-nineteenth-century Jerusalem, embattled Ashkenazim and Sephardim were pacified by French and British consuls. Where are the moral interveners from within today? Where are the keepers of Jeremiah's *brit* who admonish and warn against the abuse of Jews by Jews, and the awful consequences which could shatter both *brit* and People, bearers of the *brit am*?

Notes

1. Efraim Urbach, *Hazal, Emunot V'Deot* (Jerusalem: Magnes Press), p. 435.
2. Daniel Polish, *The Flood Myth in the Traditions of Israel and India* (Cambridge, Mass.: Harvard University Press), pp. 302, 303.
3. *The First Assembly of the World Council of Churches* (London, 1948), pp. 160–63.
4. Shlomoh Ibn Virga, *Shevet Yehudah* (Jerusalem: Schocken Books, 1947), p. 125.

Professor Ellis Rivkin is the Adolph S. Ochs Professor of Jewish History at the Hebrew Union College—Jewish Institute of Religion in Cincinnati. Dr. Rivkin's scholarship has influenced more than a generation of rabbis and contemporary Jewish thinkers. His vanguard work in the area of "The Pharisees—the Intertestamental Period" has become the foundation of works in the area. His provocative view of history continues to demand a response by Jewish and non-Jewish thinkers. He has been a lecturer at Emanuel Congregation, and he has a deep and abiding relationship with Herman that spans more than two decades.

Professor Ellis Rivkin brings his consummate skills as a historian to the central issues of Jewish theology, God, revelation, and the covenant. Rivkin has influenced a generation of Jewish thinkers with his keen mind and demand for a reading of Jewish history which is "dynamic," never static. God in history is a central tenet of Jewish thought, but understanding that history to be an always evolving covenantal dynamic adds a new dimension. Rivkin forces us to raise new questions about God within history, because the power of history is a part of the covenantal power within Judaism. As usual, Rivkin is provocative, and as such aids us in responding to the challenges of contemporary Jewish life.

The Revealing and Concealing God of Israel and Humankind

Ellis Rivkin

I

There have been critical moments in the history of the Jewish people when their conception of God was tested, found wanting, and reconceptualized. The first of these moments was when the belief that God would always make known His will to prophets gave way to the belief that God had made His will known once and for all time in a book of eternal teachings and immutable laws. The God whose future options had been open became the God whose future options were now foreclosed. The God whose demands were bespoken by living prophets was displaced by the God whose demands were to be read and reread by the Aaronide priests whom God had invested with authority over the Law unto all generations. The hearing ear gave way to the reading eye.

The second of these moments was when the God of the immutable written Law gave way to the God of the open-ended oral Law. The same God who had endowed the Aaronide priests with authority over God's written Law in perpetuity now transferred this endowment to a group of Sages who are nowhere mentioned in the Pentateuch. To this new group God gave full authority to frame oral laws, *halakhot, takkanoth, gezeroth* laws which took precedence over the literal application of the *mitzwoth, hukkim, mishpatim, pikkudim,* and *edoth* of the Pentateuch. Although this God may have been the self-same God, what He required of Israel had altered substantially, and the rewards and punishment that he meted out for the

155

keeping and nonkeeping of his unwritten laws were to be eternal, not transitory. If one now wanted to know what it was that God required, one went, not to a prophet, or Aaronide priest, but to an authoritative teacher of the twofold Law.

The third critical moment came when Solomon ibn Gabirol (1021–1070), in his *Keter Malchut,* "The Royal Crown," revealed that the traditional God of Israel was congruent with the God of the neoplatonic philosophers, and when Moses Maimonides (1135–1204), in his commentary on the Mishnah and in his Mishneh Torah, revealed that the God of Israel was congruent with the God of Aristotle. Neither the anthropomorphic nor the anthropopathic picturings of God in the Bible, the Mishnah, the Talmud, or the Midrashim needed be taken literally any longer. Even the most corporeal of words had metaphorical and noncorporeal meanings and nuances. The "one" God need not be the circumscribed, bounded, and delimited "one" that marks off each of us as an individual, but an abstract One that is infinite—unbounded by time or space as exemplified by an eternal Principle or a first Cause. That this philosophic concept of God was no academic matter was made clear not only in Yehudah Ha-Levy's attempt to confute such a concept in his powerful Socratic tour de force, the *Kuzari,* and in Moses de Leon's mystical alternatives in the Zohar, but even more forcefully in the Maimonidean/anti-Maimonidean controversies which unleashed what was tantamount to a bitter civil war.

The fourth critical moment was when first Nachman Krochmal (1785–1840) in his *Guide to the Perplexed of Our Time* and then Abraham Geiger (1810–1874) in his *Judaism and Its History* revealed that the God of Israel was the God of historical process—a God who becomes known through an unfolding through time, space, structure, process, and causality. This God could not have been fully known to the prophets, the Aaronide priests, the teachers of the twofold Law, or the medieval philosophers or mystics because the historical process is not simply replicating or cyclical, but developmental. History reveals not merely quantitative changes but qualitative changes as well. The medieval world proved to be very different from the world of antiquity, even as the modern world turned out to be radically different from the medieval. And what distinguishes this modern world from the ancient and the medieval is the role that the mind has come to play as a free agent.

Prior to the birth of the modern world there had been no Hegel; no postulating of a process by which the Absolute Idea becomes concretized and fulfilled; no divine process by which humankind attains the millennium without a divine breakthrough into the natural order. Nor had ancient and medieval thinkers been able to make that quantum leap from the philosophic to the scientific spirit—a quantum leap which was to give human minds access to those abstract mathematical formulae which uphold and sustain the universe and which can be drawn upon to serve humanly designed ends.

Of all these critical moments when the conception of God was tested, found wanting, and reconceptualized, none was more critical than the fourth. It was the most critical because the reconceptualization of God which it brought in its train was qualitatively different from the other three. Whereas the other three reconceptualizations of God reaffirmed that the Pentateuch had been written by Moses, the fourth reconceptualization subjected the claims to Mosaic authorship to a withering critical scrutiny and rejected them as groundless. Whereas the other three reconceptualizations reaffirmed that God can and does act directly in history, the fourth reconceptualization has God working in history but not as a free actor. It is true, perhaps, that if Solomon ibn Gabirol or Maimonides had openly declared themselves to be pure Platonists or Aristotelians, then a strong case could be made that their God could not act directly in history, but neither of these thinkers openly disassociated his God from such intrusion, however much ibn Gabirol's *Fons Vitae* and Maimonides' many hints and allusions may have convinced some scholars that Gabirol and Maimonides really believed otherwise.

The fourth critical reconceptualization is thus singular. By insisting that all claims to revelation be subjected to critical reason, and that no conceptualization of God which involves a demonstrable falsehood—such as the denial of operative natural law within its sphere of operation—or of a demonstrated historical fact, this fourth reconceptualization allows for postulating three modes by which God reveals Himself to humankind. The first of these is through intuitive insight. The second is through historical experience. The third is through the spirit of free critical inquiry and the scientific method. Metaphorically speaking, the first mode gives us the heart of God, the second the ways of God with humankind, and the third the mind of God.

These three modes of revelation are continuously active, since the possibility of new intuitive insights, of new historical experiences, and new scientific discoveries is to be anticipated, not foreclosed. And since each of these modes is by definition open-ended, our access to more of God's heart, to more of God's ways, and to more of God's mind is never cut off.

These modes of revelation thus serve as a continuous safeguard against false revelations, since no claim to a revelation by a single one of these modes can be accorded recognition if what is being revealed carries with it the nullification of one or both of the others. No intuitive insight can be given the status of a divine revelation if, for example, it proclaims that the past could be whatever the revelation required that it be, even if this meant the erasing of hard facts, or that the spirit of free critical inquiry and the scientific enterprise are the devil's handiwork, not God's. Similarly, historical experience cannot be drawn upon to preclude future novel insights simply because they have had no parallel in the past. As for critical reason, its function as adjudicator of claims to truth and knowledge requires that it weigh the evidence as to the degree to which an intuitive insight is sustainable and confirmable; that it likewise weigh the evidence for or against the existence of patterns, shapes, forms, paradigms, laws, and directional thrusts in history; and that it do the same with respect to the hypotheses and theories offered by scientists engaged in probing nature and nature's works.

It will be noted that each of these three modes of revelation is open-ended. There is no bar to future intuitive insights; no requirement that history repeal itself; no limitation to the spirit of free critical inquiry. It should also be noted that such open-endedness is mandated by Israel's odyssey with its God. For Israel's conceptualization of God underwent at least five major transmutations: (1) the option-free God who bespoke his ongoing will to listening prophets; (2) the optionless God whose immutable laws and doctrines were written down in a book for all time; (3) the delegating God of the teachers of the twofold Law; (4) the neoplatonic and Aristotelian God of the philosophers and the overflowing God of the mystics; and (5) the processional God of nature and history. To cut off the possibility—and the legitimacy—of a sixth or seventh or eighth transmutation is not only to fly in the face of the historical record of Israel's relationship to God through the millennia, but is a preemption of the divine prerogative. For it is evident to critical minds paying court to no adjudicating agency other than the critical mind itself to weigh the claims to truth and knowledge, that the universe thus far reveals itself to be a problem-solving universe which in the course of its history has replicated itself in part, varied itself in part, and mutated itself in part in such a way as to have become other than it had been, not only quantitatively but qualitatively. It is no less evident to critical minds that insofar as the human stage of evolution is concerned, an equivalent phenomenon has been made manifest: human thought, feeling, and interpersonal relationships have replicated themselves in part, varied in part, mutated in part.

There was thus a time when formal logic and geometry were unknown; there was a time when the sonnet and the well-tempered clavier were unknown; there was a time when $E = MC^2$ and DNA were unknown; and there was a time when atom bombs did not exist and the moon was beyond man's reach. There was likewise a time when Israel's hallmark was prophecy; there was a time when Israel's hallmark was an elaborate sacrificial cult and expiating priests; and there was a time when her hallmark was the *halakhah*. Yet the first two of these hallmarks have long since been confined to past memories and future hopes, while the third, though serving as the hallmark for many Jews, is by no means acknowledged as the hallmark by all Jews. It is thus simply a matter of historical fact that Israel's odyssey with God has been a problem-facing and problem-solving experience which has been replicated in part, varied in part, and mutated in part. In the face of hard facts such as these, one would be arrogant indeed to foreclose the possibility that in response to as yet unknowable and unforeseeable experiences of the people of Israel with a problem-facing and problem-solving universe, future reconceptualizations of God may emerge and novel forms of Judaism may be shaped.

Since the three modes of revelation are open-ended modes, they must be viewed as ongoing tools for widening our knowledge of a universe whose totality is not as yet known to us and a God who has not fully revealed Himself to us, and not as modes whose functions have become unnecessary. These tools are, so to speak, tools designed to mine a universe whose total store of precious ores is not yet known to us, and tools by which God's image can be etched feature by feature at the cutting edge of the Rock. Always limited to the findings at hand, and never knowing what the next probings may yield, each of these three modes of revelation gives us an intermixture of divine light and human shadow, and refractions, not reflections, of God and his universe. As such, what is being revealed may be true in part, false in part, blind in part.

Nonetheless, despite their limitations, these three modes are the only modes we have devised thus far which continually remind us of their inherent limitations; of the contingent status of their probings; of the likelihood of future unseen possibilities; and the likelihood that knowledge just beyond the horizon which will make the wisest of us appear to have been ignorant fools. In a word, what this triad has as one of its most salient features is an awareness of its own limitations, and of its ongoing commitment to the need for continuous self-criticism, self-evaluation, and self-rectification. At the same time, this triad of modes spurs us on by its partial successes—the light within the shadow, the truth within the falsehood, the enduring within the fragile, ever-widening the eternal and narrowing the transient. These three modes of revelation thus teach us to be both humble and proud—humble that with all our knowledge we are not God, but proud that with all of our ignorance we have angels for our peers.

II

Once one is convinced that the most reliable path to the knowing of God and to the discerning of his way with nature and humankind is to be found in these modes of revelation—intuitive insight, historical experience, and the spirit of critical inquiry and the scientific quest—then we have a revealing and concealing God, a God both knowable and unknowable, both near and far away, both mind and heart, both all-powerful and helpless, both redemptive and damning. In a word, we have a God who

159

was both present and absent in Auschwitz; who made the Holocaust a possibility but did not bring it about; who suffered with its victims but could not lift a finger to alleviate the pain, the anguish, and the heartlessness of it all; who remained true to his covenant with Israel and humankind but could not alter its conditions. Never in all of human history had God revealed himself so fully, or hidden himself so effectively. This awesome paradox becomes intelligible once one looks for God and his ways with nature and humankind through the prisms of the three modes of revelation which the spirit of free critical inquiry has vouchsafed us.

Let us take a hard, dispassionate, even clinical look at the Holocaust in the same way as we would take a look at some frightening and mystifying disease such as cancer or AIDS; or some frightening and partly mystifying natural phenomenon such as earthquakes or tornadoes; or some frightening and in part mystifying human tragedy such as war, starvation, terrorism, and homelessness. Must we not, first of all, recognize that such frightening phenomena are real possibilities in our universe, actualities that will not simply dissolve themselves by justified rage, pious pleas for divine intervention, or bitter tears? Whether or not there be a God, the only realistic option that is open to us if we seriously wish to lessen the mystery and to end the pain, the suffering, and the tragedy, is to have recourse to those laws of nature to which we have access and which, when understood and co-opted, offer us redemption from the evil which had held us in thrall. Scientists draw on these dependable laws to invent vaccines; to detect the ravaging forces of nature untamed and reduce their devastating effects; to manipulate genes to increase the food supply; to understand the workings of the brain and the trials and tribulations of the psyche and the divided self. What we do, in effect, in order to alleviate our affliction is to turn to the mind of God and tap those mathematical formulae, dependable laws, and enduring principles which made both our affliction and our healing possible. God thus is both all-knowing and all-causing, on the one hand, and not-knowing and not-causing on the other. God "knows" the formulae, the laws, and the principles, but God does not "know" how to activate them to serve human ends prior to their having been discovered by men and women through the spirit of free critical inquiry and the scientific quest. God is indeed a redemptive God, but only when the means for gaining redemption become known through the free, restless, and prying minds of men and women.

So, too, if one takes a sober and clinical look at the resources to which the individual can turn when stricken by suffering, affliction, and tragedy, for which the remedies lying dormant in the mind of God are not as yet at hand, we note that the heart and soul of God are always present. Love, compassion, hope, prayer, and spiritual resources not only are possibilities in our universe, but are actualities, actualities which throughout the ages have proved their power to mitigate, if not fully to transcend, pain, anguish, and despair, whether personal or collective. These spiritual actualities—love, compassion, justice—were proclaimed by some of Israel's prophets to be the essential attributes of God, attributes which, when assimilated by humankind, would prove to be redemptive.

No less redemptive for these prophets was the belief that God has the power to elevate humankind to a higher level of human possibility, provided that we find the means through a fuller awareness of the nature of God and of God's ways with mankind. It is thus evident that intuitive insight reveals that human beings have access to the heart and soul of God even when God is powerless as yet to prevent pain, suffering, and tragedy or to bring them to an end in response to tearful pleas, pious prayer, or righteous anger.

God's mind is thus revealed through the discovery by thinkers and scientists of the mathematical formulae, the abstract laws, and the enduring principles which nurture and sustain a universe that replicates in part, varies in part, and mutates in part, formulae, laws, and principles which may be drawn upon and utilized to attain human ends—whether they be good or evil—with confidence that they will not be willfully altered. God made thus manifest is seen to be powerful enough to sustain our complex universe, yet seems powerless to thwart its misuse by human beings who have tapped the mind of God so as to build weapons so destructive in power that they can blow a segment of the universe to kingdom come.

God's heart and soul reveal a God who makes possible not only love, compassion, mercy, grace, and righteousness, but the power to visualize what is not in existence; to yearn for the good, the true, and the beautiful; and to direct one's energies to the shaping of a future in the light of an ideal blueprint. These emotions and these capabilities bespeak a God who sustains love, compassion, mercy, grace, and justice as actualities always at our beck and call in good times and in bad and who sustains our capacity for overcoming despair in the present by visualizing a future when even death may die.

God's ways with humankind likewise are revealed through historical experience. The evidence seems to be weighty enough to support the adage that "man proposes and God disposes." All those hubristic illusions that human beings have held from time to time that history repeats itself, have been shattered not only by the transformations that have radically altered the physiognomy of even the most stable of societies and the sway of even the most dogmatic of religious beliefs, but by mutational break-throughs which were totally unanticipated and logically disjunctive. Such breakthroughs in the experience of Israel occurred when the voice of the prophet gave way to the Book; the Book to the Oral Law; the Book and the Oral Law to critical reason. Clearly, God's ways with humankind were never fully understood by prophets, priests, sages, or philosophers. The

161

divinely inspired writers of the Old Testament were wrong in their predictions; Christ-inspired New Testament writers were wrong in their predictions; and those who spoke in God's and Christ's names ever since then have been wrong in their predictions. The prophets never dreamed that they would be superseded by priests; the priests never imagined that they would be superseded by sages; and the sages never anticipated being challenged by the free critical mind. The Jesus of the Gospels never envisioned an imperial Catholic Church; the imperial Catholic Church never expected the tidal wave of Protestantism; and the Popes who reigned before Vatican II did not envisage that a day would come when the mass would no longer be read in Latin and when the windows of the Church would be opened to let in the light from Judaism, Protestantism, and the other sundry faiths of humankind.

God's ways with humankind are even more difficult to fathom than are the mind, heart, and soul of God. It is more difficult because time must pass before meaningful correlations and suggestive generalizations can be drawn from time and tide. Our spiritual and philosophic forerunners could not have discerned such meaning in the blur of time, any more than visitors from another planet, arriving before intelligent life had evolved on earth, could have postulated that the universe was in the process of becoming radically different from the universe being presently observed. After all, even Spinoza failed to see that God was a processional, not a replicating God, who had self-generated Spinoza's world out of a world in which there could have been no Spinoza or any sentient being; and a God who at that moment was in the process of bringing into existence a world which would generate minds that would become aware of evolutionary processes that had transformed a non-organic world into an organic one, and species without intelligence into a species with a mind. In a word, a prerequisite for discerning God's ways with the universe is time enough for these ways to become susceptible to tentative correlations and hypothetical generalizations.

Bearing these thoughts in mind, one can draw certain correlations and generalizations from Israel's odyssey that may throw light on God's ways with humankind. The first of these is that Israel's steadfast belief that there was a single God was powerful enough to preserve the Jewish people to this day, however powerless by worldly standards this God and this people seemed to be. For it is a matter of fact that the Jews are the only people from the ancient world to have survived the evolution of Western civilization as a living entity, despite their dependence as a minority through most of their history on the sufferance of great and mighty powers, cultures, and civilizations, and despite frequent threats to their continued existence in the form of legal discrimination, ideological harassment, pauperization, pogroms, expulsions, and the Holocaust. "'Not by might and not by power, but by my spirit,' saith the Lord" has proved to be a true prophecy indeed.

162

On empirical grounds, therefore, we can suggest that spiritual power may have greater survival power than coercive power.

The second of these generalizations is that ideological differences do not preclude peaceful, even fruitful, coexistence. Jews were granted polis rights in Alexandria despite the fact that they would not recognize Ptolemy as a God. Even though they rejected Zoroastrianism, Jews were generously treated in Babylonia by the Neo-Sassanians in the third and fourth centuries. The Jews of Andalusia were showered with privileges by caliphs and emirs and enjoyed a golden age even though they rejected the Koran. In early Christian feudal Europe, Jews were granted charters of privileges despite the fact that the Gospels held them responsible for the crucifixion of Jesus. The Jews were allowed to resettle in the Netherlands from which they had been expelled. They were granted emancipation in the wake of the French Revolution. They were accorded equal rights with non-Jews in the United States even though the Jews were a tiny minority, had no coercive means at their disposal, and were totally at the mercy of those who wielded political power and who were for the most part Christians to boot. Historical experience thus allows one to conclude that ideological differences, however deep, do not preclude harmonious coexistence.

The third of these generalizations derives from the fact that in virtually every society in which Jews have lived, harmonious coexistence has deteriorated into violent reactions against the Jews, reactions which have been justified on an array of ideational grounds; disloyal because they did not recognize the Emperor as God; threatening because they rejected Zoroastrianism, or the Koran, or Jesus; misanthropic because they are possessed of a national spirit alien to the national spirit of the Germans, French, English, or Americans; racially destructive because they are subhuman, demonic, and pestilential. It is thus evident from historical experience that ideational differences may at times make no difference, but at other times they make all the difference in the world.

The fourth of these generalizations is that a persuasive correlation seems to exist between the conditions that make for harmony despite the differences, and the conditions which exploit the differences to stir up hostility, hatred, and violence. Every society in the past where constructive interaction took place was a society which was growing, expanding, and widening opportunities for all elements in the population to attain a reasonable level of well-being and which was relatively free of objective anxieties.

Contrariwise, in every society which underwent contraction, suffered serious breakdown, and experienced a drastic lowering of living standards and of future expectations, the Jews found their previously favorable status nullified and their right to their lives, property, and right of residence rendered highly precarious. Since no past society has been able to maintain either steady economic growth or a high plateau of well-being, there is no society in the Western world in which Jews have not been singled out for hostile and lethal punishment for their difference.

The fifth of these generalizations is the revelation that these particular experiences of the Jews are an intensified microcosm of experiences universal for all humankind. All peoples have experienced the power of the spiritual to transcend and outlive the power of the material and the corporeal. One has only to look about and see how long-lived the eternal truths preserved in ancient myths still are: how Aeschylus, Sophocles, and Euripides have weathered the storms which swept away the power of Athens and Sparta; how the thought of Socrates, Plato, and Aristotle has soared above the comings and goings of classical empires, resisted the corrosive onslaughts of imperial Christianity to live on in contemporary minds; how the faith in Christ's redeeming love could not be dissolved by the wedding of the Church to wealth and power, or by the cruel and unusual punishments meted out by sadisti-Inquisitors who made mockery of the Jesus who broke bread with sinners and who pleaded with God on the cross that He forgive his tormentors for they knew not what they were doing; how the pursuit of the good, the true, and the beautiful has proven its power to survive and triumph even in the most totalitarian of modern societies.

So, too, during the periods of harmonious interaction between Jews and non-Jews, by demonstrating their capacity to dampen down the hostile potential flowing from profound ideational differences and by opening themselves to an appreciation of teachings hitherto viewed as blaspheming and frightening, all human beings have borne living witness to a remarkable human possibility, namely, a shared humanity rather than hostile confrontation, whatever the pressures of exclusive dogmas might be.

Likewise, though it may indeed be true that the Jews were singled out in disintegrating societies for singular punishment, in the end no one escaped the destructive consequences that followed in the wake of pernicious breakdown: civil wars, peasant revolts, starvation, pestilence, homelessness, despair.

Insofar, then, as the past is concerned, we can discern some of the ways of God with humankind: The spirit of God is powerful over the long run, even though there is no justification for believing that God can intervene directly to reward good and punish evil in the short run as the prophets seemed to have believed. Nonetheless, significant patterns have emerged from historical experience that give us hopeful signs that though God cannot intervene directly, he has made it possible for us to attain a higher level of human possibility.

What are these hopeful signs? It is a historical fact that human beings holding very radically different views, and according loyalty to very different values, have over significant periods of time shown their capacity for harmonious and fruitful interaction irrespective of time, place, culture, or previous conditions of discord, dissonance, and lethal conflict. It would seem to follow that if we could sort out the conditioning frameworks, and distinguish cause from consequence—economic, social, and political infrastructure from ideational superstructure—we would have some notion what must be done to create those conditions that would be conducive to perpetual harmony. This I have attempted to do by pointing out that those economic, social, and political infrastructures which have encouraged economic growth, social cohesiveness, and political stability have generated ideational superstructures which have been characterized by a lessening, if not a dissolution, of hostile and destructive interrelationships between Jews and their non-Jewish neighbors. And since, then, harmonious interrelations between communities which had been at loggerheads with each other ideationally have proved to be attainable in the past, there is good reason to believe that such transmutations are possible in the present and in the future. What is necessary, it would seem, is to activate those elements within the belief and value systems of the clashing communities which are likely to encourage harmonious interaction, and to deactivate those elements which encourage hostility.

Rhythmic activation and deactivation of harmonious and hostile elements within a tradition can be seen in the way that the Gospel story was read when the basic infrastructure was favorable to positive interaction from the way it was read when the basic infrastructure was unfavorable. Such rhythmic shifts between activating, now the harmonious and now the cacaphonic, are facilitated by the fact that the ideational and value systems that mark off one community and tradition from another are themselves so internally inconsistent and are so wracked with contradictions that at any point in time it is simply impossible to act out God-given demands which mutually exclude one another. Does Yahweh wish his people to wipe out the Amalekites man, woman, and suckling child, or does Yahweh wish his people to look forward to the day when Assyria will be His firstborn, Egypt his people, and Israel his inheritance? Does Jesus' love reach out to the most wretched of sinners, or does Jesus' wrath condemn the Scribes, Pharisees, and Christ-resisting Jews to Gehenna? Does the Church promote dialogue with the Jews, or does it imprint upon their foreheads the mark of Cain?

It would seem that historical experience reveals the laws that govern the rhythms of harmony and the rhythms of dissonance. The laws by which differences become the ear-splitting of clashing of cymbals, the deafening concussion of arrhythmic drumbeats, and a screeching jangle of instruments gone wild, or by which they are harmonized by a symphony of joyous sound. Were humankind wise enough to separate out those historical laws which work for redemption from those which work for damnation and then activate the former, then one can be confident that God will not, indeed cannot, block access to a higher stage of human possibility, any more than he can block the utilization of $E = MC^2$ for benign human ends. Contrariwise, God can no more stay a Holocaust from doing the devil's work than he can prevent an H-bomb from wiping out London, Paris, Washington, Moscow, or Jerusalem.

III

If we now take a close look at the Holocaust through the prisms of these three modes of revelation, we can see through their ghastly glow the presence of God's heart to suffer with the victims, but the absence of God's power to spare them. He could not spare them because human beings had not tapped the mind of God to build a nonlethal world, and they had not discerned in the historical record the ways of God with humankind. Had they done so, the Holocaust would have been an impossibility. The Holocaust would have been impossible had the economic, social, and political infrastructure of nation-state capitalism not broken down after 1929 worldwide, and collapsed utterly in a post–World War I Germany, a country which had never been given either the time or the opportunity to rebuild its war-shattered economic, social, and political foundations. Hitler could not have won mass support had the German people been basking in prosperity. The five fat years between 1924 and 1929 in Germany were lean years for Hitler and his followers. They waxed fat only when a sense of utter hopelessness, helplessness, and righteous despair, following on the collapse of the German economy in 1929, deluded the German people into believing that Hitler was a champion against a three-fold evil—economic breakdown, national humiliation, and Bolshevik tyranny—and that he would root it out at its source: the Jew. With evil incarnate wiped out, the good would be triumphant. Prosperity would abound; national pride and glory would swell in every Aryan heart; and the voice of Lenin would no longer be heard in the land. If, then, we wish to put our finger on the root cause of Hitler's power to transmute evil into good and be believed, then we must point to an economic collapse of such disastrous proportions that the barriers to utter evil were broken down in millions of German hearts and souls.

And if we were to ask how it came about that the collapse of the German economy turned out to be *sui generis*, we must point our finger at the Treaty of Versailles. And if we ask ourselves, how could civilized nations have imposed such brutal terms on a defeated enemy, we must point our finger at the triumph of the grand particulars of nationalism in the nineteenth century over the grand universals which had held sway in the eighteenth century. And if we ask how it was that human lives could have become so worthless and the human spirit so degraded and bereft of compassion, we must point the finger to the half million slaughtered at Verdun, to the bodies buried in Flanders Field, to the streams of blood that flowed into the Rhine, the Rhone, the Elbe, and the Seine during World War I. The Holocaust was not an evil crafted in Germany, but an evil crafted out of the failure of the grand statesmen of Europe to build a European community transcending the sovereign nation-state and a community undergirded by an economic infrastructure which recognized no national borders and which gave as much nourishment to this nationality as to that, to this denomination as to that, to this racial strain as to that, to this individual as to that.

After Verdun there is no mystery as to why there was a Holocaust. Hitler singled out the Jews as the most dangerous and poisonous enemies of the German people and the Aryan race, and therefore no punishment was too cruel or too unusual to subject them to. The Holocaust is the tragic logical outcome of that principle that elevated the claims of the sovereign nation-state to override all other claims, and nationalism to override all other values including the sanctity of human life.

There is thus no mystery as to the whereabouts of God at Auschwitz. After all, God did not create the sovereign nation-state or declare it to be the purpose of creation, at least not according to Chapter I of Genesis. For within this chapter God is pictured as a God who created a universe teeming with diversity, and capped his creation with an individual cast in his image, not a clan, a tribe, a nation, a race, a class, or privileged sex. To this individual God gave the freedom and the power to make or break God's creation. Indeed, God did not choose Abraham and his seed to be a special people until after the flood and the Tower of Babel, and then only on condition that it be a blessing to all the families of the earth.

So too God did not command the nations of Europe to confront each other as rivalrous entities or to elevate nationalism above all other gods. Nor did God dictate the Treaty of Versailles. Neither did he decree the collapse of the German economy. These were all decisions which men were free to make from that very day on which God created the first person and put the universe in his charge.

God's power was present at Auschwitz, but it was not within God's power to use it. It was not in his power because God's power is dependent on human choices as to how this power will be used whether for humane ends, whether they be angelic or demonic. God's power to act in the human sphere is no different from God's power to act in the realm of nature. So long as scientists were unaware of the formula $E = MC^2$, the power locked in that formula was self-actuating and not humanly directed. Once, however, awareness dawned, that divine power was at the disposal of humankind to enable it to serve beneficent or malevolent ends.

167

So, too, with the Holocaust. God's ways with humankind as revealed in historical experience had not been taken into account at Verdun and Flanders Field, as the Treaty of Versailles bears witness. Nor had they been taken into account when European nation-states failed to energize the sustained economic growth that would have dissolved borders, eliminated the need for imperialism and colonialism, and paved the way for constructive sharing of ideational differences. Instead they paved the road leading to confrontation and the Holocaust. God's awesome power was not drawn upon to serve beneficent ends in time. Rather it was turned over by default to serve the demonic. God's revelations through intuitive insight, through historical experience, and through the spirit of free inquiry—revelations speaking of how God's power can be activated to serve beneficent human ends—simply were not acted upon in time.

God's power thus could not be present at Auschwitz to spare the victims. The mind of God and the ways of God with humankind had not been tapped in time. But God's heart and soul were very much present at Auschwitz. His presence was to be found in the loving feelings that welled up in the hearts even of tortured victims; in the compassion displayed for those whose sufferings seemed greater than one's own; in the heroic and desperate efforts to convince oneself that life still had value; in the recollections of the joy and beauty of days and nights gone by; in the gleam of light furtively glimpsed on the uttermost fringes of darkness; in the dreams and the hopes of what might yet be realized, if only the pit would open up while there still was time; and in the tears that were shed for the utter tragedy and utter waste of it all. And it was because these soulful emotions were possible through the hell of it all that there were any survivors at all whose bodies could be resurrected and whose souls could be revived when they were snatched from the jaws of death.

God was present at Auschwitz, a helpless God, by human choice. Yet he kept love alive, compassion alive, memory alive, dreams and hopes alive, and along with the victims of flesh and blood shed bitter tears, so to speak, for the tragedy and the waste of it all.

IV

But need such tragedy and waste be the destiny of humankind? The Greeks believed so, and bequeathed us the myth of Sisyphus, the cyclical philosophies of history and the replicating philosophies of Nature and human nature. Human aspirations were believed by them to be most vulnerable when seemingly most reachable. For them, God was the Tragedian non pareil, seducing human beings by dangling before them illusions of a higher order of human existence and impelling them upward and onward to their tragic fate, mocking all the way. For such a

God the Holocaust is his ultimate achievement.

If this is the God that was revealed at Auschwitz, then humankind is doomed. It is possible, however, that the God that was revealed at Auschwitz is a God who, though powerless to redeem *at* Auschwitz, has the power to redeem *through* Auschwitz, provided that humankind heeds his ongoing revelations.

This power of redemption may be glimpsed in breakthroughs of possibilities which have occurred since the Holocaust by virtue of our being able to tap the mind of God as we have never been able to do before. Mathematical formulae, enduring principles, and natural laws have been discovered which allow us for the first time in human history to dissolve the objective anxieties that have plagued human beings from the beginning of time. Hitherto it had seemed to be impossible to produce enough food to ward off starvation; to build enough dwellings so that all might be sheltered; to eradicate pestilence, plague, and premature death; to eliminate destructive wars waged to gain possession of scarce natural resources; and to have access to the heavens above for that which was lacking and needful for humankind on the earth below.

But since the Holocaust, the prying minds of scientists heaven-bent to bring the four primary forces in nature under a single abstract mathematical formula, or enduring principle, or law of nature have glimpsed hitherto unknown dimensions of reality, dimensions which literally open up to us worlds without end where we may yet find redemption for our bodies and salvation for our souls. No longer can we say, as we might have said before Auschwitz, that Nature and Nature's God have condemned humankind to a tragic destiny by so limiting the natural resources at its disposal that objective anxieties would always be the fate of much of humankind.

There was another revelation that followed in the wake of the Holocaust, a revelation that a nation could enjoy self-esteem and the respect of other nations and economic well-being, even though it lacked the military power to defend its territory or its economic interests from the predations of a superpower. Both defeated West Germany and Japan performed economic, social, and political miracles that were the envy of victorious England and France. So, too, the emergence of a European Economic Community revealed that nation-states which had traditionally embarked on destructive wars to resolve their conflicting economic and national interests could work out constructive and congenial alternatives without loss of national dignity.

And there was a third revelation that followed in the aftermath of the Holocaust. Anti-Semitism suffered decisive defeats as objective anxieties diminished in the wake of the economic, social, and political well-being unleashed by the Marshall Plan and the Treaty of Rome. And this was nowhere more evident than in the United States, where Judaism was hyphenated to Christianity; where individual Jews were entrusted with the most sensitive secrets of the nation; and where the Jews were divested of their minority status in every respect other than numbers. The correlations of yesteryear were reconfirmed: flourishing societies diminish the power of ideational differences to block harmonious relations from emerging and dilute the hostile components that can make these differences so destructive.

And there was a fourth revelation as well. The Jews in Israel gained a state of their own, and a heightened sense of nationhood without at the same time endangering the status or well-being of the Jews living in Diaspora communities, Jews who identified themselves as Americans, or Englishmen, or Frenchmen, and not as Israelis. It was no less revealed that Jewish claims to nationhood and statehood were not thwarted on anti-Semitic grounds. Whatever problems Israel has had in gaining recognition from her Arab neighbors, these are the problems of any nation, large or small, whose claims to territory or jurisdiction are contested by other nations, ethnic groupings, and religious entities. No nation in a world of sovereign nation-states can totally insulate itself from the claims of other nations, or ethnic groupings, or religous entities, claims which frequently have lethal effects, as the American experience with international terrorism and the British experience with the IRA clearly demonstrate. Israel's future existence, to be sure, like the existence of all other nations, may ultimately be dependent on the emergence of some transnational world community, but as far as its present status is concerned, it is not likely to be in mortal danger so long as the United States, Great Britain, and the European community recognize it as a legitimate member of the family of nations.

These are illuminating revelations indeed! There need no longer be economic, social, and political breakdowns of such a magnitude that could pave the way for another Holocaust. Nations need not lift up swords against nations; profound ideational differences need not rule out harmonious human interaction; national self-esteem need not be measured in nuclear bombs, ballistic missiles, or laser beams; Jews can feel at home in the Diaspora no less than in Israel.

God's threefold mode of revealing Himself thus reassures us that the visions of an Isaiah may yet come to full realization.

But these revelations are, like the revelations in the past, not self-actualizing. They reveal possibilities, not eventualities. The ultimate outcome is dependent not on God, but on man. And here the post-Auschwitz record is murky. For every reassuring constructive breakthrough there has been a destructive failure: the superpowers still confront each other dangerously; fanatical nationalism and religious fundamentalism breed destructive wars and terrorism; economic rivalry among the United States, Europe, and Japan threatens the international economic order, while heavy debt endangers sustained economic growth in the Third World; and the spreading spirit of fundamentalism renders reasoned discourse more and more difficult. Clearly, human beings have not as yet made a clear-cut choice as to whether God's power is to serve beneficent or malevolent ends. The question is thus not whether humankind can be redeemed, but whether it will allow itself to be redeemed. Should it refuse once again, God will have no other option but to weep once again for the tragedy and the waste of it all.

V

God is a revealing God who shows us the way to redemption even in the Holocaust, but his revelation is not clear-cut. It must be discovered by our tapping the heart and soul of God through intuitive insight; by discovering His ways with humankind through historical experience; and by drawing on the mind of God through the spirit of free critical inquiry the power to shape a human destiny worthy of children created in God's image.

God also is a concealing God; for it may be that we shall never know why, with all the power in the world, God should have made himself and his universe so dependent on fragile, tempest-tossed, finite human beings who are as free to break a world as to make one.

Wolfgang Roth is the Frederick Carl Eiselen Professor of Old Testament Interpretation at Garrett-Evangelical Theological Seminar (on the campus of Northwestern University). He is a native of Germany and has attended the universities at Marburg, Tübingen, Heidelberg, and Victoria University (Toronto). He is a member of several scholarly organizations, and has written books and scholarly essays on biblical literature. He has worked closely with Herman Schaalman, as the latter has taught at Garrett for more than two decades as the Jewish Chautauqua Society resident lecturer.

Wolfgang Roth's essay raises important textual questions about the prophets. Roth introduces us to patterns within the biblical text which are themselves threads within the creative impulse in the covenant. This essay helps us to see how the covenant is more than a category of biblical thought; it is the dynamic within which we Jews-Christians read and teach our sacred texts. The covenant is that relationship within which Roth and Schaalman can and do respond to the prophets in their ongoing dialogue.

Jeremiah and Ezekiel, Moses and Joshua: Their Parallel Portrayals in "The Law and the Prophets"

Wolfgang Roth

It is a pleasure to honor in Herman Schaalman a perceptive colleague, a sensitive interpreter of Scripture and tradition, and a trusted fellow sojourner on the road of faith. His readiness to listen, ponder, and respond encourages me to offer him this exploration of the narrative presentations of four central figures in "The Law and the Prophets."

Introduction

Several features in the portrayal of Jeremiah in the Book of Jeremiah correspond to elements in the picture of Moses in the Books Exodus, Numbers, and especially Deuteronomy. They manifest themselves either through the use of the same word in analogous contexts or through broader thematic correspondences. An example of the former is the repeated employment of "mouth" in Ex. 4:10–12 and Jer. 1:6–9 within contexts which highlight the Lord's power to make a prophet's mouth the instrument of divine revelation, even in the face of a prophet's reluctance to speak in God's behalf. An example of thematic correspondence is the accompaniment of a prophet's call by visions, be they of a burning bush or of a boiling pot (Ex. 3:1–4:17, Jer. 1:13–16). In other words, the evidence of the concordance and the identification of similar topical imagery come together to suggest the existence of a special correlation between the presentations of the two figures.

Not only is Jeremiah's portrayal similar to that of Moses; also the

173

succession Jeremiah–Ezekiel, as implied in the two Books Jeremiah/ Ezekiel, is correlated to that of Moses/Joshua as found in Deuteronomy and Joshua. One example is the manner in which the beginning of each successor's activity is connected to the theme of the internalization of a book left by their predecessors (Jos. 1:7–8, Ezek. 2:8–3:3). But also the presentations of the two successor figures themselves, Ezekiel and Joshua, are literarily correlated. For instance, both are pictured as the ones who apportion to their people the inheritance set apart for them, Joshua doing so tangibly, Ezekiel through the medium of a vision (Jos. 13:1–22:34/ 6:1–11:23, Ezek. 47:13–48:29/38:1–39:29).

Some of the motif correspondences identified and discussed below are clearer and hence their cases more persuasive than others. At any rate, the argument of this paper is based on their cumulative nature. In other words, occasional correlations do not necessarily suggest the presence of a comprehensive literary design, but the coalescence of a larger number into a coherent picture does.

The Evidence

Almost twenty verbal or thematic correspondences may be identified. A dozen relate to Moses and Jeremiah and seven to Joshua and Ezekiel.

Jeremiah and Moses

1. Both Moses and Jeremiah are portrayed as "prophets" whose spheres of action are described in complementary fashion: Moses is prophet "in Israel" while Jeremiah is prophet "to the nations" (Deut. 34:10, Jer. 1:5).
2. Both Jeremiah and Moses protest their appointments, but do so with somewhat different arguments: The man from Anathoth pleads the inexperience of youth while the son of Amran pleads that he is a man "not of words." Yet the objections of both are overcome by the Lord's affirmation of their commissions (Ex. 4:10–12, Jer. 1:6–9).
3. Both Moses and Jeremiah are described as divinely destined for their missions. While Moses is miraculously preserved after birth, Jeremiah is assured that he was divinely "known" even before he was "formed in the womb" (Ex. 2:1–22, Jer. 1:5).
4. Both Jeremiah and Moses claim high degrees of immediacy in their relation to the Lord, the God of Israel: Jeremiah asserts that he has stood personally in the Lord's council while Moses is said to "know" his God "face to face" (Deut. 34:10, Jer. 23:18, 22).
5. Both Moses and Jeremiah find their appointments connected to visionary experiences: While Moses' call is preceded by the vision of the burning bush, Jeremiah's call is followed by two vision narratives, in one of which the fire motif is present (Ex. 3:1–4:17; Jer. 1:11–12/13–16).

6. Both Jeremiah and Moses are described as moving once during their activity into opposition to their divine Lord: Jeremiah accuses his God of treachery while Moses fails to "hallow" the Lord at the waters of Meribah. As a consequence Moses and Aaron are punished by being barred from entry into the land of promise but Jeremiah is offered reinstatement provided he repents (Num. 20:13–23/27:14, Jer. 15:10–21).

7. Both Jeremiah and Moses are accompanied by named adjunct figures who communicate the prophet's message when conditions make that necessary, and both are pictured as near equals of their masters: Aaron and Baruch (Ex. 4:13–16, Jer. 36:9–10, cf. 43:3).

8. Both Moses and Jeremiah commit their divinely authored words to the medium of the bookscroll, and do so for the purpose of public reading: Moses codifies "the book of the law of Moses," while Jeremiah dictates the "scroll-book of Jeremiah's words" (Deut. 31:9–13, Jer. 36:1–10).

9. Both Jeremiah and Moses are threatened with death by those to whom they are sent: The man from Anathoth barely escapes starvation in a mud-mired cistern, and the son of Amran is divinely preserved from the people's attempt to stone him (Num. 14:10 [13:1–14:45], Jer. 26:1–24, 37:11–39:18, cf. 1:17–19).

10. Both Moses and Jeremiah not only mention or affirm the rite of circumcision but also call for "the circumcision of the heart" (Deut. 10:16, 30:6, Jer. 4:3–4, cf. 9:24–25, 29:10–14).

11. Both Jeremiah and Moses are followed by explicitly or implicitly identified successors who are called to their offices in advance of the completion of their masters' missions. Ezekiel, called to office but told to remain silent, finds his mouth opened after Jerusalem's fall at the point in time when that of Jeremiah is silenced through removal to Egypt. On the other hand, Joshua becomes active as speaker and leader only after Moses' demise (Ezek. 1:2–3:15, 3:22–27/24:25–27/ 33:21–22, cf. Jer. 40:1–44:30, Deut. 34:9, Jos. 1:1–18).

12. Finally, both Moses and Jeremiah are presented as active for the period of some forty years in the vocations for which their visionary calls had set them apart. Moses' activity as prophet in Israel begins with his encounter at the burning bush and ends approximately forty years later. Jeremiah's labors as prophet to the nations begins in the thirteenth year of Josiah's reign (626 B.C.E.) and ends in the aftermath of the fall of Jerusalem, that is, approximately forty years later (586 B.C.E.; Ex. 3:1, Deut. 34:1–12, Jer. 1:3, 40:1).[1]

Ezekiel and Joshua

13. Both Ezekiel and Joshua begin their activity with the "internalization" of a book. Joshua is told not only to be strong in taking the land but

also to "observe all the law of the Lord's servant Moses," keeping it close to his "mouth," while Ezekiel is given into his "mouth" a book-scroll and then ordered to consume it (Jos. 1:7–8, Ezek. 2:8–3:3).

14. Both Joshua and Ezekiel move from the wilderness into the land of promise: Joshua through narration which describes him as leading the people into the Land of Canaan; Ezekiel through a vision which describes him being translated in the spirit to the land of promise and its holy city (Jos. 1:2–18, 2:1–12:24, Ezek. 8:1–11:25, 40:1–48:35).

15. Both Joshua and Ezekiel begin their missions standing at the banks of rivers which mark, literally or figuratively, the dividing line between wilderness and home. For Joshua it is the River Jordan which he must cross in order to carry out his mission, for Ezekiel it is the River Kebar from the banks of which he is transferred in the spirit to Canaan (Jos. 1:2, 3:1–5:1, Ezek. 1:1, 3:15).

16. Both Ezekiel and Joshua are described as those who apportion the promised land to their people, and as doing so after the opponents have been vanquished. Ezekiel in a vision allots to each tribe, to its pedigreed members as well as to its nonpedigreed sojourners, their portions, while Joshua does so tangibly through the casting of lots, excluding however the nonpedigreed (Jos. 13:1–22:34/6:1–11:23, Ezek. 47:13–48:29/38:1–39:29).

17. Both Joshua and Ezekiel are faced with the issue of the limits of human responsibility. The latter emphatically argues for the possibility of a sinner's repentance and against holding his family responsible, but Joshua's treatment of Achan and his family attests the opposite position (Jos. 6:1–7:26, Ezek. 18:1–32).

18. Both Ezekiel and Joshua bring to completion their inherited missions of possessing the land; hence, they remain without individual, named successors (Jos. 24:29–31, Ezek. 40:1).

19. Finally, Joshua and Ezekiel announce as goal of their appointed tasks their people's renunciation of apostasy and idolatry, followed by their covenantally confirmed, exclusive loyalty to the Lord, the God of Israel, and their residence in the land of promise (Jos. 24:23–24, Ezek. 36:25, cf. 34:25–26, 37:26).

The Literary Pattern

Do the correspondences suggest the presence of a comprehensive design? Is their cumulation a sufficient basis for broader conclusions? Is it appropriate to single them out for exploration? Before these questions are answered, a systematic review of their similarities and differences is indicated.

Similarities

The similarities may be summarized in this manner. Both pairs of men are related to each other as predecessor and successor, that is, the second figure is commissioned before the first figure's disappearance but remains in the background or expressly silent until the predecessor actually falls silent. Moreover, neither predecessor-successor pair has immediate predecessors or successors. Both lead figures, Moses and Jeremiah, are portrayed as prophets of the highest order, that is, as unique in their immediacy in relation to the divine. Both are, either before or after birth, preserved for their future mission, and their commissioning is (as is also the case in relation to other prophetic figures) connected with visionary experiences. Both are accompanied by named adjuncts who speak or write on their behalf, and both are together with them at least once under threat of death. Both demand a circumcision of the heart, and both commit their words to the medium of the book.

By the same token, Joshua and Ezekiel, the two successors, are bound to their predecessors not only by way of narrative plot but also as recipients of their predecessors' codified legacy (though in Ezekiel's not expressly so identified). Both move from the wilderness, real or figurative, to the land of promise, crossing rivers in order to apportion the territory. Finally, the mission of both successor figures leads to the exclusive loyalty of the people to their God in response to the divine presence in their midst. In short, such cumulation of parallel elements in the portrayals of the two pairs suggest literary counterimaging. But how do the differentiating features qualify this tentative conclusion?

Differences

A systematic review reveals their complementarity. Thus, while Moses and Jeremiah align themselves in their call for a circumcision of the heart, they are differentiated through their constituencies: Moses is prophet "in Israel" while Jeremiah is sent "to the nations," including Israel (Jer. 25:18–26). In other words, while Moses and Joshua are exclusively related to the twelve tribes descended from Jacob/Israel, Jeremiah and Ezekiel move beyond them to "all the kingdoms of the earth" (Jer. 25:26).

The subtle balancing of the two pairs is evident also in the manner in which the intimacy of the two figures with the divine is graduated: Jeremiah is admitted to the heavenly council of the Lord, but Moses sees his God "face to face" and speaks with the Lord "mouth to mouth." Or, while the book of the law of Moses is codified once and for all and must remain free from subtraction or addition, the scroll of Jeremiah's book is written twice and capable of augmentation. Or, while Moses' intercession was initially successful on behalf of his contemporaries, that same success could not be claimed for him were he to intercede in Jeremiah's time for Israel (Jer. 15:1–2, the only passage in Jeremiah where Moses is mentioned by name). But also, the intercession by Jeremiah is of little avail without the people's repentance, because their refusal to heed his words removes them from the land of promise to Egypt, the paradigmatic place of servitude, where with few exceptions they will perish.

Finally, a telling differentiation within the correlation of Jeremiah with Moses is the latter's announcement that the Lord will raise "a prophet like me" whom Israel is commanded to obey (Deut. 18:15,18). In light of the correspondence already discussed, that second Moses who is to come can only be Jeremiah! This identification of that enigmatic figure of Deut. 18 would explain the Lord's affirmation in the story of Jeremiah's commission that he "knew him even before he was formed in the womb" (Jer. 1:5). Indeed, the man from Anathoth has thus been announced by the Lord (and thus indeed been "known") through Moses' words in Deut. 18:15 and 18.

The narrative correlation of two figures is evident also in a comparison of the two successors, Joshua and Ezekiel. Thus, while Joshua leads the people physically into the land of promise and allots to them their tribal shares, Ezekiel does the same in the visionary mode, apportioning shares also to nonpedigreed sojourners. Or, while Joshua completes his mission within the boundaries of the Land of Canaan and is eventually buried there, Ezekiel returns in the spirit to his fellow exiles, telling them what he had heard and seen.

Finally, the counterimaging of the predecessor-successor pairs is uniquely suggested through the employment of that word which refers to the primary human organ of mediation of the divine will: "mouth." Both Jeremiah and Moses receive directly from the Lord "in(to) the mouth" the divine words to be transmitted to their constituencies (Ex. 4:10–12, Jer. 1:6–9), while Joshua and, it seems, also Ezekiel receive, internalize, and then give forth through the "mouth" their predecessors' legacies already committed to the medium of a book (Jos. 1:7–8, Ezek. 2:8–3:3). In other words, Moses and Jeremiah as well as Joshua and Ezekiel are mediators of revelation, but the former are so in a direct and primary fashion, the latter in a secondary and contingent manner.

Conclusions

The features of the portrayals, taken together, argue for the presence of a comprehensive design according to which Jeremiah is cast as the other Moses and Ezekiel as the other Joshua. By the same token, Moses is presented as the first Jeremiah and Joshua as Ezekiel's counterpart. Their characterizations are interdependent and thus define each other. What makes them distinct are their constituencies: Israel and the nations. Thus they are related to concentrically defined spheres: Moses and Joshua to an inner circle, Jeremiah and Ezekiel to an outer perimeter which includes the inner one. What the first pair is for the descendants of Jacob/Israel, that the latter one is for the descendants of Noah.

These findings suggest that loyalty to and service of the Lord, the God of Israel, manifest themselves in two, mutually defining forms: Both within and without the land of promise, both in body and in spirit, in circumcision both of the flesh and of the heart, through a covenant cut in stone as well as engraved on the heart, and both through the closed canon of the Law of Moses and the open canon of the scroll of Jeremiah's book. The literary doubling attests the narrative juxtaposition of a two-sided, dialectic conceptualization of Israel's heritage: an externally closed one and an internally open one, or in later nomenclature, "The Law" and "The Prophets."

Thus the questions raised earlier have found an answer. The literary correspondences are sufficiently focused on Moses and Joshua and their counterparts, Jeremiah and Ezekiel, to warrant separate exploration, and their number is large enough and their nature sufficiently varied to allow the assumption of literary patterning.

On the other hand, the conclusion supports the position of those scholars who argue that "The Law and the Prophets" emerged as one literary work and is to be read primarily as such, or at least is, as E. Auerbach put it a generation ago, the result of a *"grosse Ueberarbeitung der biblischen Buecher."*[2] In a similar vein D. N. Freedman concludes his essay on "The Law and the Prophets" with the thesis that that work "emerged as a literary entity during a comparatively brief period in Israel's history, but a decisive one during which the nation came to an end and out of the trials of captivity a new community was born."[3] By the same token, this position calls into question interpretive approaches which begin with postulated smallest text units and see in their gradual buildup the key to the analysis of the larger work. On the contrary, it seems that the conceptualization of the entire work also supplied the design of its constituent units, each of which is literarily molded to embody the perspective of the work as a whole.

Indeed, the conceptual unity of the work (the obvious and acknowledged recasting of sources notwithstanding) has suggested itself to the writer already on other grounds.[4] "The Law and the Prophets" has its own narrative plot, its set of actors, its staging in space, and, readily recognizable, its overarching chronological framework. As such it is a work of encyclopedic nature, in volume, inclusiveness, and perspective—a first "Encyclopedia Judaica-Hierosolymitica," as it were. While its traditional title reflects its double focus on "The Law" and on "The Prophets," its earlier (first?) title may be preserved at its end, in its epilogue made up of the Book Malachi. There the "writing of a book of remembrance before him [the Lord]" is described as the result of divine action in response to the God-fearers' despair over apostasy. That "book of remembrance" is not only dedicated to "the worshippers of the Lord and [to] those who think of his name," but also affirms the Lord's certain intervention on their behalf and enables them to distinguish between those who are loyal to the Lord and those who are not (Mal. 3:16–18)—an apt concluding observation concerning the both comforting and instructing nature of a work in which all is preserved which the descendants of Jacob/Israel and of Noah need to know and to remember.

Notes

1. Professor Joseph Blenkinsopp (Notre Dame) made this observation during the discussion of an earlier form of this paper at the Midwest Meeting of the Society of Biblical Literature (1984), and suggested its consideration in the context of its argument.
2. "Die grosse Ueberarbeitung der biblischen Buecher," *Supplement I. Vetus Testamentum* (Leiden: E. J. Brill, 1953), 1–10. I owe the reference to the instructive discussion in Joseph Blenkinsopp's *Prophecy and Canon* (Notre Dame/London: Notre Dame University Press, 1977), esp. 102, 178.
3. *Supplement IX, Vetus Testamentum* (1962), 250–65, reprinted in *The Canon and Masorah of the Hebrew Bible. An Introductory Reader*, ed. Sid Z. Leiman (New York: KTAV, 1974), 5–20.
4. See the writer's discussion of Joshua-Kings in "Deuteronomistisches Geschichtswerk/Deuteronomistische Schule," *Theologische Realenzyklopaedie* VIII (Berlin: de Gruyter 1982), esp. 547–50.

Rosemary Radford Ruether is the Georgia Harkness Professor at Garrett Evangelical Theological Seminary. Besides her Ph.D. from Claremont, Professor Ruether holds several honorary degrees in humane letters. She has written more than a dozen books and participated in many more scholarly anthologies and journals. She is internationally renowned for her classic work, Faith and Fratricide. *She was among the first to raise serious questions about anti-Judaism within the core of Christianity. Rosemary Ruether's relationship with Herman Schaalman has spanned this past decade. During that time they have been co-faculty members at Garrett Evangelical Theological Seminary and in several Jewish-Christian dialogue groups.*

Rosemary Ruether provides us with a historical and theological overview of Jewish-Christian encounters. The common covenant shared by Judaism and Christianity is the challenge to which Ruether wants us to continue to respond. Her criticism of Christianity and her historical analysis are all offered as her response to that essential challenge, to a life of covenant, a covenant shared equally by Jews and Christians. Her conclusion is provocative, because it forces us to remain in constant dialogue as Jews and Christians, committed to a common covenant, rooted in a shared vision of hope.

Covenant and Peoplehood in the Christian Tradition: Questions of Church, Synagogue, and Nation

Rosemary Radford Ruether

Christianity and Judaism share a common concept of covenant which they derive from the faith of Israel, but this idea of covenant has more frequently divided than united Christians and Jews due to both different and rival views of the nature and identity of the covenanted people. In this essay I plan to look at the ways in which Christianity appropriated the word "covenant" from its beginnings and then applied that term to itself as church. Then I will trace the repoliticizing of the idea of covenant by emerging Christian nations in the Reformation era and the problem of applying the concept of covenant to the American nation. Finally, I will discuss problems of Jewish-Christian relations today in terms of the theme of covenant. Can this be a term by which Jews and Christians can see each other as parallel and complementary peoples, rather than rivals for an exclusive idea of chosenness?[1]

From its beginnings, Christianity defined itself as the people of the "new covenant." Its Scriptures proclaim this idea by being called the "New Testament (Covenant)." This term was understood as both continuity and discontinuity with the people of the "Old Testament" or "Old Covenant." Christianity saw itself as inheriting the covenant of God with Israel and yet superseding the people of the Torah. The Christian covenant was conceived as a covenant on a higher level, in the sense of both greater inwardness and greater universality. In the Christian Church all nations were called together and covenanted with the God who created and is redeeming the world.

Christianity probably derived its concept of the new covenant in part from messianic sectarian types of Judaism of the first century, such as the Covenanters of the Dead Sea Scroll community. These people saw themselves as anticipating the messianic fulfillment of the covenant of God with Israel by gathering a voluntary community of righteous ones who gathered out of ordinary evil society and sought to live in complete obedience to God's laws, awaiting the final messianic advent. Christianity also originally saw itself as a messianic sect within Judaism, but one which already experienced that advent on the plane of the crucified Messiah whose sufferings brought inward redemption. It was awaiting the completion of that advent in the appearance of the Son of Man on clouds of glory to judge the world. Thus covenant for Christianity from the first had the idea of a voluntary community of personal conversion, rather than an inherited elect nation. The people of the New Covenant were both a universal people, gathered from among all nations, and a people set over against political systems as a spiritual community of the redeemed who awaited the consummation of world history.

However, as the Christian Church increasingly institutionalized itself and was adopted by the Roman Emperor Constantine in the fourth century as the unifying religion of the tottering Roman Empire, these covenantal themes tended to disappear from the center of the idea of church, even though the language remained in the Christian terms for the two parts of its Bible. Covenantal theology tended to continue primarily among apocalyptic, sectarian groups such as the African Donatists, who retained the sense of tension with the Roman Empire as the expression of the Kingdom of Satan. Monastic communities also retained the idea of a spiritual covenanted community, but this now became a voluntary community of special dedication to holiness within the Christian Church.

The Reformation, however, saw a revival of attention to the concept of covenant. The Anabaptists restored the original Christian concept of a covenanted people gathered out of the world and awaiting a messianic advent. Like their earlier Christian forebears, they not only set themselves over against worldly political systems, refusing to participate in war or political leadership, but also saw their fellow Christians of both the Catholic and the Reformed traditions, as "Churches of Satan." All churches which continue the Constantinian tradition of integration into the state were, for the Anabaptists, expressions of the Fall of the Church. Only the Christian community which gathered apart from the state, as a voluntary society of people who had experienced personal conversion, retained the true nature of the Church. In a language that echos Hosea as well as Paul, Melchior Hoffman, one of the thinkers of the first generation of Anabaptism in the sixteenth century, speaks of the covenanted community as a people gathered into the wilderness to be betrothed to the Lord:

> And now in this final age the true apostolic emissaries of the Lord
> Jesus Christ will gather the elect flock and call it through the gospel
> and lead the Bride of the Lord into the spiritual wilderness, betroth
> and covenant her through baptism to the Lord. Thus also St. Paul (II
> Cor. 11:2) had betrothed the Church of Corinth to the Lord as a virgin
> to her husband and bound it under the covenant.[2]

By this contrast to this Anabaptist use of covenant in the apocalyptic,
sectarian way as a voluntaristic messianic people, the Zwinglian and
Calvinist Reformed traditions used the term "covenant" to mean an
inherited election from God's covenant to emerging Christian nationhood. Seeing themselves in continuity rather than in a rival relation to
the covenant with Israel, Puritans generally adopted a more positive view
of the Jews than medieval Christianity had. Puritans also did not use the
Law-Grace dichotomy in the antagonistic way characteristic of Luther-
anism. Rather, law was seen as part of the inherited covenantal relation
with God which was then made inward through grace.

The New England Congregationalists inherited and fused elements
of both the Calvinist and Anabaptist concepts of covenant. Like the
Reformed theologians, they stressed the historic covenant of grace. God
throughout ages past and continuing to the present generation has bound
himself to a special covenant with his elect people. This covenant is wholly
the work of God's grace. This covenant of grace can neither be initiated
nor ultimately broken by sinful humanity. It represents the specific plan of
God for electing and covenanting to himself those whom he has chosen to
bring into the fulfillment of the promises of salvation. These people God
governs not only with special grace, but also with special chastisement, to
form them into a disciplined and godly people.

However, in addition to this emphasis on the historic and gracious
nature of the covenant, New England Congregationalists took over from
Anabaptism the concept of covenant as a voluntary pact between church
members to enter into a common fellowship and church government
together. The Mayflower compact extended this idea of covenant to
include civil society. The signers of the Mayflower pact, who included non-
church members, pledged themselves to found a godly commonwealth.
This was anticipated by the Anabaptist understanding of the church as a
disciplined community whose rules covered the whole of the lives of
believers.

The covenantal idea of church assumes rigorous standards of
church membership, including personal experience of conversion. The
covenant of the Salem community in 1629 was established with this brief
statement of their common contract:

> We covenant with the Lord and with one another and do bind
> ourselves in the presence of God to walk together in all his ways,
> according as he is pleased to reveal himself unto us in his Blessed word
> of truth.[3]

All who desired to unite with the Salem group on the basis of this covenant were examined in regard to their knowledge of the principles of religion, their personal experience of the grace of conversion, and godly conduct in their daily lives. Only those who passed these tests without serious reproach were admitted as members of the Church. Soon a large number of colonists found themselves outside the Church covenant! Difficulties particularly arose in the admission of members' children who had not yet experienced personal conversion. This led finally in 1665 to the formation of the "halfway covenant" whereby children of the baptized could be admitted to membership on the basis of their parents.

New England Congregationalists and their descendants drew on a Calvinist tradition that used the idea of covenant to mean not only voluntary converted churches but also reformed political communities. Covenant becomes not only the basis of salvation or relation to God, but also the basis of new nationhood. John Locke's concept of the social contract and the American national Constitution have their roots in this Puritan idea of a new code of righteousness by which a people enter into a national covenant. Thus Calvinism typically tries to create a coextensiveness of religious and political community. In Calvin's Geneva we find this effort to shape both a reformed church and a reformed political community ruled by the joint leadership of the ministry and the reformed magistrates. Only those who belonged to the Church could hold political office. The whole community is to submit, not only to the laws of social order, but to laws of public morals designed to shape the whole community into an expression of the reign of divine righteousness on earth.

These tendencies to interpret the covenant politically were further developed in the Federal Theology of Dutch Calvinism and found expression in the Puritan Civil War in England in the mid-seventeenth century. Puritans were the first to execute a king, thus discarding the theory of kingship by divine right and seeking to substitute for monarchy a "Holy Commonwealth." However, by the 1660s Englishmen had grown tired of civil strife and the effort to impose morality upon the body politic. Thus it was in the American colonies that exiles from the Puritan experiment were sent to continue the effort to create a covenanted commonwealth in the Massachusetts Bay colony.

This intention to found a people under God, who have specifically contracted with God and with each other to be obedient to God's commandments of righteousness, is evident in the famous sermon of John Winthrop in 1630. Winthrop was the first leader of the Massachusetts Bay

Colony, and his sermon was delivered to the colonists while they were still on board ship.

> Thus stands the cause betweene God and us. Wee are entered into Covenant with him for this worke, wee have taken out a Commission, the Lord hath given us leave to draw our owne Articles, wee have professed to enterprise these Accions upon these and these ends, wee have hereupon besought him of favour and blessing. How if the Lord shall please to heare us and bring us in peace to the place wee desire, then hath hee ratified this Covenant and sealed our Commission and will expect a strickt performance of the Articles contained in it, but if wee shall neglect the observacion of these Articles which are the ends wee have propounded and dissembling with our God, shall fall to embrace this present world and prosecute our carnall intencions seekeing greate things for our selves and our posterity, the Lord will surely breake out in wrathe against us, be revenged of such a perjured people and make us knowe the price of the breache of such a Covenant.[4]

Winthrop goes on to say that the one way to avoid this shipwreck of their common purpose is to follow the teachings of the prophet Micah to "do justly and love mercy and walk humbly with our God" (6:8–AV). To this end the community must be "knit together as one man," hold each other in brotherly affection, and be ready to "abridge ourselves of superfluities" in order to minister to each other in times of necessity. The community should rejoice together, mourn together, labor and suffer together, keeping before their eyes their common life as one Body in the Lord. If they do this, the Lord "will be our God and will delight to dwell amongst us as His own people and will command a blessing upon our ways."

Winthrop declares that the New England colony is to be like the city set on the hill. The eyes of all people are upon them, so that "if we deal falsely with our God in this work, and cause Him to withdraw his present help from us, we will become a shame to God's servants and cause them to turn their prayers to curses against us until we be consumed out of the good land where we are going." Winthrop ends his sermon with the Deuteronomic injunction of Moses in his last farewell to Israel before entrance to the Promised Land.

> Beloved there is now set before us life and good, death and evil in that we are commanded this day to Love the Lord our God and to love one another, to walk in his ways and keep his commandments and his ordinance and his laws, and the articles of our covenant with him that we may live and be multiplied and that the Lord our God may bless us in the land whither we go to the possess of it. But if our hearts shall turn away so that we will not obey, but shall be seduced and worship other gods, our pleasures and profits and serve them, it is pro-

pounded unto us this day, we shall surely perish out of the good Land whither we pass over this vast sea to possess it.

Therefore lett us choose life that wee and our Seede may live, by obeying his voyce and cleaveing to him, for hee is our life and our prosperity.[5]

The Puritan extension of this concept of covenant to the political community drew upon and, in turn, became an important source for theories of constitutional government. The contract theory of government was a revolutionary idea in the seventeenth century. It was used to overthrow ideas of government based on natural or inherited hierarchy or divine right of kings. Feudal and royal ideas of government argued that the prince and his subjects were related to each other much as children were subject to their parents, or creatures subject to the paternal power of God.

Puritanism rejected the idea that any political leadership represented natural or divine fatherhood. Political leadership was a function within a community's agreement to form a society. No man inherited the right to rule by nature. Just as humanity contracted with God voluntarily to enter the covenant and to obey God's commands, so human government was based on a voluntary contract entered into willingly by all partners. In this contract humans pledged themselves to adhere to common disciplines of law and order and to receive thereby the blessings of peace and security.

It was the boldness of Puritan theory to try to bring together as one these theories of the covenant between humanity and God and the political contract of society. They postulated a Christian commonwealth founded upon the covenantal bond. In so doing, Puritan thought gave America a double-sided legacy. On the one hand, it gave America a high consciousness of itself as an elect nation, specially favored by God, called to a higher mission than the rest of humanity, destined to prosper and succeed beyond all other nations because of this divine election and favor. On the other hand, it exposed America to a higher level of criticism and judgment for our failures to live up to these high standards of covenanted life. Not for America the mistakes, pride, greed, or naked power that the unregenerate nation might claim as the natural law of politics. Establishing itself as an elect nation under God, it must manifest a higher righteousness and be judged accordingly.

In the Puritan preaching of the seventeenth-century New England divines, we see this judgmental side of the concept of the covenant. God is said to have a controversy with New England. Like the prophets of the Old Testament, the New England Jeremiahs inveigh against their people for failing to live up to the strict terms of the covenant. God had rewarded their former piety with an abundance of material blessings. But now these same material blessings have allowed the people to grow fat and wanton and to neglect the terms of the covenant. Worldly manners have crept in among them. Standards of piety and frugality have become relaxed.

The ministers never openly imply that the people might become so unrighteous as to lose their covenanted relation to God completely. But they strongly hint that the covenanted relationship implies not only God's blessings upon obedient compliance but also God's severe wrath and punishment upon its infraction. Moreover, God is soon to bring his controversy with New England to a crisis. His patience is wearing thin. Only a short time remains for the people to repent and return to strict standards of life before some culminative act of divine vengeance will catch them. Natural catastrophes, droughts, floods, military defeats, and raids from hostile French and Indians are all God's "medicines" of chastisement to bring the people to recognition of their laxity and return to full adherence to covenanted life.

Well into the eighteenth century, legislators as well as churchmen were exhorted to recognize that while a covenanted people enjoyed great privileges from God, this also entailed great duties and obligations.

> A covenant people are not left at their liberty, whether they will Love, Fear, Serve and Obey the voice of God in his Commands, or not. They are under the highest and most awful obligations imaginable to the whole of the Covenant duty; not only from God's express Command and Precept, who is their King, Lord and Lawgiver, but also, by virtue of their own Professed Subjection unto God. . . . They are therefore most Solemnly cautioned to take heed to themselves and beware, lest they should forget and forsake the Lord, his Worship, Fear and Service, because by this means they would surely forfeit all those desirable blessings, which a course of obedience would crown them with, and pull down upon themselves the just rebukes and terrible revenges of Heaven.[6]

The ideas of America as a New Israel are the source of much that is good and bad in American history. On the one hand, the idea of America as an elect nation, specially blessed and favored, easily lends itself to extreme nationalism. On the other hand, those who take seriously the idea that covenant means a higher standard of righteousness take upon themselves the prophetic role in society. They castigate America for failures of justice, goodness, and righteousness, exhorting Americans again to rededicate themselves to the high standards of covenantal life.

In 1776 the thirteen colonies revolted against the rule of English monarchy and contracted with each other to form a new government. Only a few of the New England states shared the Puritan concept of political life under God. They too had had to adjust their originally exclusive concepts of the Christian commonwealth to a more diversified and less disciplined reality. Other states, especially Virginia, were Anglican in foundation and thus represented religiously the Puritan Antichrist. Rationalist deism sat more easily with statesmen from this region than Calvinism. Yet leaders from these various colonies shared political ideas from the English and French Enlightenments propounded by thinkers such as John Locke and Baron Montesquieu. These thinkers had developed secular versions of the idea of the social contract.

The establishment of a constitution as the basis of the American nation reflects this concept. Americans, in forming a new nation, were not merely rejecting dependence on England. They were rejecting one concept of government for another. They were declaring that the rules of law in a society are binding upon all only when all can be seen as voluntary parties to the social contract. The leaders and agents of social enforcement represent collective authority collectively assented to by all citizens.

But who really are the citizens? Who are the parties to the contract? The leaders of the colonists who assembled in Philadelphia were ready to apply the principle of the consent of the governed, instead of monarchical rule from England, to themselves. But were they willing to apply this same principle to many other persons in their midst who also had not been consulted about their government? What about the many people who had come to America as bondservants? Were the servant and propertyless people to have no voice in government? What about Negro slaves? Who consulted them about their government as they journeyed to a land, not of freedom, but of bondage, in fetid slave ships?

What about the American Indians whose lands were being progressively forfeited by the expansion of the European colonists? They were viewed as separate nations with whom the American nation made treaties, but these treaties were soon broken as the colonists expanded to yet other parts of this new country. As their numbers dwindled into enclaves surrounded by the white nation, the anomaly of their situation remained. Finally, what about women? On what basis are they excluded from the Rights of Man so boldly proclaimed in the American Declaration of Independence? These questions were to continue to haunt the American experiment as the Abolitionist Movement, the Civil War, the eighty-year Women's Suffrage Movement, and the Indian Wars sought to resolve the contradictions left by the Framers of the Constitution.

But these bloody or bloodless struggles still have not resolved all the questions about the racial, religious, and ethnic inclusiveness of the American covenant. Are Catholics, Jews, and Muslims really included? Is there something intrinsically Protestant about the nature of American social institutions that makes it difficult to absorb Catholics? How Christian is the American Commonwealth? Can Jews be included? What about those whom Christians would have called "pagans"? If the covenant belongs to the "converted," how can it include those who do not share these Protestant or Christian principles of religion?

Furthermore, how Anglo-Saxon is the covenant? The English Puritans wove a close relationship between Protestantism and Anglo-Saxon or English peoplehood. God had made a special covenant with them to represent his favored people. Americans inherited this idea of the Anglo-Saxon Protestant as the core of America's identity. Nineteenth-century Americans even referred to WASPs as "native Americans" in contrast to immigrant peoples of other nationalities. To become an American was to assimilate into this Anglo-Saxon Protestant cultural identity. This provided the mold into which the other peoples were to "melt" in the American melting pot, giving up their own languages and cultures and identifying themselves with the New England colonists as their "ancestors."

As more and more Irish Catholics, Italians, Poles, Jews from Eastern Europe, Greeks, Armenians, and Asians poured onto these shores in successive waves of immigration, this latent ethnocentricity was to be strained to the breaking point. The Anglo-Saxon racism that asserts itself throughout the nineteenth century against Blacks, Indians, Asians, Jews, and other so-called ethnics also surfaces in these latent assumptions about the religious-racial exclusivity of the covenanting people of the United States.

Blacks have been the group most rigorously regarded as "beneath" the level of American peoplehood racially, although religiously they early adopted versions of evangelical Protestantism. A bloody Civil War was fought to abolish the institution of slavery—something the United States Constitution had failed to do. But many of the abolitionists had not yet come to terms with the idea of the equally *human nature* of Blacks and whites. The implicit whiteness or Anglo-Saxonness of American nationhood was expressed in reactions to many other groups. Some groups melted into this white Anglo-Saxon Protestant mold much more easily than others.

The post-Civil War period saw increasing stress over the growing ethnic, racial, and religious pluralism of America. The potato famine brought wave upon wave of immigrants from Ireland. The pogroms of Russia filled New York and other cities with Jewish refugees. Rapid industrialization was shaping huge urban ghettos of tenements and sweatshops. Much of this new factory labor was not being furnished by people of the old racial stocks. What would happen to Anglo-Saxon manifest destiny if the Elect Nation itself came to have only a minority of Anglo-Saxons and Protestants? White Americans responded to the immigration crisis in two ways: with an increasing cry to limit immigration of nonwhite populations, and with efforts to keep disenfranchised and socially inferior those people not yet assimilated.

Orientals, especially Chinese, began to immigrate to the western side of the continent with the Gold Rush and the building of the continental railroads. They were the first people treated to an explicitly racial ban on immigration. In the 1880s and 1890s the Immigration Restriction League campaigned for legislation against so-called non-Aryan settlement. John Burgess, professor at Columbia University, expressed the League's view that the very nature of the American commonwealth, its political institutions and cultural consensus, demanded such exclusion:

> What folly, on the part of the ignorant, what wickedness on the part of the intelligent, are involved in the attempts . . . to pollute the United States with non-Aryan elements. . . . We must preserve our Aryan nationality in the state, and admit to its membership only such non-Aryan race-elements as shall have become Aryanized in spirit and in genius by contact with it, if we would build the superstructure of the ideal American commonwealth.[7]

This statement leaves unanswered the question of which nations can become Aryanized in spirit and which cannot. Can a Frenchman do it but not a Jew? Are blacks, Orientals, and Indians excluded by their very biology? Although contemporary Americans have accepted both a more secular and a more plural conception of national identity, struggles over public prayer and English as a second language show the extent to which we still have not resolved the relationship of unity and diversity in the American covenant.

Part of what has allowed the American covenant to evolve to accommodate itself to this growing ethnic, religious, and racial diversity and to more inclusive and egalitarian concepts of civil rights has been the dynamic aspect of the idea of the covenant. The covenant can be understood in two ways. On the one hand, it can be seen as a gift of God that confers a special elect status on a particular people, the descendants of the original colonists. On the other hand, it can be seen as a mandate to create a just nation. This mandate has suggested to waves of American reformers a process of continual revolutionary renewal whereby the covenant unfolds, disclosing new dimensions of what a community of justice means. To include all members of the body politic as equal sharers both in civil liberties and the blessings of shared opportunities demands continually breaking the imposed limitations of special privilege for whites, for Protestants, for males, for Christians. This vision impelled Americans down a path of adaptation to new constituencies.

Thus in the 1840s abolitionism began to agitate for abolition of that greatest contradiction to the idea of a covenant of freedom, namely, the retention of chattel slavery. Only with a bloody civil war was this "peculiar institution" abolished, but it would be another hundred years before the civil rights legislation of the 1960s sought to clean up the legacy of restricted civil rights for American blacks. In the 1840s there also began the long struggle for full civil rights for women, that half of humanity traditionally excluded from the exercise of political rights in patriarchal societies. The civil rights struggles of the 1960s continued these earlier struggles for blacks and women and began to apply them to unfinished business among other ethnic minority people, as well as questions of economic unprivilege for the "other America" of the poor.

The era of the social gospel and the New Deal struggled with questions of rights of workers and basic welfare legislation for groups not able to support themselves, such as indigent elderly, mothers of dependent children without fathers, and handicapped people. But the massive cuts in this welfare budget under the Reagan administration show how far most Americans are from accepting these social principles of corporate responsibility for the economically deprived as part of a shared vision of the role of government. Reaganomics has been based on an individualist concept of classical liberalism which recognizes the military and police powers as the only legitimate sphere of the state. Thus the struggle over the claims of justice implied by the American covenant remains an area of acute conflict in the 1980s.

I began this essay with the discussion of the appropriation by the Christian Church of the covenantal idea. The Christian view of Christians as the people of the New Covenant not only proliferated into many churches, each thinking of themselves as people of renewed covenant over against their Christian as well as Jewish ancestors, but also setting up new nations which think of themselves as New Israels. How is the original Israel, the original covenanted people, the Jews, to respond to this Christian proliferation of their identity whose rights to such an identity they do not acknowledge? Such concepts of New Israels have usually been used in a hostile and supercessionist way by Christians. Even when they are appropriated in a more complementary way, as in the Puritan tradition, Jews can only feel ambivalent about such a wholesale use of their identity by people who, in their view, have never received permission either from God or themselves to become "New Israels"! The long history of anti-Semitism and Christian power has meant that this issue has never been appropriately discussed by Jews and Christians.

There have been various attempts to mediate this dispute between Jews and Christians over the inheritance of the covenant. One important dialogue took place between the Jew, Franz Rosenzweig, and the converted Jew, Rosenstock-Huessy. Rosenzweig's reasoning is relevant to us, for he argued that Judaism and Christianity should be considered related to each other as a fire is related to its rays. Judaism is still the center of God's election, through which the central messages of monotheism and ethical life are transmitted. Christianity is the expression of the mission of Israel to the Gentiles. Through the Church this message of Israel is

193

transmitted to the world. Christianity is the universalization of Israel for the sake of all nations. A Christian theologian, Paul van Buren, has recently adopted this same paradigm for the relationship of Judaism and Christianity.[8]

Such a concept of the relationship of the Jewish and Christian dispensations has much to recommend it, but it doesn't quite do justice to the reality of either group or their distinctive views of their identities. It makes Judaism sound too limited to a particular people, in a racial or ethnic sense. In fact, Judaism, widespread as a faith and a community, has gathered people from many nations. The ethnic pluralism of that people called Jews is evident to any visitor to Israel. On the other side, Christianity has taken on elements of particularism and has become identified with particular peoples. In the English and American traditions especially, the idea of the Christian covenant has become identified with the national identities of particular peoples; it has been used to chart and judge their national destinies.

Thus covenantal theology remains an important unresolved area of Jewish-Christian relations. It has not been easy for Jews and Christians to engage in dialogue at all. This is because Christians have generally assumed that there could be only one authentic end of the dialogue—Jewish conversion to Christianity. All else was hardness of heart on the part of the Jews. Jews have regarded this conclusion as totally unacceptable, tantamount to the annihilation of Judaism. Today, in a more open ecumenical relation that has developed between the two faiths, especially in the United States, a new dialogue might be mutually fruitful. This would be a dialogue based on the assumption that each faith would recognize the integrity of the other. There may be no better place to start such dialogue than on the topic of covenantal theology.

Notes

1. This essay is summarized from the chapters of my book, *The Liberating Bond—Covenants, Biblical and Contemporary*, Rosemary Ruether and Wolfgang Roth (New York: Friendship Press, 1978).
2. "The Ordinance of God," in the *Library of Christian Classics*, vol. 25, *Spiritual and Anabaptist Writers*, ed. G. H. Williams (Philadelphia: Westminster Press, 1957), p. 188.
3. Peter de Jong, *The Covenant Idea in New England Theology: 1620–1847* (Grand Rapids, Mich.: Eerdmans Publishing Company, 1945), p. 84.
4. Conrad Cherry, *God's New Israel: Religious Interpretations of America's Destiny* (Englewood Cliffs, N.J.: Prentice-Hall, 1971), pp. 42–43.
5. Ibid.

6. Grindal Rawson (1709), in Perry Miller, *The New England Mind* (Cambridge, Mass.: Harvard University Press, 1939), pp. 483–84.
7. Thomas Gossett, *Race: The History of an Idea in America* (New York: Schocken Books, 1965), p. 307.
8. Paul van Buren, *The Burden of Freedom: Americans and the God of Israel* (New York: Seabury Press, 1976), p. 81.

Alexander M. Schindler is the rabbi that Time *magazine once called "the most prominent spokesman for American disparate Jewish groups." Schindler is president of the Union of American Hebrew Congregations, which is the parent body of the Reform Movement in North America, which includes over 1 million Jews in 780 congregations. In 1978, Alexander Schindler received the coveted Bublick Prize at the Hebrew University. He also currently serves as vice-president of the World Jewish Congress. Alexander Schindler and Herman Schaalman have been close personal friends for more than three decades. This was particularly true when Herman served as president of the Central Conference of American Rabbis and worked closely with Alexander Schindler on the Conference of Presidents of major Jewish organizations.*

America has always been a secure home for Jews, because the civil covenant has always been open and pluralistic. Alexander Schindler raises some difficult and painful questions about religious rightists who are challenging America's covenantal openness. This has been a topic of increasing concern among those who understand the covenant as an always open and expansive community. Among many contemporary issues, Schindler demands we recognize the "Christian right" as threatening the very vitality of the covenant, as we have experienced it in America.

Thunder from the Right:
A Jewish Perspective

Alexander M. Schindler

Itzik the landowner, a leading citizen of Chelm, startled his wife, Chashe, by storming into the house with the news that the Messiah was coming—was at that very moment only a few hours from Chelm.

But the news dismayed Itzik somewhat. "I have only recently built this home, and have invested our funds in cattle, and besides, I have just finished sowing our crops!"

Chashe calmed him, declaring philosophically, "Don't worry! Think of the trials and tribulations our people have met and survived—the bondage in Egypt, the wickedness of Haman, the persecutions and pogroms without end. All of these the good Lord has helped us overcome, and with just a little more help from Him, we will overcome the Messiah, too!"

From *A Treasury of Jewish Folklore*, NATHAN AUSUBEL, ed.

Jewish life, for all of its heralded historical continuity, has been constantly marked by sudden, rupturing change. Whether we speak about the ebb and flow of conquerors in ancient Israel or the unparalleled frequency of war during modern Israel's short existence; whether we discuss the transplantation of over 2 million Jews to the New World from 1881 to 1920, or the destruction of two-thirds of those who remained in the Old World within the horrifyingly brief span of the *Shoah*—history, for our people, has been a terribly swift sword. Yet as individuals, and as a community, living within familiar landscapes and with comforting assumptions, we are always startled when we realize that the backdrop

197

which we call history actually moves, shifts, or changes within our own lives. The effect can be as shocking as feeling the earth shake during a quake. We have taught ourselves to accept the fact that time marches on, but we do not expect to see the clock's hands moving. When we do, the result can be disorientation.

Such disorientation has struck the American Jewish community's liberal mainstream during the Reagan years. We, along with other liberal sectors of society, have seen and felt the American political center of gravity lurching markedly to the right. We have witnessed the almost violent ending of the New Deal era, while subsequent or ancillary movements for social progress have before our eyes been plucked from the mainstream of conscience and concern to be redefined as "special interests." We have seen ideological forces whom we once comfortably and condescendingly named the "rightwing fringe" emerging from offstage and taking over center stage. Standards of freedom and opportunity that we thought were well rooted in the American soil are being toppled by standards of so-called Christian morality, and the Constitution and Bill of Rights themselves are facing exposure to dangerously corrosive elements of the new political climate.

Yet while we fight defensive battles on many social action fronts, we must also, as *truly* progressive Jews, be willing to accept the challenges of self-examination and reaffirmation of our ideals which the insurgent, triumphal New Right provokes within us. This challenge to liberal Jews is strongest and most direct from that element within the Fundamentalist/ Evangelical Christian movements, headed by such leaders as the Reverend Jerry Falwell of Moral Majority and the Reverend Pat Robertson of the Christian Broadcasting Network.

The strength of this kind of fundamentalist Christian challenge is built upon several premises. First, they are *actively* soliciting organized Jewish support for their political agenda and social vision. Second, they are already deeply in league with our own fundamentalist, rightist elements. Third, they have a theologically rooted, abiding interest in the welfare of the Jewish State of Israel. Fourth, they effectively mirror our own weaknesses and refocus our attention on concerns that we have neglected: the deterioration of the family, the debasement of sex, the indiscriminate permissiveness of our society, the spiritual superficiality of many nominally religious lives. These issues have not evoked an adequate moral response from our liberal Jewish community, and we might as well admit it.

Since the 1984 presidential election campaign (during which Jerry Falwell greatly alienated the Jewish electorate by calling for the "Christianization of America"), leaders of the Christian Right have been campaigning hard to create a more moderate image of themselves in Jewish eyes and to effect a truce between the two communities: at worst, an agreement to disagree; at best, a quid pro quo arrangement. In this campaign, they are notching their trips to Israel on their belts. They are prefixing "Judaeo-" to their "Christian" agenda. Confident of scoring a knockout against punchdrunk liberalism, confident of capturing the driver's seat of the Republican Party, and adhering to the fundamentalist belief in the "chosenness" of the Jews, the Christian Right is witnessing to the Jewish community with vigor. "Join us," they are saying, "while the door is open. Abandon your traditional alliances—they're bound to fall."

"If they give you," says a Yiddish proverb, "take. If they take from you—yell!" In this spirit, we, in turn, have been undertaking responsible dialogues with leaders of the fundamentalist Christian movement. "Responsible dialogue," however, does not mean that those who engage in it are compelled to voice platitudes. A responsible dialogue demands frankness as well—it requires that divergent views be openly explored and that perceptions be freely stated. We can't lift the curtain of stereotypes without first examining the stereotypes.

First, however, we must uphold the right of fundamentalist preachers to speak out on public policy. American Jews cherish the First Amendment separating Church and State, but we do not see that principle as precluding a political involvement by the religious community. Indeed, the right to such an involvement is secured by the Free Exercise Clause of that Amendment itself.

We *Jews* claim this right for ourselves with a passion, and we will *not* deny it to others, however divergent their views. If Eisendrath could thunder against the war in Vietnam and Schindler can hold forth on nuclear disarmament and economic justice, why, then, Pat Robertson and Jerry Falwell have every right to take the stump for prayer in the public school and against abortion.

In fact, I am confident enough of the liberalism and conscience of my own community to feel that the more free speech exercised by the fundamentalist Christian leadership, the better. I believe that Jewish ears will in general find the scope of the fundamentalist manifesto entirely too narrow, ethically inadequate, and unfaithful to the fullness of religious witness.

Perhaps my own conception of religion is at fault. But I cannot understand how an agenda that calls itself *religious* can oppose our government's ratification of the Genocide Convention.

I cannot understand how a *religious* agenda can concern itself almost exclusively with personal rather than with public morality, more with what happens in the privacy of the bedroom that with what happens in our urban ghettos.

I cannot understand how a *religious* agenda can identify itself with a particular economic theory—clearly secular in its essential nature—which leaves it up to God to take care of toxic waste dumps, and rent gouging, and unemployment, and unequal pay for women, and all those other scarcely self-corrupting by-products of the rigid laissez-faire approach.

I cannot understand how a believer in the Christian spirit of humility, as detailed in Jesus of Nazareth's magnificent Sermon on the Mount, can make a trip to South Africa, virtually endorse the status quo in the most racist society on earth, and presume to tell the oppressed black majority who their true leadership should be. This is Ugly Americanism, not Christianity, at work.

Finally, while I yield to no one in my love for this land for which I fought and bled, I cannot understand how those who speak in the name of a religion that claims adherents in every corner of our world can nonetheless be so narrowly nationalistic as to attain a blatant chauvinism. The embrace of the Christian Right is scarcely global! And its preachments about nuclear disarmament make it almost impossible for me to believe that the more traditional Christian quest for peace on earth emerged from the same Holy Scriptures in worship of the same Lord.

Forgotten is the injunction about "turning the other cheek" to one's enemy. No inspiration is derived from God's promise to Noah, sealed by the rainbow sign, that God would never again destroy the world. Foreign policy decisions are made with reference to an approaching Armageddon. All countermeasures to Soviet influence appear condoned by that camp, dictatorships and death squads and grinding proverty and apartheid right on up to nuclear brinkmanship—all condoned, if not blessed, by the Christian Right. It *is* a puzzlement!

Of course, many Jews will disagree with one or another of the views implicit in my critique. Few, however, will disagree with me when I say that the American Jewish community is most perturbed about the centerpiece of the Moral Majority's national agenda: "prayer in public education." We are exceedingly sensitive on this subject, and the reason is not far to seek: we see the public classroom as the very first line of defense in our struggle to maintain separation of Church and State on the American scene.

This is a "gut issue" for American Jews that more than likely cost Ronald Reagan the large minority, if not the majority, of the Jewish vote in 1984. We hold the principle of Church-State separation to be our fundamental protection, the ultimate ground of the unique freedom that we have experienced in this land. Elsewhere in our wanderings we always suffered persecution—never here. In all other countries there was an established faith—never here. That is why we prize the First Amendment as the very cornerstone of our liberties in this blessed country.

Even the slightest chip in that separating wall evokes our anxious concerns, and properly so. For instance, could there be anything more innocuous than the "equal access" program adopted by Congress last year? It seemed so harmless! American's secondary schools were to be opened to a wide variety of religious activities, no more; and everything was to be voluntary, nothing was to be required. Yet look at what happened across the land! In Illinois, the Jews for Jesus established chapters in various high schools. In one West Coast community the Moonies asked for equal time and space; in another, it was the American Nazi party. On Long Island so many cults and missionary groups are competing for available resources, the despairing local school officials are actually recommending the closure of *all* extracurricular activity, including sports, just to get out from under.

Thus it is that the American public school, which always was and should be the primary unifying force of our country's divergent religious and ethnic life, is threatened with becoming a battleground for competing sectarian interests. This is why we American Jews will continue to resist vigorously the Moral Majority and its allies on their every suggestion to introduce religious into the public schools—lest the separating wall crumble into a moat where the sharks of intolerance thrash about and sharpen their teeth for victims.

Now, the fact that we are opposed to many aspects of the Religious Right's manifesto does not really go to the root of our distrust. We oppose many other groupings on diverse issues without holding those groups suspect, without fretting and fuming as we do about the Religious Right. Only with them do we Jews take on the persona of Itzik the Jew who, in my opening tale, is leery of the arrival of the Messiah.

Then again, look at the messianic manner in which Christian Right arguments are advanced! There is entirely too much hyperbole. Extremist solutions are often endorsed. Everything is cast in apocalyptic terms, as a struggle between good and evil, between God and Satan, between the forces of light and darkness—terms that go way beyond the bounds of a reasonable democratic discourse. In effect, the Religious Right's rhetoric forecloses such a discourse, for if a political opponent is wrong, misguided, or even stupid he can be dealt with in the marketplace of ideas, but when he is immoral or a sinner, the case can be made that he does not deserve to be in the debate at all.

When we hear that those who favor ERA are "anti-family," that those who insist on civil rights for gays and lesbians are "perverts," that those who oppose school prayer are "anti-Christ," that those who believe in free choice in reproductive matters are "murderers," "Nazi-like perpetrators of another holocaust"—when we hear all this we somehow get the feeling that somebody is out there who would rather not have us about.

It is in this context that I made comments some years ago that were later misrepresented to imply that I hold Jerry Falwell and other leaders of the Christian Right to be anti-Semites. That simply is not so. What I did say—I repeat—is this: that the extreme and absolutistic language of the Christian Right "creates a climate of opinion which is hostile to religious tolerance. Such a climate . . . is bad for civil liberties, for human rights, for interfaith understanding, and for mutual respect among Americans. . . . Therefore, it is also bad for Jews. . . . I do not accuse Jerry Falwell and Bailey Smith of deliberately inciting anti-Semitism. But I do say that their preachments have an inevitable effect. Jerry Falwell tells us that only one brand of politics is acceptable to God, and Bailey Smith tells us that only one brand of believer is acceptable to God. It is no wonder, then, that those who hold different political views should be branded 'Satan' and those who hold different religious beliefs should become the victims of vandals. . . ."

That's what I said, and I stand by every word. The health of the American democratic process requires civility, temperateness, and a genuine respect for divergent views, even if these views involve a different interpretation of Holy Writ.

Too often the leaders of the Christian Right invoke God's name to sanctify their positions. This problem is more than stylistic, in fact—it is theological. We respect the fact that Christian ministers draw on Scripture for inspiration as they make their life decisions, and that they believe Scripture to be the revealed word of God. But can we really know God's will on all the issues facing our nation through scriptural study? Can *any* being of flesh and blood know with certainty just what God Almighty wills on a particular policy matter? Surely that is a knowledge that neither Christian nor Jew, however learned or pious, has the right to claim!

In his elegant speech at Liberty Baptist College in Lynchburg, Virginia, Senator Edward Kennedy made a similar point when he asked the Reverend Falwell for respect "for the independent judgment of conscience." "Those who proclaim moral and religious values," the senator said, "can offer moral counsel, but they should not casually treat a position on a public issue as a test of fealty to faith."

Illustrating the problem, the senator quoted Falwell's own statement that "to stand against Israel is to stand against God." Said Kennedy: "There is no one in the Senate who has stood more firmly for Israel than I have. Yet, I do not doubt the faith of those on the other side. Their error is not one of religion but of policy."

Kennedy's example is particularly well chosen. Many Congressional leaders who receive extremely high marks on the "morality index" of the Christian Voice, because of their conservative positions on such "holy" subjects as gun control and United States relations with Zimbabwe, have only mediocre, if not poor, voting records on Israel. Thus, for instance, more than 90% of the senators who co-sponsored the Prayer Amendment also voted in favor of selling AWAC's to the Saudi dictatorship. Were they saints on some issues and sinners on others? Did their religion lapse on the AWAC's vote?

Surely not. They had other considerations that came to play in their decision, such as the extension of United States influence in the Middle East, the dampening of Syrian power, the need to recapture petrodollars. If this be so, it is a confession that the AWAC's sale was a complicated matter that involved *many* moral and political considerations at once. And, if *that* confession is made, it must apply as well to domestic gun control, to United States relations with African nations, and to all the other issues that the Christian Voice simplemindedly decides, assigning the halo of divine approval to rightwing policies.

Let me make it crystal clear here, that Jerry Falwell and Pat Robertson, the two most outstanding leaders of the Christian Right, did *not* line up with other conservatives on the AWAC's sale. They opposed it, as they oppose the delivery of those planes now. Nonetheless, the hazard—indeed, the blasphemy!—of proclaiming "God's will" on specific policy issues is demonstrated by this example.

Less abstractly, the example also illustrates the flimsiness of the Fundamentalist Right's strongest playing card vis-à-vis the Jewish community: support for Israel. Often it goes no deeper than rhetoric. In much of its political lobbying and electoral work, for instance, the Moral Majority violates it own much-touted concern for Israel. In 1980, Moral Majority support for Steven Symms—whose involvement with Libyan interests was neck-high—was crucial in fueling the defeat of Senator Frank Church, one of the most consistent and influential supporters of Israel in the Senate. Most recently, the Hunt-Helms race for Senate in North Carolina showed one of the most obdurately anti-Israel members of Congress receiving crucial support from the Religious Right to defeat his rival. Apparently, on the single-issue hit lists or "morality" indices of the Religious Right, Israel takes a low priority.

Worse and more frightening is when the Religious Right's support for Israel takes the form exemplified in the Temple Mount Plot, in which Christian fundamentalist funds were fueling an ultra-orthodox Jewish plot to wrest control of the Temple Mount from the Moslem world. Had such a fanatical madness succeeded, it would have brought equally fanatical revenge and disaster to Israel—all in the name of prophecy fulfillment! The Jewish community thus needs to examine the content of the Fundamentalist Christian "concern" for Israel before being seduced by silvery words. Better that the Religious Right should show support for the Jewish state by following *our* leadership, the leadership of Jews in America. We are Israel's tested and proven supporters, and in the huge majority our support is for pluralism and democracy in the Jewish state, not for the kind of extremism that threatens to tear the fabric of Israeli society into shreds.

Now, in one respect my critique of the Religious Right hasn't been fair at all. I freely intermingled the views of the Moral Majority with those of the Christian Voice, the Religious Roundtable, and many other conservative political action groupings. I tossed them all together under the rubric of the Christian Right. That isn't really fair play. The Christian Right is *not* a monistic grouping, all of whose followers are of one mind on each and every issue or approach.

Yet in truth, this *is* the way we see the Religious Right. This is the way *we* hear them. And this is the burden of politics for the more responsible leaders of the Christian Right, those who are trying to present a more moderate and, we trust, accurate image of themselves to our community. As long as there are haters in the camps of the Reverend Pat Robertson and the Reverend Jerry Falwell, as long as there are the Reverend Jim Swaggarts and the Reverend Tim LaHayes around who say that God rejects the Jews because of their sins, that in rejecting Jesus the Jews have placed themselves "under Satan's domain who kills and steals and destroys"—so long as such voices are heard, "moderate" assurances about the integrity of Jews and Judaism in fundamentalist Christian eyes will be scrutinized and doubted by our community.

The task of the leaders of the Religious Right, therefore, is to tame the extremism within their own ranks. This must precede any political or religious missioning to the Jews, any agreement to disagree. We Jews are simply too grateful for, and attached to, America's democratic system to abandon the traditional alliances in which we have helped shore up and expand that democracy. "Punchdrunk" liberalism may be, yet we remain in its corner. We are prepared to face our opposition on each and every point of contention—but is the Religious Right prepared to fight by the rules? That question, and the doubts it entails, constitute the greatest gulf between the Jews and the fundamentalist Christian movement.

Steven S. Schwarzschild is professor of philosophy and Jewish studies at Washington University in St. Louis, where he has served as chairman of the Jewish Studies Department. He served on faculties at the Hebrew University and Notre Dame University. He lectured at many universities. He was ordained at the Hebrew Union College—Jewish Institute of Religion. He served as a congregational rabbi in both America and Germany. He has pursued his academic career for more than two decades. He has been editor of Judaism, *a quarterly journal. He has written two important, scholarly works. Steven Schwarzschild and Herman Schaalman's relationship spans an entire lifetime. Their family ties go back to Germany. Their personal and professional lives are intertwined. Professor Schwarzschild has lectured at Emanuel Congregation, and his work has been a formative part of Herman Schaalman's own philosophical interests.*

Steven Schwarzschild shares with us his critical philosophical mind in an introduction to Hermann Cohen's most important work. Cohen continues to represent one of *the* essential modern Jewish thinkers, whose views on covenant deeply influenced contemporary understandings of the covenant. Philosophical thought—with a commitment to practical reason—is in and of itself a covenantal form of thought, according to Schwarzschild. Schwarzschild brings Cohen's depth to us in order to reclaim some of the dynamics of German Jewish philosophy, as a challenge for today. This essay adds much to our contemporary review of Hermann Cohen's greatest work, *Religion of Reason out of the Sources of Judaism.*

The Title of Hermann Cohen's "Religion of Reason out of the Sources of Judaism"

Steven S. Schwarzschild

Hermann Cohen devoted the long introduction of his *Religion of Reason out of the Sources of Judaism (R.o.R.)* to what he called "An Explication of the Title and of the Structure of the Task: A. Reason—B. Religion—C. The Sources of Judaism." Even now it is still worth the trouble to give an explication de texte of the title of the work.

In the first place, the work is correctly entitled "Religion of Reason," not "*The* Religion of Reason." The latter was the title when the book was first published, while in all later editions, though unfortunately not in all later references to it, this fundamental mistake was rectified.[1] It had truly been a fundamental distortion, for Cohen held that there can be only one rational religion, which would have to be as universal and necessary as pure reason itself, and that consequently all human beings, at least regulatively speaking, would subscribe to it. This one religion of reason could and should be crystallized from Judaism, to be sure, but also from Christianity and from other religious, historical, and cultural configurations. Whether and to what extent, on Cohen's conception, Judaism might be the most favorable climate in which to nurture the universal religion we shall have occasion to see shortly.

The phrase "out of the sources" in the second part of the book's title refers, in the first and obvious place, to the fact that, in matters of religion as in every other area of philosophic truth, reason has to extract a priori truth from historical realities by means of the transcendental method, and this entails, of course, that the historical realities need to be studied and analyzed. Cohen would always say: "One has to square away one's

philology before doing one's philosophy."[2] More concretely, this conception of the relationship between religion, history, and philosophy was
formulated by Cohen in his *Ethics of the Pure Will*,[3] but also in his *Religion
and Morality* (1907), and finally in the present work, as the thesis that
religion produces notions in history, and philosophy's task is in the course
of time to refine and to validate them. (With all the important differences
between them, there are thus significant parallels between Hegel's and the
neo-Kantian approach to history.) Thus, for example, biblical religion
produced the very notions of history[4] and of a universal humanity (which
Greek philosophy was never able to do),[5] though it was Enlightenment
rationalism that finally brought them to their fullest conceptual and social
exfoliation. Specifically in the present work, "the (historical) sources of
Judaism"—that is, first the Bible, along with the Bible authoritative
rabbinic/talmudic and medieval Jewish philosophical sources, and then
the texts of the Jewish liturgy, must be shown to justify the claims being
made in the name of theologico-philosophical religion. (Those sources
are abundantly adduced in Cohen's text itself and then supplemented in
the appendix, in the original, compiled by Leo Rosenzweig.)[6]

The phrase "out of the sources" should, however, also be interpreted
on a second level of philosophic discourse. "Source" and "origin" are very
close synonyms in any language, and Cohen used them as such (*Quelle* and
Ursprung). "Origin" (*Ursprung*) was so decisive a technical, philosophic
concept in his fully matured thought that he called his entire system a
"philosophy of origin."[7] Here "origin" does not primarily mean historical
beginning; rather, it means the transcendentally logical ground, the
rational presuppositions, which are the only conceptual basis from which
the subsequent historical events could transpire.[8] This rational origin is
perhaps best symbolized by "O"—the letter O for "origin" and zero for its
mathematical significance: it is empirically nothing, because purely, a
priori, rational, and it is also the infinitesimal, which, though de facto
zero, is a differentiated zero, with the potentials of all the various
"functions" that are derived from it and that produce the natural and
other numbers, which are then treated as names of actual phenomena, as,
indeed, is the case in the mathematico-physical sciences.[9]

The Jewish theological background to this conception is only
intimated by Cohen: what in Western scholasticism is known as the
doctrine of *creatio ex nihilo* is known in Jewish scholasticism as *yesh me'ayin*—
that is, "what-there-is (the given) from nothing"—and in both traditions,
by both rationalists and mystics, God himself is then often regarded as the
nihil, the *'ayin*, the Nothing by which all is produced. This "originating"
(productive, "constructionalist") power then also actually manifests itself
in the concrete life of religion. For example, in the climactic, concluding
chapter of *R.o.R.*, entitled "Peace"—written, *nota bene*, at the height of
World War I—Cohen writes: "Peace, which is the *goal* of the moral world,

must also be valid as its *own originating power.* God is peace. (Cf. *Meg.* 18a, *Lev. R.,* 9:9: "Rabbi Yudan b. Rabbi José said: 'Great is peace, for God's name is peace, as it is said in *Judges* 6:24: "And he called him God-peace."'") God stands for *harmony* between the moral powers of the universe and their material conditions" (Cohen's typical italics).[10] Or, for another example, the people of Israel are the "pure [i.e., atemporal] origin" of monotheism, which, naturalistically considered, would be a "miracle."[11]

We may thus substitute the word "origin" for the word "source" in the title of this work. In this way the implicit claim is put forward that biblical Judaism and the later talmudic Judaism that evolved consistently from it are in fact the historically closest instantiation of the pure, a priori, rational conception—indeed, of the "construction"—of God and all that this conception entails—primarily an ethic.[12] To be sure, other historical religions and cultures also partake of that universal, rational "ethical monotheism" (as nineteenth-century Jewish philosophers favored speaking of Judaism), but they attained to it with neither the same philosophical purity nor the historical immediacy that distinguishes Judaism. (Historical immediacy is here of logical significance, since, to use Cohen's infinitesimal notation, $O + (dx/dy) = O$ still.) In order to crystallize the universal "religion of reason" out of their respective sources, these other religions consequently are compelled to work harder at shedding the mythological, immoral, pagan, irrational, and other barnacles that they accumulated on their voyage through history, by means of the process called "idealization" in Marburg neo-Kantianism,[13] and they were well advised to use Judaism as their (relatively) ideal model in performing this task.[14] "Judaism is an indispensable historical force 'toward' moral progress" together with "practical [!] Christianity, which is literally and historically practical Judaism."[15] And it is part of Israel's mission to mankind in turn that Jews must continue to help Christianity "idealize itself" and thus "come nearer to Judaism."[16]

Cohen, passionate and outspoken Jewish believer that he always was, did not then shrink, in an age and place far from receptive to candid discussions between what nowadays are called "faith communities," from arguing publicly, fully, and often very polemically, about Christian theology and history.[17] On the positive side, he believed that Protestant Bible scholarship, Bible "criticism" (as preeminently conducted by his colleague at the University of Marburg Julius Wellhausen, and which discerned the height of religious development in "prophetic religion") together with contemporary Protestant theology (as practiced most persuasively by his other local colleague and intimate fellow worker Wilhelm Herrmann, and which resulted in a liberal, social Christianity) constituted very valuable contributions toward religion of reason out of the sources of Christianity.[18] But his vision encompassed much more than

Judaism and Christianity. He quarried building blocks for the edifice of a universal culture of reason in all of his works primarily also from German culture, as he conceptualized it (the culture of Luther, Leibniz, Mozart, Kant, Beethoven, and social democracy), and as well from Greek, scholastic, French, Spanish, and other societies.[19] Thus, for example, in *R.o.R.* (p. 282), the Bible, Christianity, the Renaissance, the French Revolution, scientific humanism, and Kant's categorical imperative are cited as precursors of modern ethical humanism. On the other hand, Cohen did not hesitate to level biting criticisms at those traditions (those other than the Jewish and the Platonic-Kantian) that, on his philosophico-ethical analysis, went in wrong directions and therefore required fundamental "purification."[20] Even a century later so-called interreligious dialogue still has a lot to learn from the debates that took place in and beyond his circles.

It is further useful in this connection to realize that the place that *R.o.R.* occupies in Cohen's philosophic system is precisely analogous to the place that *Religion within the Bounds of Reason Alone* occupies in Kant's. It can be argued that Kant's system was not formulated only in the three *Critiques* but actually in four: though overtly the title of his philosophical theology has a different form, when "reason alone" or "mere reason" *(blosse Vernunft)*[21] is seen to be synonymous with "a priori reason," and when "within the bounds of" is seen to be a paraphrase of "critique," then the title of the fourth work turns out to be conceptually translatable as "Critique of Practico-Religious Reason."[22] As Kant's *Critique of Pure Reason* then becomes a *Cognition of Pure Reason* at the hands of Marburg-neo-Kantianism—its constructive function emphasized more than its critical function by also reducing sensibility to functions of originating, pure reason—and as similar treatment is bestowed on the other two *Critiques*, so his "Critique of Practico-Religious Reason" is transformed into a *Religion of Reason.*[23] Neither the one nor the other breaks with its respective system. Each extrapolates and crowns the system, contrary to the bulk of interpretations and uses to which they have been put subsequently.

The theory that the *R.o.R.* is the work of "the last Cohen," that is, that it is post-neo-Kantian and pre-existentialist, was dreamt up by Franz Rosenzweig and canonically expounded in his introduction to Cohen's collected *Jewish Writings.*[24] Jews and non-Jews have taken up and spread this misrepresentation, until it has become accepted wisdom.[25] One genus of this species holds that Cohen did not actually take the step out of the neo-Kantian system but that logically and philosophically he should have taken it. Either way, this has served as a basis on which to make larger ontological claims on behalf either of some Hegelian/Marxist form of "realism,"[26] or of quasi-Husserlian ontology,[27] even of Christian incarnationist doctrines,[28] or of a sort of Jewish metaphysical naturalism.[29]

The fact is that no ontological claims about God or man or the world are made in this work. For one thing, the title itself stresses with indubitable clarity the intension to provide a religion of *reason*—as, indeed, do all the other titles of Cohen's writings even in the last decade of his life. More specifically, Alexander Altmann has shown canonically that "the concept of the correlation signifies a methodological concept for Cohen, in the pregnant sense that methodology possesses in idealistic thinking. It is and remains a concept of origin and of production and cannot, therefore, in any way be interpreted in the sense of dialogical thinking. God as a member of the correlation is then no personal Thou but an idea . . ."[30] In other words, religion produces out of its a priori rational "origins" the concepts, the ideas, of God, creation, revelation, redemption, the human self, and so on, all of which entail rational and religious obligations for human beings.

We have earlier noted the religious backdrop to the neo-Kantian notion of "origin." Here the notion of "correlation" should be seen as a variant on the biblical notion of *b'rit/Bund*.[31] In this correlation/ covenant, empirical man obtains ethical imperatives from his ideal partner through reason, which is what the two share. The latter is, of course, an entrenched doctrine in philosophical theology; it is systematically explicated by Cohen under the term "the spirit of holiness" ("the holy spirit").[32]

The ideality of God in the correlation is even further abstracted by Cohen: if man and God are held to stand in relation, in "correlation," with one another, and though it even be kept in mind that it is ethical man that stands in relationship with the idea of God, not two empirical terms, it might nonetheless be inferred that God and man are members of one and the same class of concepts (for otherwise would their asserted relationship not be a "category mistake"?), and such an implication would bring God altogether too close to some form of immanentization. Cohen, therefore, goes on to argue that (the idea of) God is not *in* the relation but is its (rational) ground.[33] In other words, what was done typically in the history of neo-Platonism by way of ontological claims—namely, to build new, additional rungs into the ladder of emanations in order to keep spirit and matter as far apart as possible and yet to relate them—is here done in conceptual terms: God is now (Kant and Kantians would say "even"; traditional religionists and realists would say "only")[34] the regulative idea of universal ethical reason, which in Cohen's fully articulated philosophy of religion is then functionalized through the ideas of creation (from which the scientificity of nature is "correlatively" derived), of revelation (from which the imperatures of ethics are derived), and of redemption (from which the program of the good society, socialism, is derived).

A diagram should here be helpful:

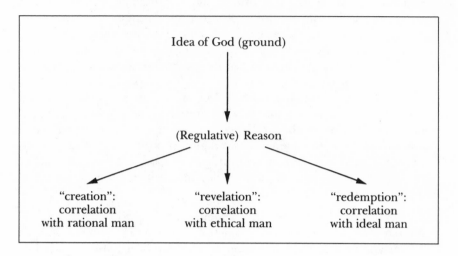

All in all, thus, Cohen's theological concepts are justified/validated by him not as possessing any kind of cognitive status but, in line with Kant's own "primacy of practical reason," as transcendentally necessary presuppositions for man's total ethical life—ethics themselves having, in turn, been rationally, philosophically, validated. As he says in *R.o.R.*, "God is not real, and He is also not alive in the sense of human beings being alive. Maimonides put a clear stop to this. Only the truth is the valid value which corresponds to the being of God."[35] And the ethical ultimacy of that being is stated in the somewhat earlier *Religion and Morality:* "Thus the Jewish idea of God is exhaustively defined by the ethical meaning of the idea of God."[36] We are thus still dealing with "ethical monotheism," as was the case all along in Cohen's earlier Kantian and neo-Kantian works. Cohen's religion is strictly ethical religion or, better, religion of ethics.[37] Indeed, he wanted to incorporate this truth into the very title, or subtitle, of his final work: the Society for the Advancement of the Science of Judaism, which was the patron of the book, wanted it subtitled "Jewish Philosophy of Religion," but Cohen was ready to concede only "Jewish Philosophy of Religion and Ethics."[38]

That *R.o.R.* is a consistent extrapolation of, not a deviation from, Cohen's formal philosophic system can also be shown in other ways. For one thing, religious doctrines in general and Jewish ones in particular interlaced his *Ethics of the Pure Will* and other earlier works so frequently and so systematically that one cannot but be reminded of how a professed theology also underlay Kant's *Critiques* and other writings (though in Kant's case this theology was an explicitly, however rationalized, Protestant one).[39] For another, the last third of Cohen's *Ethics* consists of chapters in which he goes through what might appear as the very old-fashioned ethical, indeed, the moralistic exercise of reciting the table of virtues (though what he does with them is philosophically, culturally, and even politically very sophisticated); and he does precisely the same thing, though this time in unabashedly Jewish, rabbinic, traditional terms, in the last third of his *R.o.R.*[40] Indeed, the parallelism between *R.o.R.* and "the system" is all-pervasive: for example, Cohen's treatment of the religious doctrine of "creation" not only recapitulates his analysis of "nothing," infinity, the infinitesimal, "infinite privative judgments" of his *Logic of Pure Cognition*, but also explicitly cross-refers to it (as he cross-refers to "the system" and its appendages throughout).[41]

The analogy between the places of their respective *Religions* in the total systematic oeuvres of Kant and Cohen then also extends to the fact that religion is for both of them a rationally necessary consequence of, emphatically not the basis for, ethics. Cohen calls religion a philosophical *Eigenart* (a subspecies)[42]: it stays within the philosophical realm of rational ethics, although it adds to and retro-affects the latter.

In sum, then, "Religion of Reason (1) out of the Sources of (2) Judaism" (3) is intended to convey briefly that (3) historical Judaism will be treated as the empirical matrix, out of which (2) the rational, a priori (necessary and universal) concepts are transcendentally educed, which (1) are in turn the "synthetic" producers of the universal human religion of ethics.

It is finally then only proper that we cast a glance at two other items that precede the text of this work: the motto and the dedication.

The book is dedicated by the author to his deceased father.[43] Gerson Cohen was the long-time cantor and Jewish teacher, the de facto rabbi, in the philosopher's small native town of Coswig/Anhalt. From the local schools and his father's Jewish training Cohen went to Breslau, in order to study primarily not at the local university but at the rabbinical seminary. As long as his father lived, and indeed in a sense afterward, their warm relationship centered on their common Jewish devotion.[44] It was then fitting that what turned out to be the philosopher's posthumous work, a Jewish philosophical theology and, by general consent, the most important and seminal such work in the century (with two or three possible competitors), be dedicated to his father.[45] This dedication was not, as is sometimes claimed, an act of contrition for having for many years allegedly strayed from the path of Judaism but, as we have by now sufficiently seen, a summation of his entire life and work.

The epigraph is a famous passage from the Talmud: *Mishnah*, tractate "Day of Atonement," 8:9: "Rabbi Akiba said: 'Well off are you, oh Israel! Who purifies you, and before whom do you purify yourselves? It is your Father in Heaven.'"[46] (This is in fact the coda and climax of the mishnaic tractate, which, for the rest, like almost all of the *Mishnah*, is a technical legal code.)

The passage displays a number of important religious and literary aspects. Here we have to be concerned with the chief point that Cohen wanted to make—a point which, from another angle, we have discussed previously. The passage raises two questions, to both of which one and the same answer is given. Actually, Cohen has reversed the sequence in which the two questions are posed in the original text, but he explains in the body of the work, where he uses what is here the epigraph, what he takes to be its logical sequence: God purifies you, but, on an higher level of truth, you purify yourself, albeit exclusively "before" God. "God purifies no more than he forgives"; you yourself do this, ethically.[47] (Cohen continues in the text by emphatically distinguishing this from Christianity and other forms of pantheism: "No man purifies you, and also no man who is supposed to be also a god. No son of God is to purify you. . . . An unbridgeable gap must loom before [man]. . . . Truly, the Day of Atonement is the day of monotheism."[48] Man is the agent of his self-purification, though he executes this act only within the correlation. A dialectical relationship is humanly enacted between morally acting human beings—in fact, human beings striving for the ideal of "purity"—and the *idea* of the morally acting God, and the moral actions of this God, are uniquely predicated of him in the sense that human beings could not logically perform their acts if there were no second person in ideal, not empirical, relationship to whom ("before whom") those acts are performed.[49] (The sentence before the one that Cohen quotes from the *Mishnah*—that only "before God shall you be pure" on the Day of Atonement—declares in the name of Rabbi El'azar ben Azaryah: "Sins between a man and his fellow [as distinguished from sins between man and God] the Day of Atonement does not forgive until [!] he has reconciled him"—and from here Rabbi Akiba's exclamation takes off. In other words, temporal or other empirical relations between human beings come first ethically, and then only does the logical relation of standing "before God" begin to operate as the superstructure of ethics.)[50] In short, atonement does not precede but is in fact constituted by the moral action of repentance.[51] (At the end of the full study in which this paper is the first section the massive impact of Cohen's philosophical theology of repentance on contemporary Jewish Orthodoxy, namely, Rabbi J. B. Soloveitchik and the late Rabbi I. Hutner and others, is illustrated at some length—not to speak of Rabbi Nehemiah Nobel, the Orthodox community rabbi of Frankfurt o/M, who took a year off from his rabbinical duties to study with Cohen in Marsburg.) "Pure" in the classic Jewish sense has been joined by "pure" in Kant's sense.[52]

Notes

This is the first part of my introduction to Cohen's *Religion of Reason* . . . (*R.o.R.*—here always cited in the second edition, unless otherwise indicated) in the forthcoming respective volume in H. Cohen's *Werke* (Hildesheim, N.Y.: Olms). I dedicate it gladly to my friend Rabbi Hermann Schaalman on his professional retirement. Not only have he and his family and my family been good friends all our lives, but his parents and mine were lifelong friends before us. All of us, as thorough-going "Yekkes," devoted German Jews, share some fundamental values. This short paper is, therefore, appropriate to the purpose. It even, as it happens, has occasion to deal with the concept of the Jewish covenant, the theme of this volume. I wish Herman and Lotte a long life of continued satisfaction and productivity.

1. The first edition was published in Leipzig in 1919. Later editions have been published as follows: 2d ed., Frankfurt, 1929 (reprint, Cologne, 1959); 3d ed., Wiesbaden: Fourier, 1966; 4th ed., Bonn: Bouvier. The English translation by Simon Kaplan, introduction by Leo Strauss, was published in New York by Ungar, 1972. A Hebrew translation by T. Wislawsky, annotated by S. H. Bergmann and N. Rotenstreich, introduction by S. Ucko, epilogue by J. ben-Shlomoh, was published in Jerusalem by Mossad Bialik, 1971. In a lecture delivered by Ernst Cassirer on "Hermann Cohen's Philosophy in Its Relation to Judaism" before the Franz Rosenzweig Memorial Foundation in April 12, 1931 (Verene cat. no. 207/a, b, e), the original, first title is surprisingly still used. Verene says that it was "apparently not published." Since it is unknown, I want to give a summary of it here. It consists of forty-four manuscript pages, in English and for an English audience. The lecture may be said to consist of four parts: pp. 1–9, a long, beautiful, and very personal introduction about Cohen; pp. 9–15, about Cohen's Kant interpretation; pp. 15–23, about religion in general in Cohen's systematic works (pp. 22–25 about "idealized religion"); and pp. 23–44, about Judaism as universal ethics, by way of Cohen's Maimonides interpretation. Two small points strike the attention of a Cohen expert: Cassirer quotes Cohen's posthumous work by its first and false title: "Die (!) Religion der Vernunft . . . " (pp. 9, 43), and he uses the notion of "mind" in a rather un-Cohennian, psychologistic, quasi-Natorpian way. Comp. Verene catalog no. 78, also designated as "apparently not published," undated, which handles exactly the same subject more briefly, soberly, and technically, in German. For the problem of the horrible condition of the text of the first edition, cf. Bruno Strauss's epilogue in the 2d ed., pp. 623–29. (*Re* Bruno Strauss, cf. his entry in *International Biographical Dictionary of Central European Emigrés* 1933–1945 [Munich: K. G. Saur, 1983], 2, pt. 2:1137. What does not come out in this article is how closely knit the world of the German-Jewish intelligentsia was: B. Strauss's father was a close friend of H. Cohen's when the former was a Jewish teacher in Marburg, and Bruno's brother married Ilse Hahn, sister of Edith, who in turn was Franz Rosenzweig's wife [Edith Hahn Rosenzweig Scheinmann]; in other words, Bruno Strauss was also *me'chuttan* to Rosenzweig. [B. Strauss lectured on Cohen in Rosenzweig's Lehrhaus in the 1923–24 semester.])
2. Franz Rosenzweig quotes Robert Fritzsche as reporting Cohen's refrain: *"Das Philologische muss immer in Ordnung sein"*: "Vertauschte Fronten," in *F. Rosenzweig—Der Mensch und sein Werk—Gesammelte Schriften*, vol. 3, ed.

R. and A. Mayer (Dordrecht: Martinus M. Nijhoff, 1984), p. 235. (Rosenzweig's essay, in which this sentence occurs, is the centerpiece of my forthcoming study "M. Heidegger and F. Rosenzweig: The German and the Jewish Turn to Ethnicism." The Heidegger connection is the most interesting aspect of this last essay of Rosenzweig's, but actually it is a renewed discussion of Cohen's *R.o.R.*)

3. Cf. *Ethik des Reinen Willens* (*Werke*, vol. 7) (Hildesheim/New York: Olms, 1981).

4. *Jewish Writings* (Berlin, 1924), 1:249; cf. also 33, 120, 175f.

5. *R.o.R.*, 278, 282. M. M. Findley puts forward the same thesis: cf. *History and Theory* 4/3 (1965):294.

6. Ibid., 535–43. Leo Rosenzweig is an unfortunately neglected figure in modern Jewish intellectual history. Born and educated in the talmudic Judaism of Lithuania, he studied with Cohen, earned his Ph.D. with *La Restauration de l'a priori Kantien par H. Cohen* (Paris, 1927), and ended his life, unappreciated, as a teacher of *midrash* in the Jewish Theological Seminary of America in New York. To me he was a teacher and a friend.

7. Cf. Cohen's *Logic of Pure Cognition*, 1:8 and 2:2, on "the logic" and "the judgment of origin."

8. Cf. *R.o.R.*, p. 83: "cause" in the sense of "prerequisite/condition" ("Vorbedingung").

9. Cf. Cohen's *The Principle of the Infinitesimal Method and Its History—a Chapter in the Foundation of the Critique of Cognition* (1883); *Logic*, 2d ed., pp. 32, 79 ff.; *R.o.R.*, paras. 9, 14, 15, and p. 76. (In order to "logicize" the still partially mythological notion of "beginning," Cohen prefers to speak not of *creatio ex nihilo* but of *creatio ab nihilo* [Logic, p. 84].)

10. *R.o.R.*, p. 517.

11. Ibid., pp. 301, 284.

12. Cf. B. Kellermann, "Die philosophische Begründung des Judentums," in *Judaica: . . . H. Cohens 70. Geburtag* (Berlin, 1912), p. 94: Judaism as "the originating concept" of ethics.

13. For "idealization" cf. S. Schwarzschild, "'Germanism and Judaism': H. Cohen's Normative Paradigm of the German-Jewish Symbiosis," in *Jews and Germans from 1860 to 1933: The Problematic Symbiosis*, ed. David Bronsen (Heidelberg: Carl Winter, 1979), pp. 142–54.

14. *R.o.R.*, pp. 39 f., the end of the "Introduction," *Jewish Writings*, p. 168.

15. "Dem 50jaehrigen *Doctor medicinae* Herrn Sanitaetsrath Dr. S. Neumann ein Festgruss," *Allgemeine Zeitung des Judentums* (September 16, 1882), pp. 447 f. (Cp. Marx's famous and notorious statement in "On the Jewish Question" that Christianity is practical Judaism!)

16. *Jewish Writings*, 2:308 f., and in "Religiöse Bewegungen der Gegenwart," 1:64, and *The Concept of Religion within the System of Philosophy* (1915), 120. F. Rosenzweig, then, in *The Star of Redemption*, assigned precisely this role to Judaism—to keep Christianity on the straight and narrow, as it were! (Cf. *The Star of Redemption*, trans. W. W. Hallo [New York: Holt, Rinehart & Winston, 1970]), pp. 399–402.

17. Cf., e.g., *Neue juedische Monatshefte*, 1:106–11, 135–38 (on Gunkel); 1:509–14 (on Wm. Herrmann); 1:652–54 (on Troeltsch); 2:45–49 (on Luther); 2:178–81 (on Wellhausen), etc. (My copy of *N.j.M.* was given me, with his extensive marginalia, by Leo Rosenzweig—cf. n. 16.) Cp. Walter Jacobs, "H. Cohen on Christianity," *C.C.A.R. Journal* (January 1970), pp. 61–69 (also published as *Christianity through Jewish Eyes: The Quest for*

Common Ground [n.p.: Hebrew Union College Press, 1974], chap. 9).
(Cohen's personal library, now in the National Library in Israel, comprised
a large number of books on Christianity and Bible criticism.)

18. For Herrmann, cf., e.g., *Schriften zur Grundlegung der Theologie W.
Herrmanns*, Theologische Bücherei . . ., vol. 36 (Munich: Chr. Kaiser, 1965).
Cohen's discussions with Paul Natorp, which are implicitly also a Jewish-
Christian polemic and which centered on Natorp's *Religion within the Bounds
of Humanity: A Chapter toward the Foundation of Social Politics* (1894), 2d 1908
ed. with a new epilogue that addresses Cohen, are analyzed in greater
depth in the second section of my introduction to *R.o.R.* Some people
never learn: Christoph v. Wolzagen, "Schöpferische Vernunft: Der
Philosoph P. Natorp und das Ende des Neukantianismus" (!), *Frankfurter
Allgemeine Zeitung* (March 17, 1984), no. 66, apostrophizes the Natorp-
Heidegger line at the expense of Cohen.

19. Cp. Schwarzschild, "Germanism and Judaism," pp. 145f.

20. For Cohen's argument against Tröltsch, cf. n. 17 above. Cohen's close
disciple and friend, Benzion Kellermann, the radical Reform rabbi, wrote a
whole monograph in this sense, *The Ethical Monotheism of the Prophets and Its
Sociological Evaluation* (German), but it was turned down by the journal
Logos in the same spirit in which the *Kant-Studien* published Bruno Bauch's
racist doctrine of a "German Kant" vs. a "Jewish Kant" at the time, so that
Kellermann had to publish it separately (Berlin: Schwetschke, 1917). Cf.
H. Liebeschütz, *Von Georg Simmel zu F. Rosenzweig* (Tübingen: Mohr
[Siebeck], 1970), pp. 198f.; and cf. Wendell Dietrich, *Cohen and Tröltsch: Ethical
Monotheistic Religion and Theory of Culture*, Brown University Judaic Studies
(Providence, 1985), chap. entitled "H. Cohen's Objections to E. Tröltsch's
Interpretation of the Prophetic Ethos." (Comp. *Jewish Writings*, 2:481.)

21. Cf. Grimm's *Wörterbuch*, the etymology of "mere" ← Latin *merus* in
relationship to *purus* ("pure"). (*"Blosse"* = "naked") ideas require
phenomenal garb, "naked virtue," "chaste."

22. One has to keep in mind, of course, that, unlike the *Critiques,* Kant's
Religion . . . was not originally composed as one continuous work; it is a
compendium of several essays. Under these circumstances a degree of
imprecision is understandable. The textual misfortune that befell Cohen's
last work, as we have noted, may then be regarded as another partial
analogue.

23. Cf. N. Rotenstreich, "Religion within the Limits of Reason Alone and
Religion of Reason," *Leo Baeck Institute Year Book* 17 (1972); 187—for the
rest, a misinterpretation.

24. Op. cit., vol. 1 Cf., however, Schwarzschild, "F. Rosenzweig's Anecdotes
about H. Cohen," in *Gegenwart im Rueckblick—Festgabe f. d. Jüdische Gemeinde
zu Berlin*, ed. H. A. Strauss and R. K. Grossmann (Heidelberg: L. Siehm,
1970).

25. Cf. Hugo S. Bergmann, *Faith and Reason* (Washington, D.C.: B'nai B'rith,
1961), chap. 2; Paul Gruenewald, *H. Cohen*, Schriftenreihe d.
Landeszentrale f. bürgerliche Bildung (Hannover, 1968), pp. 32, 35, 48;
Nathan Rotenstreich, *Jewish Philosophy in Modern Times* (New York: Holt,
Rinehart & Winston, 1968), p. 64; Eugen Rosenstock-Huessy, *Judaism
Despite Christianity* (University: University of Alabama Press, 1969), p. 40;
Karl Loewith, "Philosophie der Vernunft und Religion der Offenbarung,"
*Sitzungberichte d. Heidelberger Akademie d. Wissenschaften, Philosophisch-
Historische Klasse* (1968), p. 7. Abhandlung; Joseph Klein, *Die Grundlegung*

der Ethik i.d. Philosophie H. Cohens u. P. Natorps—eine Kritik d.
Neukantianismus (Göttingen: Vandenhoeck & Ruprecht, 1976), pp. 8, 23,
137f., 146, etc., which has to be used with the greatest wariness: cf.
Schwarzschild, "'Germanism and Judaism' . . .," p. 208, n. 36; even
Henning Guenther, *Philosophie des Fortschritts: H. Cohens Rechtfertigung der
bürgerlichen Gessellschaft* (Munich: W. Goldmann, 1972), pp. 5, 80 ff., 110.

26. Cf. on Ferdinand Toennies, "Ethik und Sozialismus," *Archiv f.
Sozialwissenschaft v. Sozialpolitik* 25 (1909): 895–930, and the Cohen-
Toennies correspondence, 1893–1918, in the Cohen-Archives of the
University of Marburg, nos. 127–79, 1109; Guenther, pp. 44–46, 95f., 111,
116, "Geschichte und Dialektikverweigerung." (Joachim Kahl writes stupid
bolshevik attacks on the Marburg School: "Joseph Dietzgen und der
Neukantianismus," in *"Unser Philosoph" J. Dietzgen,* ed. H.-D. Strusing
[Frankfurt: Marxistische Blätter, 1980], pp. 146–160, and "F. A. Lange und
H. Cohen—Begründer der Marburger Schule des Neukantianismus und
philosophische Wegbereiter des Revisionismus," *Universität und
demokratische Bewegung—Ein Lesebuch zur 450-Jahrfeier der Philipps-
Universität,* ed. D. Kramer and C. Varija (Marburg: Verlag
Arbeiterbewegung und Gesellschaftswissenschaft, 1977), pp. 123–47.

27. Cf. H. Holzhey, *Kants Erfahrungsbegriff* (Basel, 1970), pp. 13, 199–244.
Basically this historical line can be described by the names Ortegà y
Gasset—Natorp—Nikolai Hartmann—Heinz Heimsoeth (cf. Heinrich
Knittermeyer, "Zu H. Heimsoeths Kantdeutung," *Kant-Studien* 49
[1957–58]: 293ff.)—Knittermeyer himself—Husserl—Heidegger—
Bultmann—Barth, etc. (An important post-World War II link in this chain
is also Hans Wagner, *Philosophie und Reflexion* [Munich/Basel: Ernst
Reinhart, 1967]; cf. his pp. 50, 60, 124f., etc. for Wagner's self-defined
genealogy.)

28. Cf. Guenter, pp. 116, etc.; Hans Ludwig Ollig, *Religion und Freiheitsglaube—
Zur Problematik von H. Cohens später Religonsphilosophie,* Monographien zur
philosophischen Forschung, no. 179 (Königstein/Ts.: Forum Academicum,
1979), e.g., pp. 4 f., 106 f., 163, 171 f., 354.

29. E.g., Martin Buber, "The Love of God and the Idea of Deity," in *Eclipse of
God* (New York: Harper & Bros., 1952)—though Buber admits that Cohen
never changed his mind on the ideal character of "God" (cp. also Buber's
famous attack on Cohen's anti-Zionism, "Concept and Reality" [*Der Jude,*
1:281–89, and "Zion, the State, and Mankind . . . " [ibid., pp. 425–33]);
ben-Schlomoh's ideological attack on Ucko's insistence on "the God-idea,"
pp. 15 ff., 20 f., 489 ff., 508; Eliezer Schweid, "The Foundations of H.
Cohen's Religious Philosophy" (Hebrew), *Jerusalem Studies in Jewish Thought,*
vol. 2, no. 2 (1982–83), which rightly, if in a pedestrian fashion, arrives at
basically the same conclusions as do we here and yet, at the end (p. 306),
extrapolates Cohen via Rosenzweig and Buber to a "Land of Israel"–lesson.
Cf. also Mordecai Kaplan, *The Meaning of God in Modern Jewish Religion*
(New York: Jewish Reconstructionist Foundation, 1937), p. 244: "For God
must not merely be held as an idea, He must be felt as a presence, if we
want not only to know about God but to know God"; Emil Fackenheim,
*Encounters between Judaism and Modern Philosophy—a Preface to Future
Jewish Thought* (New York: Basic Books, 1973), pp. 131 ff., 248; and
H. Cohen—after 50 Years, Leo Baeck Memorial Lecture, no. 12 (New York:
Leo Baeck Institute, 1969), pp. 5, 10f., et al.

30. "H. Cohens Begriff der Korrelation," in *In Zwei Welten—Bishnay Olamot: On*

S. Moser's 75th Birthday (Tel-Aviv, 1962), p. 397; cf. also Schwarzschild, "Truth: The Connection between Logic and Ethics," in *Judaism* 15 (Fall 1969):466; and "The Tenability of H. Cohen's Construction of the Self," Journal of the History of Philosophy 13 (July 1975): 368, n. 30, 371, n. 39; Sinai Ucko, "Compassion: Notes on H. Cohen's Philosophy of Religion" (Hebrew), *Iyyun* 20 (January 1969): 24 (Ucko was an editor of the 2d ed.; cf. n. 1 above, and, for his treatment of Cohen, cf. ibid., 7–30).

31. Cf. *Concept of Religion*, pp. 103 f.
32. *R.o.R.*, chap. 7: and "The Holy Spirit," *Jewish Writings*, 3:176–96.
33. *Jewish Writings*, 1:265f.
34. Cohen, *Kants Begründung der Ethik*, 74f.: we should say "'only a phenomenon,' not 'only an idea.'"
35. *R.o.R.*, p. 480. Cp. Maimonides' *Code*, "Book of Knowledge," 2:10, and his Guide for the Perplexed, 1, chaps. 53, 68.
36. *Jewish Writings*, 3:135. If anything, Cohen wrote to his disciple and intimate Benzion Kellermann to the contrary, on February 16, 1908: "For me the ontological valence *('Seinswert')* of God does not coincide with the ideal of eternity. Therefore, I can ethically demand the adoration of the idea of God in addition to moral action. Thus I affirm cult. And thus also the bulk of ritual. Why do we always think of the dietary laws when we speak of ritual and not rather of holy communion? (A private letter in the possession of the Kellermann family. It contains also Hebrew notes by Cohen in script.)
37. Cf. *Ethics*, pp. 528 f. "(The prophets') religion is morality."
38. Strauss, p. 625.
39. Cf. my introduction, Olms ed., VIIIf.
40. Compare the table of virtues in the last third of Cohen's *Ethics* and *R.o.R.*, chaps 18–22, to Alistair MacIntyre, *After Virtue* (University of Notre Dame Press, 1981), and W. F. Frankena, *Ethics*, 2d ed. (Englewood Cliffs, N.J.: Prentice-Hall, 1973), 62–70. Cf. H. Holzhey, "H. Cohens Weggang aus Marburg," *Neue Zürcher Zeitung* (March 21, 1971), pp. 49f., which describes Cohen's moving farewell lecture at Marburg University in 1912, again devoted to the virtues; and Leo Strauss, "Introduction" to Kaplan's English trans. of *R.o.R.*, XXIV, XXXVI, K. Loewith, p. 9. Wm. Kluback, *H. Cohen— the Challenge of a Religion of Reason*, Brown Judaic Studies 53, Chico, CA: Scholars Press, 1984, devotes itself entirely to Kant's and Cohen's treatments of the virtues. Unfortunately, he comes to the wrong conclusion—in line with the Rosenzweigian thesis discussed above. (Cf. my review in *Idealistic Studies*, forthcoming.)
41. On creation, see *R.o.R.*, chap. 3, esp. paras. 7ff., and chap. 5: "The Creation of Man in Reason." For cross-reference, see, e.g. *R.o.R.*, p. 73.
42. *Concept of Religion*, 1915.
43. Cf. Schwarzschild, "Germanism and Judaism," 130f.
44. Cf. Schwarzschild, "F. Rosenzweig's Anecdotes about H. Cohen," 213f.
45. Cp. Mrs. Cohen's original introduction, para. 2. Jews usually refer to their fathers in Hebrew as "my father and my teacher."
46. The epigraph is missing in the 3d ed. Cf. Lev. 16:30, *Yoma* 85b. (Cohen preferred to quote the *gemara ad locum*, rather than its text in the *mishnah*.)
47. On the reversal of the two questions, cf. Strauss, 625; cp. also L. Rosenzweig's correct Hebrew text, ibid., 539, *ad locum*.
48. Ibid., 260f. On 260 he includes pantheism in this.
49. Cp. J. Guttmann, *Die Philosophie des Judentums* (Munich, 1933), 361f. (the end of the book).

50. D. Silverman, in his English translation of Guttmann's chapter on Cohen in *History of Jewish Philosophies*, 260ff., misses the point entirely by mistranslating the *mishnah*, Guttmann, and Cohen!

51. Cp. Maimonides, *Code*, "Law of Repentance," 2:2, etc., and Schwarzschild, "On Jewish Eschatology," in *Human Nature in Jewish and Christian Faith*, ed. F. Greenspahn (New York: Ktav, 1985), 26. Notice, in particular, *Code*, "Laws of Ritual Baths," 11:12 (the climax not only of this section but of the entire "Order of Laws of Purity") where (1) a Hebrew pun on *"mikveh"* ("hope") and *"mikvah"* ("bath") is operative throughout, (2) Ezek. 36:25 is silently collocated with Lev. 16:30, and (3), while the laws of ritual baths are designated as divine fiat *(khok)*, they are then daringly interpreted as "the waters of pure reason" *(da'at hatahor)*! Herman Cohen picked up this pun: cf. *Jewish Writings*, 21:1ii.

52. Cf. Loewith, p. 6.

Professor Lou Silberman is one of those classmates at the Hebrew Union College—Jewish Institute of Religion who was ordained with Herman Schaalman in 1941. Silberman spent more than three decades in academia, primarily at Vanderbilt University. He served on various faculties, including the University of Vienna, Emory University, the University of Chicago, and the University of Arizona in the Department of Oriental Studies. He has also served as president of the Society of Biblical Literature. Lou Silberman's close personal and professional relationship with Herman Schaalman spans the latter's entire adult life, since he emigrated from Germany in 1935. They share many of the same perceptions of covenant and the challenge that covenant brings to Judaism.

Lou Silberman raises some critical questions about an inherent dialectic within rabbinic Judaism: *aggadah* and *halakhah*. This creative tension is in and of itself another expression of the covenant's dynamic. Silberman uses this inherent dialectic to suggest some important roots within rabbinic Judaism for ethical standards. This critical scholarship adds an important element to how ethics is a *living* response to a life of covenant. Silberman's view of rabbinic process is an example of a life of covenant.

Aggadah and Halakhah: Ethos and Ethics in Rabbinic Judaism

Lou H. Silberman

The focus of this paper is the question of obligation, of responsibility and our response in the multifaceted situations of our lives within the nexus of the divine-human and the human-human and the human-other-than-human structures and processes of existence. Our first inquiry is, therefore, what is the source and ground of our obligation? Whence come our responsibilities? What responses are called for?

The verses at Deut. 26:5–10 are as satisfactory a place as any from which to look toward the Jewish answer to these questions. In the chapter we have a description of a ritual act—the bringing of the first fruits of the land to the sanctuary—together with an acknowledgment: "My father was a fugitive Aramean. He went down to Egypt with meager numbers and sojourned there; but there he became a great and very populous nation. The Egyptians dealt harshly with us and oppressed us; they imposed heavy labor upon us. We cried to the Lord, the God of our fathers, and the Lord heard our plea and saw our plight, our misery, and our oppression. The Lord freed us from Egypt by a mighty hand, by an outstretched arm and awesome power and gave us this land, a land flowing with milk and honey. Wherefore I now bring the first fruits of the soil which You, O Lord, have given me."

If we listen carefully, we hear the declaration of obligation: "wherefore"—for this reason. For what reason? For this saving, this redeeming act in history, an act that occurred in the past and is yet not past. Notice the way in which the third-person singular "he" suddenly becomes "we," the first-person plural, and at length places responsibility on the first-person singular "I". And by whom was and is that act performed? By the God of our fathers. But we ask, Why did He act? And in seeking our answer, we are led back to the fathers and to that relationship that called for divine responses to "our plight, our misery and our oppression." It is to this relationship, *berit*—covenant—that we look if we are to understand the obligation of Israel.

Much recent biblical scholarship has indicated that many of the legal structures and forms found in scripture may have their counterparts in the political actualities and legal systems of the ancient Near East. Among these is that just referred to—*berit*—the establishment of a relationship between individuals, states or their representatives, kings and their subjects, husbands and wives. Two of these in particular claim our attention. The first is the suzerain-vassal treaty, or obligatory *berit*; the second, the royal grant, or promissory *berit*. In the former the sovereign, freely and out of goodwill, acts toward the subordinate, taking him under his protection and receiving a pledge of loyalty in return. In the latter, no obligation is imposed, yet loyalty cast its light over the situation.[1] Our concern is not, however, to examine the history of these forms in their literary expressions in scripture, but to recognize that they are the vessels into which even more ancient doctrine was poured. Martin Buber in his book *The Prophetic Faith* points to "the three great articles of faith . . . God's accompanying leadership, the people's 'loving' devotion, and the zealous demand for decision." These appear again and again, most forcefully in the opening of the Decalogue—the Ten Words: "I am the Lord your God who brought you forth from the Land of Egypt, from the slave house"— divine leadership; "showing kindness to the thousandth generation of those who love Me . . ."—the call the loving devotion; "you shall have no other gods besides [or perhaps—standing in front of, hence obscuring] Me"—the demand for decision (Ex. 20:2, 6, 3). Here, we are told by scholars, is a fragment of a text formed after an ancient suzerainty treaty—and well it may be as a form. As to content, the explanation is as yet insufficient, for once again this text points behind itself to an even more ancient scene—one that is not necessarily historical but certainly is protohistorical—in which the themes appear. "The Lord said to Abram 'Go forth from your native land [not the slave house] to the land I will show you'"—divine leadership; Abram, called by Isaiah, *ohavai*, "my [God's] lover," went forth in loving devotion. He went forth, Buber wrote, "to the final test, [the binding of Isaac on the altar] in which it is demanded from him to return to God what has been promised and given to him [Abraham], and 'goes' again in silence to perform that which was laid upon him. . . . Here too . . . there prevails the atmosphere of decision."[2]

Here we are in the realm of *berit*, of relationship—but on a plane not encountered elsewhere—between Deity and people and with un- paralleled intensity excluding the possibility of dual or multiple loyalties.

Weinfeld has noted the way in which "this idea of exclusive loyalty" is expressed in prophetic literature through the exchange of the language used to describe *berit*. In place of that of sovereign-vassal we find the relationship of husband and wife: "I passed by and saw you and I knew you were ready for marriage so I spread my cloak over you covering your nakedness and made my vow and my *berit* with you—the Lord God's word—and you were mine" (Ezk. 16:8). "If," Weinfeld argues, "the idea of marital love between God and Israel is not mentioned explicitly in the Pentateuch it seems present in latent form." His evidence is drawn from the use of language in the Pentateuch indicating the breaking of the marriage relationship, and from the occurrences of the phrase, "you will be my people and I will be your God"—reflecting a legal formula taken from the sphere of marriage.[3] Again, our central interest is not in the details of biblical scholarship—important though they be—but in the overarching conclusion toward which they point and indeed which has been brought more clearly into focus by that scholarship, the centrality of *berit* in the faith of Israel.

Thus behind the language of vassal treaties binding people in loyalty the ultimate motive of obligation: " . . . it was because the Lord loved you and kept the oath he made to your fathers that the Lord your God is God, the steadfast God who keeps his gracious covenant [*berit*] to the thousandth generation of those who love him and keep his commandments" (Deut. 7:7–9). Here again we see the three basic affirmations: divine leadership, loving response, and decision. But it is the ultimate source of obligation—God's love for Israel—that must ever be held in mind when one turns to pay heed to the response that *berit* calls forth.

It is important for us to recognize that one ought not speak, in our context, of covenant theology in the formal sense in which it has been presented by such a distinguished theologian as Eichrodt on the Christian side and Buber and some who have taken their cue from him on the Jewish side.[4] This is not to suggest these contemporary formulations are unimportant or are to be disregarded. Rather must we be careful not to read back into the past our own structure of thought and then "find" it in the Bible. The covenant theology of the Bible as an intellectual structure is far more implicit than explicit, and the same is true of its continued presence throughout the development of Jewish thought in the talmudic and medieval periods. It is there as a pervading ethos, as the "given" that need not be expressed in the context of intellectual discussion. It is present, too, in the whole liturgical life of the community, the life that provides the background against which intellectual endeavor takes place. I shall be returning to this question of the ethos of ethics shortly, but I am anxious at this point that it be understood in our context. The concept of *berit* must be understood as providing the horizon for biblical and for all subsequent Jewish thought. Its verbal presence may or may not be observed, but its effective presence is almost everywhere apparent. Certainly there are times and seasons when it seems to have faded into such a shadowy presence as to be thought of as of little or no effectiveness, yet when the whole context of the community's situation is attended to, one cannot help but recognize that it is there, informing the life structure and processes of that community.

The analytic approach of biblical scholarship has, on occasion, contributed to our failure to recognize *berit* as the horizon of biblical thought. However valid literary or traditio-critical undertaking may be— and I would most certainly affirm them as requirements for our understanding of biblical texts—we must not lose sight of the totality of the texts as they have achieved a gestalt and function together. This is evident in the Pentateuch where *Torah* (i.e., divine instruction) is set within the historical narrative so that the clear inference is called for that the variety of laws enumerated and expounded are for the community obligatory because of their setting within the historical nexus. Further, the prophetic endeavor—whatever else may be said of it—can hardly be understood without the presence of the *berit,* setting both the problem of retribution and that of redemption.

Before, however, we continue with the development of this theme as it provides the scene for our examination of obligation and response, we are called upon to face a critical issue. The *berit,* however multi-faceted it may be, is a covenant between a singular people—*'am Yisrael*—and Deity, however narrowly or widely one understands Deity. Again, I do not intend to dismiss lightly the question of the emergence of monotheism in ancient Israel, only to put it into its perspective. Whatever the steps in its development—if there was a development—at some point, be it late or early, the affirmation was made that the Deity with whom the people of Israel stood in relationship was singular—the only truly divine being—and thus unique. Further, that as the only God, He stood in relation within history to all mankind not only Israel: "Are you not the same as the Ethiopians to me, O Israelites, says the Lord. Did I not bring Israel forth from Egypt and the Philistines from Cyprus and the Arameans from Kir?" (Am. 9:7). All are the object of divine solici-tude. Yet this people who had experienced within history the same divine leadership as other people nonetheless stood in a unique and thus an exposed relationship that had made it vulnerable as the others were not. The Hebrew particle *raq* at the beginning of verse 2 of Amos, chapter 3, singles out this people whose historic experience was, on one level, the same as the others: "You *only* among the families of the earth have I known intimately." The verb *yada'* reflects the intimate relationship of the marriage *berit.* Israel is the unique *berit* partner of God. This is a relationship imposing, as we have seen, obligation and calling for response. But then, what of the other nations? How do they stand in relation? Or what obligation if any and what response if any is called for from them?

Part of our problem as we are confronted by these questions is the fact that beginning with the twelfth chapter of Genesis the concern of scripture is with the unique relationship—the particular *berit*—between God and Israel. Nonetheless, as the verses from Amos suggest, however unexpressed the divine relationship with others may have been, it was not absent. That the nations somehow were under obligation, albeit other or somewhat other than that of Israel, although not formulated, seems to be presupposed within the historical narratives. It is because of their failure to respond to that obligation that the nations who had been the recipients of divine assistance become the objects of divine wrath. One thinks at this point of the verses in Deut. 9, "And when the Lord your God has thrust them from your path, do not say to yourselves, 'The Lord has enabled me to occupy this land because of my virtue'; it is rather because of the wickedness of those nations that the Lord is dispossessing them before you." Because scripture did not formulate this in any consistent fashion, it became a systematic task for later Jewish thinkers who sought to lay out the nature of the obligation of mankind in general. It is striking to observe that rabbinic Judaism saw this relationship between God and mankind in covenanted terms—the *berit* proclaimed in Gen. 9 between God, Noah and his offspring to come, and "every living thing that is with you." The obligations that devolved upon mankind through this covenant were understood by rabbinic Judaism to be those that had already been commanded Adam and were here reaffirmed in a covenantal context. While the "exegesis" establishing this may appear to our modern eyes as fantastic, the intent—that of sensing within the biblical text obligations that fall on all mankind—cannot be faulted. In an interpretation of Gen. 2:16: "And the Lord God commanded the man saying . . . 'Of every tree of the garden you are free to eat . . . '" we read, "R. Levi said, He commanded him concerning six obligations: 'commanded' refers to idolatry; 'the Lord'—refers to blasphemy; 'God' refers to judges; 'upon the man,' refers to bloodshed; 'saying' refers to sexual license; 'from all the fruit you are free to eat' refers to theft."[5] A seventh obligation, to refrain from eating flesh torn from a living animal, was understood to have been imposed upon Noah, since only from his time onward was the eating of any flesh permitted. The discussion of these laws in rabbinic literature is complicated, and there is no need here to become too deeply involved in its various strands. What is evident is that the seven commandments—understood to be the obligation of the sons of Noah (i.e., all mankind) fall into the three categories of divine-human, human-human, human-other-than-human relationship.[6] Under the first are the prohibitions against idolatry and blasphemy; under the second, the prohibitions against bloodshed, sexual license, theft, and the affirmative command concerning judges, that is, to establish courts of justice in order to make sure that the other commandments are observed. One may interpret this to mean the establishment of a just social order. Under the third is the prohibition against eating flesh torn from a living animal. This latter may be understood to subsume man's obligations toward a variety of other-than-human things, and—without reading our own concerns into the past—may well refer to mankind's obligation to its environment. One recognizes this theme in the specific obligation imposed upon Israel: "When in your war against a city you have to besiege it a long time in order to capture it you must not destroy its trees, wielding the axe against them. You may eat of them, but you must not cut them down . . . " (Deut. 20:19).

To sum up the argument thus far: I am asserting that the ethos of ethics in Judaism, the genius of the system, is the sense of the *berit,* the covenantal relationships between God and Israel (and between God and mankind) seen as the paradigmatic situation of the Jew. My argument is based upon what seems to me to be the Gestalt of Scripture, the exposition of the pattern of existence over against or, perhaps better, within the sense of existence.

I propose now to examine the way in which this twofold Gestalt continued to inform the life of the Jewish community in a subsequent period. Here we find ourselves engaged with the works: *Aggadah* and *Halakhah.* Etymologically the first of these derives from the Hebrew root *ngd* with the meaning "to declare," "to tell," "to proclaim," "to announce." The root of the second is the stem *hlkh,* "to walk." But etymology, while interesting, is hardly—as James Barr has argued—decisive.[7] Of greater interest is the function of the words; toward what realities do they point?

Aggadah is, after all, not merely a word, not even a literary genre. It is a continuation, albeit on another level, of the historical narrative that provided the ethos within which the legal structures and processes of Scripture were set down. *Aggadah* is not, however, particularly concerned with history, or at least not in the same way as scripture is. Rather does it provide the ethos—the sense of existence—of the Jewish community by means of a wide variety of narrations, historical—to be sure—but legendary, mythic, personal anecdotal, lyrical, etc. These narratives are themselves complex entities whose dynamics must be understood. Let me note at this point that what I am about to suggest with regard to *Aggadah* is germane as well to our second item, *Halakhah.*

The aggadic process is composed of three elements: the given tradition, in our case, scripture; the socio-political-economic situation at any particular time (called the "World" as a convenient symbol); individual sensibility of a singular person or of the group—the Jewish community in its totality, or its several parts. We must recognize at once that the givenness of scripture—that is, the tradition—is of crucial importance, for one of the specificities of Judaism is the essential role of tradition:

scripture and the oral tradition that both proceeded and continued it. The oral tradition, as it is the continuation of scripture, represents a conversation, an interchange between scripture and the contemporary situation of the community as perceived, apprehended, understood, and responded to by the sensibilities of the community or some of its components, group or individual. Now this process must be understood not necessarily as a self-conscious undertaking—although it has its self-conscious aspects—but as the ongoing flow of the community's life. The emergence and formulation in rabbinic Judaism, in the period following the destruction of the Second Temple in the year 70 C.E., of liturgical patterns meant that more and more members of the community fell under the influence of the pharisaic-rabbinic ethos with its particular interest in and emphasis upon the covenantal chosenness of Israel. The regular public reading of scripture, both the Pentateuch and the Prophets, underscored this perception of Jewish existence. The absorption of many Psalms into the order of worship added to this way of viewing the nature of the relationship of God and Israel. Thus scripture—however it had functioned earlier and in other parts of the Jewish community and however else it was functioning in the rabbinic community—was an active presence. To this presence the community was called to respond through the preaching of the synagogal teachers who by means of a variety of devices offered *midrash,* that is, the investigation into, the searching out of the meaning of scripture. Those searchings out were, of course, stimulated by the "World," the situation in which the community found itself, and represented the way in which the sensibility of the community or of its teachers responded to the challenges and demands the interfacing of Tradition and "World" engendered. In this active process the covenantal ethos of the community was continually renewed, refurbished, refashioned. Thus antecedent, psychologically if not chronologically, to any pattern of communal life was an implicit but often explicit expression of the presupposition of what that pattern was to be. So far as we are able to determine from the literary remains of the first three or four hundred years of Jewish life in the period following the destruction of the Commonwealth, there did emerge a sense of the expected quality of life in both its communal and individual structures. This is not to suggest that the expected quality was always concretely actualized, only that it did exist and that it was—whatever else contributed to it—widely and deeply informed by the ethos of *berit,* with its divine call, Israel's loving devotion and the decisive activity flowing therefrom.

An example of the way in which this occurred may serve to bring these ideas into focus. Deut. 11:22 reads: "If, then, you faithfully keep all this Instruction that I command you, loving the Lord your God, walking in all His ways, and holding fast to Him. . . . " The *Sifre*—a midrash whose basic material dates from the second century of the Common Era—

interprets it in the following fashion understanding the word translated "loving" to mean "for the sake of love." "Perhaps," says the *Sifre*, "you may say, 'I will study Torah that I may be called wise, so that I may take my place in the academy, so that I may live long,' Scripture says: 'for the sake of love!'" The next words commented upon are, "walking in all His ways." "*These* are the ways of God," says the *Sifre*, basing its enumeration on Ex. 34:6: "The Lord, the Lord, God, compassionate and gracious." "Just as God is called compassionate, so be you compassionate. The Holy One blessed be He is called gracious, so be you gracious . . . God is called the righteous one, be you righteous. God is called steadfast lover (*Hasid*) so be you a steadfast lover." Still further, "holding fast to Him." "How is it possible for man to ascend to the heights and cleave unto flame?—for God is called elsewhere 'a devouring flame.'—Cleave, therefore, unto the scholars and their pupils and it will be accounted to you as though you had ascended on high and received Torah."[8] It is not difficut to sense the ethos this interpretation profers: disinterested study of Torah (the text does a moment later suggest that unsought honors will be added thereto); *imitatio Dei;* the significant role of the Torah scholar. That the disclosing nature of *Aggadah,* as here argued, is not the reading back of any contemporary interest into the text, is evidenced by the very next and concluding interpretation in the passage, that returns to the problem of cleaving to God: "If you wish to recognize Him by whose word the world was created learn *Aggadah* for thus will you recognize Him and cleave to His ways." The divine-human relationship expressed in *berit* and disclosed in *Aggadah* was the a priori of the way—*Halakhah*—in which Israel was to walk. Which brings us now to the pattern of existence, *Halakhah,* as it expressed the sense of existence, *Aggadah.*

We have seen that the Pentateuch contains within the narrative setting a number of legal collections whose obligatory nature is understood to be rooted in the narrative. In addition to these scriptural laws there existed—whether one wishes to argue the case from a traditional or a "scientific" point of view is not here germane—an even larger body of oral laws that only slowly and latterly precipitated into literary form. Pharisaic-rabbinic Judaism understood this part of the tradition—the *Torah Shebealpeh*—the Oral Torah—to be obligatory for the same reason as Scripture—*Torah shebiktav.* Indeed, some of the conflicts within Judaism in the pre-Christian period reflect this Pharisaic claim and its rejection by other segments of the Jewish community. *Halakhah*—"His ways," as we have seen, was for rabbinic Judaism composed of both these strands— written and oral—as coordinate members. These were together, in terms of the earlier analysis of the aggadic process, the Tradition that interfaced with the "World," which interfacing was "perceived, apprehended, understood and responded to by the sensibilities of the community," to repeat the phrase used earlier. But while the aggadic process created or expressed the ethos of the community, the halakhic process was concerned with pattern, with structure, with paradigm for behavior. For that reason it had to be more precise, more sharply defined. Its methodology had to be more vigorously observed, its results more specifically applied. The problems that emerged out of the interfacing of Tradition and "World" were not left to the individual to solve within the horizon of the community's ethos, for this was indeed a community, not a mere collection of individuals. Thus the sensibilities of the community were disciplined by the hermeneutic process by which answers to the problems posed by the interfacing were sought. The world of *Halakhah* was thus, never coterminous with the world of *Aggadah,* nor did it always manage to crystallize the sense of existence into the pattern of existence.

Let me turn to examples to indicate the twofold relationship between "sense of existence" and "pattern of existence." Deut. 21:18 ff. (i.e., scripture) deals in very clear language, so we may think, with the case of a wayward and defiant son, "who does not heed his father or mother and does not obey them even after they discipline him." Such a son is to be brought before "the elders of his town at the public place of his community" and charges are to be laid against him: "This son of ours is disloyal and defiant; he does not heed us; he is a glutton and a drunkard. Thereupon the men of his town shall stone him to death." By the time the Mishna—the collection of the oral legal tradition—was codified around 200 C.E.—the *terminus ad quem* of the development—the ethos of the community had rejected the pattern. Yet it was a given of scripture. How did the *Aggadah,* the ethos of the community, deal with the *Halakhah*? What is for us clear language is for aroused sensibility far less clear, or perhaps is far clearer than we recognize. First the word "son" is attended to. Exactly when does that term apply? Its specificity indicates exclusion. A daughter is not mentioned but only a son. Carrying the principle of exclusion further, it must mean only during the period when he is not a man, that is, when he is a child. More than that, not when he is a minor, that is, before the age of 13 years and a day, for he is not yet obligated to the commandments. Hence this commandment is effective only during the boy's puberty. It is not necessary to examine in detail the process of definition by which the limitations involved in "glutton and drunkard" were arrived at; the further requirements that both parents—as the biblical text indicates—must lodge the complaint, and must be physically capable of bringing him before the elders, nor the composition of the court, and so on.[9] All that is necessary is to indicate that *Aggadah,* the sense of existence, has apparently provided fertile soil in which *Halakhah*—the thicket of the law, to use that admirable phrase placed in Thomas More's mouth in *A Man for All Seasons*—may spring up to offer a hiding place even for the wayward son.

On the other hand, *Aggadah* is not always able to mitigate *Halakhah* but at least it has its say and in some sense may be thought to reprove the pattern it finds offensive. Thus, we refer again to Deuteronomy, this time chapter 23, verse 3: a mamzer (translated in the NJPS as "misbegotten" against the inadequate "bastard" of King James and RSV) is prohibited from entering "the congregation of the Lord." Our concern is not with the definition of *Mamzer* in Jewish law—the offspring of adultery or incest within the Jewish community—but with *Aggadah's* protest against the exclusion. In *Vayikra rabbah* 32 (a fourth-fifth century C.E. midrash on Leviticus) we find an interpretation based on Eccl. 4:1. "Said Kohelet: 'and behold the tears of such as were oppressed, and they had no comforter.' Daniel the Tailor applied this verse to *mamzerim*. Said he: 'Behold the tears of the oppressed, their father sinned; why should these poor creatures suffer? They have no comforter, but their oppressors have power in their hands'—there is power in the hands of the Great Sanhedrin of Israel that comes against them with the power of Torah and sets them off afar because of the verse: 'a mamzer shall not enter into the congregation of the Lord' 'They have no comforter'; said the Holy One blessed be He: 'I shall comfort them, for although in this world they are stained, in the future—as Zachariah said, I see it all of gold'—this being the interpretation of Zach. 4:2, 'I looked and behold a menorah entirely of gold . . . ' *i.e.,* they shall be cleansed of their blemish."[10]

What we have seen in these two passages represents the dynamic intertwining of *Aggadah* and *Halakhah* and suggests the constructive tension that enveloped them. *Halakhah* is thus not to be understood as an automatic and mechanical solution of legal problems but rather as the search for a pattern of existence governed by a sense of existence.

In a brilliant essay "Halakhah and Aggadah or Law and Lore" published in 1917,[11] Hayyim Nahman Bialik, the great modern poet of Hebrew reborn, discussed the relationship toward which I have pointed, with that particular insight which a poet brings to his task. It is filled with striking aperçus, any one of which would provide a more than suitable conclusion for this paper. "We are not interested here in this Aggadah or that Halakhah" he wrote, "but in the concept of Halakhah, in Halakhah as a great legal sanction, as a tangible shaping, complete in itself, of concrete life—a life not floating in the air or hovering in the mist of beautiful feelings and phrases, but with a beautiful body too and a beautiful substance . . . I maintain that this Halakhah is the integral complement of Aggadah, the logical period at the end of the sentence. Indeed the greatness of Aggadah lies in the very fact that it leads to Halakhah. Any Aggadah which does not so issue is a mere sentimental bauble."

But: "A people that has not learned to combine Halakhah with Aggadah delivers itself to eternal confusion and runs the danger of forgetting the one direct way from the will to the deed, from the effort to the realization." That the perception of this relationship has not always been recognized and understood is, sadly, evident in the long and tangled history of the Jewish people. That it was and is, nonetheless, with all the implications here suggested, the ultimate dynamic of Jewish existence is the affirmation of this paper.

Notes

1. See *Encyclopaedia Judaica* 5, *s.v.* "Covenant," 1012–22; bibliography, 1021–22.
2. Martin Buber, *The Prophetic Faith* (New York: Harper & Bros, 1949), p. 31.
3. *Encyclopaedia Judaica* 5, 1021.
4. Walther Eichrodt, *Theology of the Old Testament* (Philadelphia: Westminster Press, 1961).
5. This exegesis of Gen. 2:16 occurs in a number of rabbinic texts: *Genesis rabba* 16:6, *Pesikta de Rab Kahana* 12:1, etc.
6. For a concise discussion of the Noachide laws—the first six as we have seen are actually commandments directed to Adam—see *Encyclopaedia Judaica* 12, *s.v.,* 1189–91.
7. James Barr, *The Semantics of Biblical Language* (London: Oxford University Press, 1961).
8. *Sifre* to Deut. 11:22.
9. See Mishna Sanhedrin, chap. 8, paras. 1–5. In Danby's English translation pp. 394–5.
10. Bialik (see next note) uses this same midrash but my reference to it derived immediately from my reading of Vayikra [Leviticus] rabba. It was only when I was checking the citations noted below that I realized he had used it. Apparently it was latent in my memory.
11. Cited from *Contemporary Jewish Record VII* 6 (December 1944): 662–80. The two passages quoted are found on pp. 677 and 678, respectively.

Professor Elie Wiesel is the Andrew W. Mellon Professor in the Humanities, University Professor, and professor of religion at Boston University. Elie Wiesel is internationally renowned as an author of more than twenty-five books. His writings span the forms of novel, play, short story, and critical essay. He is chairman of the United States Holocaust Memorial Council. He has taught at Yale University, Florida International University, and the City University of New York. He has lectured throughout the world. Elie Wiesel was virtually unknown when Herman Schaalman brought him to Oconomowoc with a group of covenantal theologians in the sixties. Their relationship spans more than a quarter of a century. Elie Wiesel has lectured several times at Emanuel Congregation.

Elie Wiesel is noted for his sensitive approach to the world of Torah. He brings his masterful qualities of storytelling to the process of contemporary Midrash. Here Wiesel offers us yet another example of contemporary challenges to the text and his loving response on behalf of the text. Two biblical characters, Ishmael and Hagar, and their destinies become the foils for a delicate critique of Abraham and Sarah. Elie Wiesel knows how to tell the story, because he can hear the story being constantly retold, relived within the covenant. Sometimes just telling the story is the challenge of the life of covenant today.

Ishmael and Hagar

Elie Wiesel

Who hasn't heard of Abraham and Sarah? Everyone loves them. They radiate goodness, nobility, human warmth. Who doesn't claim kinship with them? One could even argue that humankind's destiny was shared by them. He is the father of our people, and she the mother. Everything leads us back to them. The promised land bears their seal. Our faith was kindled by theirs. Unlike any other couple, they arouse joy and hope. When we are tormented by our own troubles, we recall their trouble and gain a transcendent understanding of our own. Abraham was the first to be chosen by God and the first to choose God and crown Him God of the Universe. Abraham is synonymous with loyalty and absolute fidelity; his life a symbol of religious perfection. And yet a shadow hovers over one aspect of his life. In his exalted biography, we encounter a painful episode which puzzles us. This is a situation in which Abraham, the husband, is an agonizing enigma. We refer, of course, to his behavior toward his concubine Hagar and their son Ishmael.

Let us read the text. It tells us that Sarah is barren. She cannot conceive, and thus, unhappy above all for her husband, who desires a son, an heir, she proposes that he have one with his Egyptian servant Hagar. The *shidukh* is successful. Abraham and Hagar are together, and Hagar becomes pregnant—which is when the problems start. The servant becomes arrogant toward her mistress, who then takes offense. Hagar feels persecuted and takes flight. She is proud and therefore prefers to die in freedom in the desert rather than remain a slave in Sarah's house. By chance, an angel notices her and advises her to return home and wait to

235

see what happens. Hagar obeys, goes back to Abraham, and gives birth to Ishmael. Later the narrative recounts that, like any older brother, Ishmael will try to play tricks on Isaac. What ultimately must happen, happens: Hagar and her son are sent away for good.

The text, of course, is more detailed and contains some astonishing descriptions: Sarah's mentality, Hagar's character, Abraham's behavior. Sometimes a single word suffices to paint a vivid picture, while at other times a single word describes a silence to portray the ambiguity of a situation. The more we reread the story, the more it troubles us. The story makes us feel ill at ease. We wish the events had happened in another book, in someone else's "memory." How can Jewish history begin with a domestic quarrel between a rich elderly mistress and her young servant? Why did the Bible preserve it? Naturally, none of this would have happened, had Sarah not been barren for so many years. Why did she have to be so afflicted?

All the matriarchs have the misfortune of being unfruitful at first. One Midrashic author offers a generous explanation—generous, that is, to the husbands, the patriarchs. This author says that pregnant, even the most beautiful wives appear less attractive because of the loss of their figures. So, to be more desirable to the patriarchs for as long as possible, the matriarchs had no children for years and years. The Midrash adds that Sarah, who became a mother at the very advanced age of ninety, still had the beauty of a young bride on her wedding night. Can we allow the Midrash to sweep away the tragedy of Hagar and Ishmael as if it would not have happened if God had not decided to cater to masculine pride? Is this possible? For let us not forget: If Sarah had had a son earlier, immediately after her marriage, Hagar would have remained a servant, and Ishmael would not have been born. This Midrash leads to extraordinary fantasy; and this story belongs on a higher level—it has a deeper meaning. Nothing in the beginnings of Jewish destiny is frivolous. All doors open on metaphysical dilemmas and conflicts.

Let us begin at the beginning. Abraham is not yet called Abraham but Avram. Sarah is known as Sarai. They are a lonely couple whose life seems rather turbulent. Avram has left the home of his parents to follow the path leading to God, a dangerous path, filled with obstacles and traps. Famine and wars succeed each other, as do divine promises, but the earthly troubles are more real. Avram does not stop—his life is one long battle: against neighboring kings, against the powerful unbelievers, against the cruel nature of some people, against drought. Nothing comes easily to him. Everywhere he must fight, but everywhere he wins. After all, isn't God on his side? Yet he feels beaten: He has no child. But God has made promises—solemn promises! We can imagine his grief; with no son, no heir, what kind of future is there? Who will continue his work? We can imagine Sarah's grief. When they were young, they had hope. Each day, each night could bring good news. Now, after so many years, the waiting is more difficult, more improbable; there seems to be uncertainty, anguish, agony without end.

It is only then that Sarah, in a characteristic gesture of compassion, offers to lend her servant Hagar to her old husband. Hagar is young, and she will bear him a child, perhaps a son. Thus Abraham will be a father of a child even if she, Sarah, will not be a mother. Abraham does not refuse. The text recounts that Hagar, once pregnant, becomes arrogant; Sarah makes her pay dearly. Hagar flees, returns, gives birth to Ishmael, remains for fifteen years, long enough to see the birth of Isaac, whose presence dominates the scene. Then comes the drama, the human confrontation, the break-up, the explosion between two women, two brothers, and, above all, between father and son. Sarah demands that her husband expel Hagar and Ishmael, who provoke her, but Abraham hesitates. Ishmael is his son; he feels he has neither the right nor the strength to drive away his son and to send him into the unknown. Divine intervention is needed to make him decide. Where is pity, compassion, the human heart, and Jewish morality in this story?

These are troubling, painful, baffling questions. All of these questions and so many others are inevitable. They force us to judge all the characters in the story. Whom are we judging? A father—Abraham; two mothers—Sarah and Hagar; two sons—Ishmael and Isaac. Is that all? Surely not. God—He too—plays an important if not an essential role in the evolving plot. Except for Him, all the characters seem to be real, living beings, so full and colorful is their description.

Abraham is submissive in his relationship to God, sure of himself in his relationship with those around him. He obeys heaven but is obeyed on earth. We perceive him as moody, impulsive, demanding. He shows himself vulnerable and flexible only with Sarah. Abraham was able to resist his father, but Sarah is irresistible. Whatever Sarah desires, she obtains. It is Sarah, not Abraham, who comes up with the idea of a match with Hagar. Abraham never would have dreamed of living with another woman. He loves Sarah. She is his strength and perhaps equally his weakness. Remember the strange episode in Scripture (Gen. 12:10–20) where they traveled to Egypt and he had introduced her as his sister. She is too beautiful. Later in the text (Gen. 20), she attracts King Avimelekh, who, in theory, could eliminate a husband who happens to be in the way. These are unpleasant, dark episodes that leave a bad taste in one's mouth. Instead of separating the couple, they strengthen their bond. We don't understand Abraham; was he fearful for his life? And what about his honor? How can he abandon his wife—his adored, beloved wife—to the whims of a king who has an eye for a woman's beauty, especially that of a stranger? How can a hero like Abraham, who has defeated five kings, yield to a single one without so much as a fight? How is it possible that a man of his stature thinks only of saving his own skin? Admittedly, he is preoccupied with theological questions, but is there nothing of the romantic in him, nothing of chivalry?

We shall ask these same questions about Abraham with regard to Hagar and Ishmael. Abraham drives them away, yet he is famous for his hospitality. Does he sacrifice his son for love of his wife? Sacrifice is what we are talking about! He sends them into the desert, where death awaits the parched wanderer. How can he be so cruel toward a woman who has loved him—be it for one night only—and toward a child—his own child at that! Sarah doesn't like them—why doesn't Abraham suggest they stay at a neighbor's, or let them go and live with some distant tribe? Why condemn them to death by thirst and disease? How are we to explain these flaws in Abraham's character, and to what shall we attribute them? Is this the same Abraham whose faith and goodness remain models for all time? Did he commit such acts of weakness?

We read once again the passage about the second character in the drama—Sarah—and see that she also suffers from the rereading. Negative traits make an appearance. In Egypt, she is a willing accomplice in her husband's lies. Like a couple that illegally cross some dangerous border, they are united in trying to evade the police. Have the police nothing better to do than wait for Sarah? Thousands upon thousands are without doubt pouring into Egypt in search of food. Is Sarah alone threatened? The answer is yes, because Abraham tells us Sarah is very beautiful. She accepts Abraham's compliment without protesting. What about humility and modesty? Couldn't she, shouldn't she answer her husband: "Really, you are very sweet, but there are women more beautiful, more attractive. Let's not play such a charade. We are married, let's remain so in the eyes of the whole world! Besides, what good is such a game? Why not ask God to save us?" In other words: Sarah's role in Egypt does not become her.

This is even more evident later on in the conflicts with Hagar. No sooner has Sarah persuaded Hagar to accept Abraham, when she seems to regret it. One would say that she is suspicious; she keeps close watch over her servant and looks for a quarrel. As soon as Hagar is pregnant, Sarah finds her arrogant. What if she's mistaken, and the servant's behavior is simply due to her pregnancy? Pregnant women have strange desires, whims. Everybody knows that—everybody, it seems, but Sarah! Is it possible that the text is mistaken and that we are mistaken, because Sarah is herself mistaken? Hagar meant no disrespect toward her mistress; it is Sarah who imagined terrible things of that sort. In other words, Hagar is Sarah's victim and Sarah was wrong to impose a role upon her and then begrudge her for playing it too well.

The issues become inflamed later in the story. Hagar comes back, she has a son, then Sarah has a son; and instead of making peace with the servant, instead of being grateful that her innermost wish has come true, that she has become a mother—Sarah continues to torment Hagar and *her* child. The servant now acts out of consideration, she watches every gesture, every word; Sarah no longer complains—now Abraham's wife picks on little Ishmael! Now it is he whom she observes, scrutinizes, and suspects! This too is clearly indicated in the text: she sees Ishmael playing with Itzhak and she gets upset. Why does that make her nervous? What could be more natural, more beautiful than to see two children, two brothers, play together? Sarah finds this neither beautiful nor touching. Had Ishmael done the contrary, had he avoided his little brother, had he chosen not to play with him, Sarah foolishly would have accused him of something else—of bad education, for example, or selfishness. She seems to detest him. Nothing about him pleases her. She probably dislikes his way of eating, of speaking, of sleeping, of waking, of washing. Finally, she turns to her elderly husband and demands that he expel the servant and her son. She speaks of them without mentioning their names. She reduces them to their functions. "Send them away," she says, "for I refuse to let the son of the servant share my son Isaac's inheritance" (Gen. 21:10). Her son has a name, the other does not. The apparent reason for her demand is the inheritance. Is Sarah concerned with material things? Here is another trait we would hardly have associated with Sarah. No, Sarah is not likable here; we cannot like her. Our sympathies go rather to her victims, Hagar and Ishmael.

Only there, too, we meet obstacles. In rereading the text, our enthusiasm gets dampened for the servant and her son. Hagar and Ishmael are no saints either.

A closer look at Hagar suggests she has an unpleasant side. She is young and vibrant, and she *knows* it. She knows many things. She knows of her mistress' misfortune, but instead of showing some gratitude to this family which has taken her in, she sows discord between husband and wife. The text confirms it. There is muffled anger in Sarah's tone—not only against Hagar but also against her own husband. "*Khamassi alekha . . .* may God be the judge of which one of us is right." The talmudic commentators agree with Sarah, who reproaches Abraham for his silence. "Oh yes," Sarah says to her husband, "you have seen Hagar behave badly toward me and you *said* nothing, *did* nothing to put her in her place; you didn't take my side; you remained silent . . . " Because of Hagar, the couple no longer appear so united, so harmonious.

Instead of humoring her mistress, who Hagar knows is unhappy, she irritates her. Rashi argues in his commentaries—in no uncertain terms— that Hagar lacked respect for her mistress; she gossiped about her, she let it be known that Sarah was a hypocrite, for otherwise she would have had children. Is that the way to repay kindness and generosity? The Midrash teaches us: "At first, Sarah introduced Hagar to her neighbors and friends, saying: 'Look at this poor girl, let's help her to adjust, to find her bearings.' Later, Hagar visited those same neighbors and friends to tell them malicious stories about her mistress." No wonder Sarah felt she had to do something about it.

Later, we see Hagar and her son in the middle of the desert. There is no water, and Ishmael becomes ill. What does Hagar do? She casts her son far away from her so as not to see him die. Is this the attitude of a mother? Surely, she loves him and cannot bear his illness or his slow and cruel agony. But why doesn't she think of *him*, of *his* needs? Doesn't Ishmael need her? The Midrash interprets the verse "She went astray in the desert" in order to emphasize the generally negative side of Hagar. The Midrash teaches us, "She strayed far from the faith and the customs she had learned in Abraham's house; she returned to her pagan ways and to her pagan gods." According to the Midrash, it was her way of protesting against her fate. This was her personal "response" to what she had suffered: to refute, to reject faith in God. In this too she is different from our ancestors, who were able to draw greater strength from their suffering and additional reasons to believe in God. Hagar bends in the face of suffering, so much so that one almost understands why the Torah turns against her.

Now for the fourth character—Ishmael. No one can fault him: he is almost outside the play. Object rather than subject of a story which is beyond him, he could have remained uninvolved. He could have not been there. He is there by accident. A model victim, there is no way he can be happy. One could say that happiness escapes him. He knows very well that it was not he his father desired for a son; and if he did not know, he is constantly reminded. What is he called at home? "The son of the servant," but not the son of Abraham. Yet, he too is linked to a divine promise— which his mother received from an angel during her pregnancy. But the same angel had predicted the nature and the social standing of the son to be born: *Pere adam*—he would be wild. *Yado bakol veyad kol bo.* He would have his fingers in everything. The commentators did not hesitate to explain: He would be a thief. Violent. Poor thing: He isn't even born yet and already he is being accused of crimes and sins as vague as they are unfair. He is not even born yet and already he is being made an antisocial being. From the moment he arrives, what does he see? Helpless, he is witness to some painful scenes: His mother is humiliated without end. What must he think of the system in which he grows up? What must he think of the patriarch Abraham whose reputation transcends borders? Or of his God who permits so much injustice within His human family? And later, in the desert, what must he think of his own mother who casts him far away to let him suffer alone, agonize alone, die alone?

However, Ishmael too had a bad press among the commentators, who cannot admit that Abraham and Sarah are capable of gratuitous cruelty toward him. And when the text says that Sarah saw Ishmael *metzahek*—have fun—the Talmudic commentators say that *metzahek* means something worse: Ishmael indulged in idolatry and even murder. In other words: *metzahek*—Ishmael ridiculed the faith and the laws of Abraham. He indulged in debauchery by word and deed, including a taste for hunting. He never went without his bow and arrows, the most deadly weapons of the time. Did he try to teach Isaac how to use them? Sarah caught him shooting an arrow in the direction of her son, without touching him. Frightened, Sarah decided to get rid of Ishmael. A more charitable commentator translates *metzahek*: "He discussed with Isaac the question of the inheritance," saying that as firstborn he would receive the larger portion of Abraham's estate. In short, Ishmael's role is less glorious than one might have thought. The victim, he victimized Isaac, who indeed was innocent in this whole drama, for he was too young.

There remains one more character about whom not much has been said: God. What is His role in all of this? Is He also innocent? Why did He prevent Sarah from conceiving? And why did He advise—no, command —Abraham to obey his wife and banish Hagar and her child? God could have abstained. He did not have to be directly involved in this business. In fact, Abraham and Sarah could have put the whole blame on Him! It is His fault, and the human beings could do nothing! It is God who holds the secret of human suffering, He who dispenses joy and happiness, He also who takes them away from whomever and whenever He wishes. If Abraham and Sarah had committed an injustice toward Hagar and Ishmael, it is because they were caught in a situation willed and ordered by God.

After this review, it is clear that in this drama none of the characters is entirely without guilt. All are wrong, because each and every one of them finds himself at a certain moment and for various reasons in conflict with the others.

Where does this tragedy begin? At which crossroad does it darken the horizon? Who committed what first mistake? When does the conflict begin? When Hagar accepted Sarah's suggestion? Is Sarah in conflict simply by making the suggestion? When Abraham submitted with surprising passivity to all of this, does his conflict begin? Does the conflict begin when God made too many promises to too many people at the same time?

Probing deeper into the text, we realize that the tragedy unfolds on more than one level. At first sight, it is the drama of a childless couple. On a more social level, the text tells us about a servant's troubles. A third reading gives psychological implications: a couple is affected by the presence of a stranger. And then, on the theological level, God appears and disappears in order to convey in simple gestures and words a hidden meaning that justifies exaltation or despair. Here everything is compli-

241

cated. Everything is complex. The angel orders Hagar to name her son Ishmael, but it is Abraham who gives him the name. Hagar weeps, but it is the voice of her silent son that God hears. First it is an invisible angel who speaks to Hagar, but she speaks of a vision. Miracles play an important part in this tale. By a miracle, Sarah becomes a mother; by a miracle, Ishmael is saved from death. One might say that God, in a good mood, has decided to help everybody, to ward off evil from everywhere, to intervene in favor of all His creatures and lead them toward a bright future.

There is however another way to read the story: one relating to scientific facts. In the eyes of secular scholars, the plot is natural and accurate, for it reflects the spirit and the law of the Code of Hammurabi, as illustrated by documents originating with the Nuzzi in the Northeast of Iraq. For example: "If Gilimninu bears her husband Shennima children, he will not take another wife. But if Gilimninu is unfruitful, it is she who will choose a woman for her husband." This is exactly what Sarah did in giving Hagar to Abraham. The Code of Hammurabi adds another provision to this law: "If the woman chosen by the wife becomes arrogant, she loses her new status and becomes a slave again." Here again is exactly what happened to Abraham's family. Seen from this angle—that of the ancient culture and environment to which Abraham belonged—the biblical story evolves according to the logic and the law of the time. All the characters are right—except, of course, for Hagar. On a purely anthropological level, she is guilty. She got only what she deserved. She had only to respect the rules of the game. Arrogance must get its due, and social transgressions must be punished. Had Hagar not shown disdain toward her mistress, she would have remained in her home, respected and happy. By violating the customs, she put herself in jeopardy. Sarah was right when she turned to Abraham—the master of the house, the supreme and all-powerful judge—to mete out just punishment to the guilty woman. Since she knew the law, she also knew the nature of the punishment, and she was right to remind him of it. We therefore have here a clear and simple situation. Dramatic, no doubt, but without any problems.

We prefer to follow our own tradition. Our story is studied in terms of the values which come from its own depths. The Code of Hammurabi is of interest to us, but the Torah alone can explain the Torah. *Moshe kibel torah misinai* is what characterizes Judaism: Everything connects us to Sinai, because everything comes from Sinai. Our enlightenment must come from the text itself. *Hafokh ba vehafokh ba dekoula ba* means: The questions and the answers are all in the text.

We must read the text once more to take a closer look at Hagar. The Code of Hammurabi aside, Hagar seems to us the most attractive of the characters in the cast. She is beautiful, young, dynamic, and proud. The moment she feels offended by her mistress, she goes away. It has nothing to do with the fact that she spent a night with Abraham. That is the way she is: proud by nature, maybe by birth. Hagar is not a nobody.

As a matter of fact, there is a Midrash which describes her as an Egyptian princess. This legend links the adventures of the biblical couple in Egypt to the drama of Hagar. Briefly: When Abraham misled the Egyptian king, Avimelekh, by presenting Sarah as his sister, Avimelekh, we remember, fell ill and could not approach Sarah. Having learned the truth, he apologized the next day to Sarah and gave her his daughter as a gift. Her name was Hagar. Lest we judge the royal father too harshly, the Midrash attributes this thought and sentence to him: "It is better, my daughter, that you be a servant in the house of Sarah and Abraham, than a princess in my palace." Consolation or reward—Hagar's servitude carried no humiliation for this young woman in love with freedom.

That is why she refuses to yield to Sarah's wishes. In fact, Sarah had to make considerable efforts to convince her to accept Abraham as lover. Hagar had no taste for such an arranged, hasty match or blind dates. Once persuaded, Hagar continues to bear herself with dignity. Although a servant and a "stand-in," she does not forget that she is a royal princess. When Sarah is too hard on her, she chooses freedom. She goes into the desert—the desert she knows, for it is her homeland. The desert, to her, means total freedom—for her imagination, for her dreams, for her memories. Better to die in the desert—in freedom—than to live in security and in servitude.

Imagine Hagar alone with her anger, alone with her wounded pride, in the desert, near a well. "And God opened her eyes, and she saw a well of water . . . " (Gen. 21:19). In Hebrew, the word is *"ayin"*—eye. Is this word used because an eye reflects images? Does the eye, like the well, attract friend as well as stranger? One cannot live without water, without light, or without hope. Thus, the eye and the well represent the cry of hope and hope itself. Hagar in her extremity—with no hope left—gazes at her image in the well. Suddenly, a voice calls to her. An angel has found her. It is a beautiful line: "She fled her mistress and was found by an angel of God." This is not one of those wandering angels who roam around the cities looking for surprises, or who crisscross the desert measuring its wonders. No: This angel is on a special mission. Must he find the fugitive to save her? Not exactly. The mission of the angel is to bring her home first—that is, back into servitude—and then to console her. Consider the dialogue: "Hagar," says the angel, "servant of Sarah, where do you come from, and where are you going?" And she answers: "I am running away from my mistress Sarah." Our commentators try to explain this answer by emphasizing Hagar's slave mentality: She ought not to have said "I am running away from my mistress Sarah," but simply "I am running away from Sarah." The Talmud comments: "When one calls someone an ass, he could use a saddle." This answer is evidence of frankness and of sincerity: Hagar does not lie. She is a slave and she says so. If the slave feels ashamed, her owner must feel even more so. Hagar's response is therefore an accusation pointed against Sarah: She treats me as a servant, she humiliates me. That is why I decided to run away! Consider the text more carefully. Hagar answers the first part of the question and not the second. She says where she is coming from, but not where she is going. The Malbim comments: "This is the fate of the fugitive; he knows where he comes from, but not where he may go." In this respect, nothing has changed since then: In our time, refugees cannot tell for sure whether they will find a place to rest and establish roots. With this difference: The refugees of my generation did not even know where they had come from: they came from so many countries, persecuted by so many oppressors, tormented by so many destructive angels. Unlike us, Hagar had but one enemy—and had been exiled from only one place.

But her divine messenger surprises us with this answer: He sends her back into servitude and at the same time predicts that she will continue to suffer. He finds a way of reassuring her: her suffering will have a purpose. She is pregnant, she will bear a son whom she must call Ishmael, because "God has heard your pain." Hagar is moved and overwhelmed and suddenly expresses herself as a poet, a mystic: She seems to refute the angel. Surely God hears, but that is not all: God sees. Rashi adds: God sees the pain of the afflicted. "You are the God who sees all," says Hagar, "and I myself have seen it here." That is why she calls the well—or the spring—*B'eer Lakhai Roii.* Is this the well of the living vision? Of one who sees life? Yes, Hagar is somebody.

Rabbi Shimeon bar Yohai, a very great sage, envies her and says so in public. When he is in Rome on behalf of his brethren in occupied Judea, he exclaims: "Hagar, a servant of my ancestors, was three times privileged to see an angel bearing a blessing—and I am here on a humanitarian mission and have seen no angel at all! Is that fair?"

Actually, the promise given to Hagar recalls that one given Abraham. Hagar, too, receives the assurance that her offspring would be numerous, even innumerable. According to the Midrash, Balaam, poor prophet that he was, understands this very well: of the seventy nations created by God, only two will bear His name: Israel and Ishmael. And at the end of days, says the Midrash, it will be the sons of Ishmael who will wage wars in the Holy Land and ravage its cities.

Stimulated and encouraged by the angel of God, Hagar returns to Abraham and Sarah. She has a son and Abraham names him Ishmael. He is an old man, our grandfather, when this son is born—eighty-six years old. Thirteen years later, God tells him that, for a second time, he will become a father. Abraham laughs. Sarah laughs. God changes their names: Avram becomes Abraham, Sarai is called Sarah. Meanwhile, things are happening in the world. Sodom attracts a little too much attention and then disappears. Lot and his two daughters are saved; his wife, too curious, is unwittingly discovering sculptures, and she turns into a pillar of salt. Abraham again leaves for Egypt and returns from Egypt. Isaac is born, and the second chapter of the drama brings back Hagar, who during these last year has dwelled somehow behind the scenes. The plot unfolds during the great feast, which Sarah and Abraham are giving to celebrate the weaning of Isaac. While the adults are drinking and eating and singing, or telling funny stories, Ishmael *metzahek*—literally, he laughs—with Isaac, or "makes him laugh." Sarah gets angry and the servant and her son are thrown out of the house. Let us add another interpretation of the word *metzahek*: Ishmael tried to pervert Isaac by initiating him into idolatry. This is Rabbi Akiba's view, but his disciple Rabbi Shimeon bar Yohai takes the liberty of contradicting him. "This is one of the rare times when I disagree with my master," he says. It is inconceivable that Ishmael, Abraham's son, could have practiced idolatry in the house of his father—our grandfather.

Whatever the relations between the two brothers, it is more important that Hagar and Ishmael become exiles, refugees. We imagine them abandoned, in danger, at the threshold of death. Ishmael is ill, he has a fever, and his mother is sick with despair. So, she leaves her child in the bushes. Is this cruel behavior? Let us not judge her too severely. She distances herself so she can cry out loud. As long as she is near her son, she manages to hold back her tears—so as not to frighten him, not to distress him. What could be more natural, more human, on the part of a mother? There is an interesting detail in the text: Hagar always refers to Ishmael as a *yeled*, a child; for the angel, and the text, Ishmael is a *na'ar*, a boy. Though he is seventeen years old, he is, in his mother's eyes, a child—a sick and unhappy child.

We love Hagar in the Bible and also in the Talmud. We cannot help but love her, because with all her faults she remains a perfect mother—though not a Jewish mother.

She is not like Abraham. Ishmael is his son, yet he banishes him. What kind of father is he then, this father of the Jewish people?

Let us not be too hasty. Who are we to judge Abraham? Caught between his duty as a husband and that of a father—between two loves—he wavers. It is the first time in his life when he cannot make up his mind. It is also the first time we detect a misunderstanding between Abraham and Sarah. There is a painful rift. Sarah calls Ishmael "the servant's son"; Abraham continues calling him his son. In the end, it is God Himself who must prompt him to act, to act against his own heart and his own conscience. "Listen to the voice of your wife," God tells him. Had God not insisted, Abraham would not have given in to Sarah. Even so, he feels uncomfortable. He *knows* that he is making a mistake. The text says: *Vayashkem Abraham baboker*—"And Abraham rose early in the morning," very early; he took some bread and a pitcher of water and handed them to

Hagar. Like a thief, one might say. Why did Abraham get up so early in the morning? For two reasons. First: he wanted Hagar and her son to set out before sunrise, before the great heat—when it is still possible to walk on the sand. Second: Abraham wanted to say farewell to his son and the boy's mother without Sarah being present. Sarah was still asleep. This was the right moment to see his son off. What if he were to get too emotional? If he were to burst into tears? Worse: what if Sarah were to look for a quarrel and say that he was giving them too much bread, too much water? No, it is better that she is not there.

Our talmudic sages are extremely generous and understanding with regard to Abraham. They find a lot of excuses for him. Besides, they are convinced that Abraham continued to think lovingly of his son even after he and Hagar had left.

One Midrash says that Abraham tied the heavy pitcher to Hagar's hip so it would drag in the sand and leave traces. Thus Abraham would be able to find his son. He often thought of him, and Sarah did not like that. Three years after the dramatic separation, Abraham could bear it no longer, and he decided to find Ishmael. Sarah must have made a jealous scene, because she extracts from Abraham a promise to go only as far as Ishmael's house, but not to enter it. In fact, he promised Sarah he would not get down from his camel. So Abraham set out, following the traces in the sand. He reached his destination toward noon. A woman welcomed him: Aissa, the Moabite wife of Ishmael. "Where is your husband?" he asked. "He has gone to gather fruit and dates." "I am thirsty and hungry," said Abraham, "and exhausted from the journey. Please give me some water and a bit of bread." "I have neither bread nor water," said Aissa. Then Abraham said to her: "When your husband comes home, tell him that an old man came to see him from the land of Canaan, and the old man sends him the message that he was displeased with the threshold of his house." When Aissa gave her husband the message, he understood what it meant and at once repudiated his wife. Hagar then sent him to Egypt to find a new wife, which he did: Fatima. Three years later, Abraham, overwhelmed with yearning, came back: "Where is your husband?" he asked Fatima. "He is not here," she said. "His mother and he went to look after the camels in the desert." "I am hungry, I am thirsty," said Abraham, "and exhausted from the journey." "Of course," she answered, and she went quickly to bring bread and water. Then Abraham prayed to God on behalf of his son, and at once Ishmael's home was filled with every possible good thing. "When your husband gets home," said Abraham to Fatima, "give him this simple message: an old man came from the land of Canaan. He very much liked the threshold of your house." The moral of this Midrash? Abraham cared for his son whom he loved, though he never saw him again.

Some sages believe that he even cared for Hagar. The proof: after

Sarah's death, he remarried. A woman named K'turah who bore him six sons. Who was K'turah? Rashi reveals her identity: Hagar. K'turah and Hagar are one and the same. To quote the Midrash: Abraham took Hagar back, for she was a woman of distinguished bearing. Can a former servant have a distinguished bearing? Abraham rehabilitated her by marrying her. The Midrash adds: During all those years, Hagar had remained faithful to him. She had not taken up with any other man. Abraham was the only man in her life. The circle is now closed. Abraham and Hagar were reunited—and were happy, perhaps.

Did they ever think back to their first encounter? It took place when Hagar was still a little girl and Abraham a young man. In Egypt. Remember that unfortunate Egyptian adventure? Abraham and Sarah play a dangerous game. They pretend to be brother and sister. Because of their lie, Avimelekh, king of Egypt, is punished: he and his entire royal house are sick. That night they are all victims of Abraham and Sarah, who had lived in disguise. What was *their* punishment? The tragedy of Hagar and Ishmael. Had they not lied, the king would not have offered his daughter to Sarah. And the history of the Jews—and of Islam—would have been different.

The *akeda,* too—the binding of Isaac, which is a high point of the Jewish experience throughout the ages—is considered a punishment for the sufferings of Ishmael. Here again we find a Midrashic text that says Abraham was wrong when he preferred Isaac to Ishmael: no father has the right to favor one child over another. Thus, when God orders Abraham to take Isaac and bring him to Mount Moriah, the sentence reads: *Kakh na et binkha et yehidkha asher ahavta et Itzhak.* "Take your son, your only son, the one you have loved, Isaac." But that is wrong! Isaac is not his only son! The punctuation needs to be changed. The sentence should read as follows: *Kakh na et binkha,* comma,—"Take your son"—*et yehidkha asher ahavta*—"the only one you have loved," comma, "Isaac." Thus the command contains a reproach as well as an explanation.

The *akeda*—the supreme test a father and a people can face—is therefore the result, the consequence, of the injustice committed by the father and by his wife toward an unloved son, Ishmael. Did Sarah hate him? What a pity. Abraham should have explained the situation to her. Did God side with Sarah? What a pity. Abraham should have argued with him as he had done for Sodom. But Ishmael did not bear a grudge against his father at all. That is clear from the text itself. Having lived a rich and full life, Abraham died at the age of 175. And his two sons Isaac *and* Ishmael came to bury him in the cave of Makhpela. Isaac *and* Ishmael were both there for the funeral. They were together, reconciled for this one event. For the Talmud, this is proof that Ishmael had repented. There is additional proof: Ishmael allowed his brother to precede him in the biblical description. Had Ishmael seen his father again while he was alive?

No doubt he had. After all, Abraham did marry Ishmael's mother. But the text says nothing of such meetings. Ishmael reappears only at Abraham's death, as if to remind us of the eternal truth: Death often smooths out the most difficult problems. In the face of death, many conflicts look childish. More than that, the reunion of the two brothers before their father's grave also reminds us of a truth too many generations have tended to forget: both Isaac and Ishmael are Abraham's sons.

It is sad to say—and even sadder to repeat—that the so-called villain in this story is Sarah, our beautiful and noble grandmother. She is so warm toward strangers, so hospitable to the needy, so welcoming to all women seeking faith. Is she too intense and too jealous a mother? Of course she desired a glorious future for her son! But she was wrong to do so at the expense of another mother and another son. The great Rabbi Moshe ben Nahman—the Ramban—Nahmanides—comments that when our ancestress Sarai (or Sarah) persecuted Hagar, she committed a sin. Abraham, by not preventing her, became an accomplice to that sin. That is why God heard the lament and the tears of Hagar and gave her a wild son whose descendants would torment in every way the descendants of Abraham and Sarah. The sufferings of the Jewish people, said the Ramban, derive from those which Sarah inflicted on Hagar.

The Radak—Rabbi David Kimhi—also does not hesitate to blame Sarah for her immoral behavior, for her lack of charity and compassion. The term *Vateaneha*—"And she, Sarah, made her suffer"—was to haunt our history for centuries upon centuries.

Of course, one could invent—or formulate—all kinds of excuses to whitewash our grandmother. We have mentioned a few. Hagar's arrogance, the bad influence Ishmael had on his little brother, the fate and future of Israel: If we try hard, we can exonerate Sarah. But apologies no longer have a place in our tradition. We are sufficiently mature to admit our shortcomings—especially since the Torah itself chooses not to conceal them. The patriarchs are neither infallible saints nor angels. They are human beings with impulses of grandeur and weakness. They love, they know fear, they hate and say so, they try to go beyond their condition and share in God's vision of creation: when Sarah is hurt, she admits it; when she is jealous, she shows it. Whatever she is, she is no hypocrite. There, Hagar is unfair toward her mistress: Sarah was never two-faced. She loved her husband and therefore gave him Hagar. Sarah believed in God and in His promise; therefore, she suffered for her own kindness. And because Sarah suffered, she inflicted suffering. Was she wrong? Maybe, but we love Sarah nevertheless. Maybe we love Sarah even more. In other words: Because Sarah was wrong and knew it but could not help it, it becomes our duty to do the impossible and correct her fault without diminishing her. We are her children, and that is the least we could do for her.

If only Sarah could have shared her love between Isaac and Ishmael!

If only she could have brought them together instead of setting them apart! Maybe some of today's tragedies would have been avoided. The Palestinian problem is rooted in the separation of these two brothers. As always, we must ask, Is it the mother's fault?

Having read the text and all its commentaries, having studied the question and all its ramifications, we cannot but feel sorry for Hagar—but we love Sarah.

Rabbi Ira S. Youdovin is the rabbi of Temple Beth El in St. Petersburg, Florida. He is the past director of ARZA—the Association of Reform Zionists of America. He has lectured widely on concerns of Israel and contemporary Zionism. He is Herman Schaalman's son-in-law, and their beautiful relationship with one another is well articulated within the personal foreword to his essay.

Ira Youdovin was a part of the Reform movement's initial attempt to synthesize Zionism and Reform Judaism into a new ideology, Reform Zionism. His critical enquiry into the relationship between Zionism and the Reform movement is essential to Israel and the Jewish people as a whole. There can be no covenant today without a commitment to Israel as a nation rooted in Zionism and Judaism as expressed in a pluralism of ideological movements. Youdovin's view is a valid and necessary response to the challenge of contemporary Jewish life.

Reform Zionism and Reform Judaism: A Creative Encounter Waiting to Happen

Rabbi Ira S. Youdovin

A Personal Foreword . . .

My first real conversation with the man who would become my father-in-law was occasioned by a trip I made to Chicago in March of 1981 to organize a membership drive for my organization, ARZA—the Association of Reform Zionists of America. Herman had been the unanimous recommendation of associates in Chicago as the rabbi who had the greatest influence with his local colleagues.

Although he had already been selected as the next president of the Central Conference of American Rabbis, I knew Herman only as a distant and somewhat forbidding presence: with a mane of brown hair that stubbornly refused to gray, and his affection for white turtleneck sweaters worn under blue blazers.

The meeting was memorable for two reasons. First, although we met in Herman's office, it was I who provided the lunch. More accurately, I *schlepped* sandwiches—corned beef on rye with mustard, extra pickles, cole slaw and potato salad on the side, and Dr. Brown's diet cream soda— 700 miles from New York to Chicago, which is not bereft of perfectly respectable delicatessens. To this day, Herman claims it was all a mistake resulting from miscommunication between his office and mine. But I prefer to believe that I was an unwitting participant in a conspiracy to smuggle calories and cholesterol past the watchful eyes of Lotte

251

Schaalman, whose mission in life is to make people healthier than they want to be.

The session was memorable for the questions Herman asked. Like many other Reform leaders, he was concerned over the implications of joining the World Zionist Organization, whose once-lofty reputation had become badly tarnished. Beyond that, Herman—and uniquely Herman—was concerned that political activity might distract Reform Zionism from addressing the profound theological questions that lie at the heart of Reform Judaism's still unresolved relationship to a Jewish State in our time. He asked when we planned to confront these issues.

It should be noted for the record that Herman, despite his reservations, agreed to host what turned out to be a very successful session with his Chicago colleagues. Although an idealist, Herman understands the importance of political process and even enjoys participating now and again. The meeting was initially scheduled for his home, but was changed at the last minute to his office when Lotte was called away to Milwaukee to help with the birth of the young lady who is now my five-year-old niece.

This essay is an attempt, however belated, to address some of the questions Herman raised at that meeting.

The Creative Encounter

When the Union of American Hebrew Congregations initiated a year-long period of study and discussion to determine the feasibility of establishing Zionist affiliates, ARZA—Association of Reform Zionists of America and Kadima—Canadian Council of Reform Zionism, it was not aware that the process would also generate a new ideological movement within the pluralism of Reform Judaism. Reform Zionism came to life almost as an afterthought. Nearly a decade later, its potential as a creative force within the Reform movement has yet to be tapped.

It is not surprising that an appreciation of this potential is elusive. Long before ARZA/Kadima, Reform Judaism had become imbued with a deep love of Zion and had compiled an ever-expanding catalogue of Israel-based and Israel-oriented activities, including its own kibbutz in the Arava and *aliya shlichim* working out of UAHC offices. Where Reform leaders had once denounced Herzl and his colleagues as "prophets of evil," UAHC president Rabbi Alexander M. Schindler had proclaimed, "Whether we spell it with a big 'Z' or a small 'z', we are all of us Zionists." In this thoroughly "Zionized" environment, it is easy to see how the new organizations were perceived as a means for intensifying and expanding current programs, rather than as vehicles for blazing new ideological trails.

To be sure, ideological investigation was an important aspect of the process leading to ARZA/Kadima, but its focus was retrospective, inquiring as to whether the World Zionist Organization's interpretation of its own stated positions on *aliyah* and Israel's centrality had moderated over the years to a point of compatibility with North American Reform Judaism, which has a primary commitment to Jewish life on these shores. Insofar as it addressed the future, discussion focused on practical concerns such as ARZA/Kadima's potential for strengthening Reform's voice in the World Zionist Organization, a forum generally viewed as being an important bridge linking Israel and the Diaspora, thus bolstering the movement's demand for equality in Israel and a more equitable distribution of WZO-Jewish Agency funds designated for religious purposes. Reform's participation was seen also as invigorating organized Zionism by introducing the untapped resource of a worldwide movement embracing more than a million people. Moreover, establishing formal ties with organized Zionism would be a symbolic final step in Reform's long march away from its anti-Zionist past, an act that would discredit once and for all some lingering stereotyping.

That the process must also initiate consideration of Reform Zionism as a new ideological formulation was first suggested by Rabbi David Polish during a two-day meeting of the Ad Hoc Committee on Zionist Affiliation, which had been mandated by the UAHC's Executive Committee to develop a formal recommendation. At the Committee's urging, Rabbi Polish wrote a draft for consideration the next day. It was accepted enthusiastically, and later became the core of ARZA's Ideological Platform, which was also drafted by Rabbi Polish and adopted by delegates to ARZA's first National Assembly in September 1978 as the first officially sanctioned statement of a distinctive ideology within the framework of Reform Judaism.

The ARZA Platform is a brilliant philosophical treatise which synthesizes Reform Judaism with the WZO's Jerusalem Platform. It is, however, markedly conservative when suggesting an agenda for ARZA within the Reform movement, seeing its role more as supporting existing programs than initiating new ones. To a great extent, this orientation is both inevitable and admirable. Unlike other Zionist groupings, which were created ex nihilo and built their programs from scratch over a period of years, ARZA was born into a Reform movement that was already offering a wide range of Zionist activities. Supporting and expanding these ongoing efforts is certainly an important aspect of Reform Zionism's work. On the other hand, it is both curious and disquieting that the Platform refrains almost entirely from citing, either explicitly or by implication, items of existing policy or program that Reform Zionism, as a distinct ideological movement, might strive to change.

Missing from Reform Zionism's posture is an awareness of its potential to continue the process of ideological development that was initiated by Reform's first encounter with Zionism during the early years of this century. At the time, American Reform Judaism perceived itself as being something of an American sect having no relationship to other Jewries or Judaisms anywhere in the world. Sensitivity to the plight of Zionist pioneers challenged that isolationism, expanding Reform's image of itself, and instilling in its adherents a consciousness of Jewish peoplehood.

Although Reform's relationship to Israel has changed radically since its passage from anti-Zionism to non-Zionism, in one subtle way it has remained almost totally unchanged. Even as Reform Jews have grown closer to the Jewish State, and have figured ever more prominently in community-wide efforts to support it financially and politically, they have done little to foster the growth of their own Reform movement in Israel. This attitude prevails among Reform leaders, who assign a very low priority to fund raising for *Yahadut Mitkademet*, Israeli Reform Judaism, and among members of Reform congregations, who contribute approximately 40 percent of the UJA's revenues and have their names on buildings of various description throughout Israel (as well as on Reform temples here in the United States), but who have yet to provide significant funds for Reform synagogues, educational facilities, and community centers in Israel, which cannot be financed in any other way because of Orthodoxy's monopoly on government allocations to Jewish religious institutions.

The only satisfactory explanation for this disparity is that Reform Jews are indifferent to their own Reform movement in Israel because they do not see Reform Judaism as having any particular relevance in the Jewish State, and certainly not as a potentially significant element in its spiritual future. In this sense, Reform's perception of itself has changed little over the years. The oft-told tale of the American visitor who refuses to believe that an Israeli synagogue is really Reform because it has no English prayers is not at all apocryphal. The reality of Israel, together with the impact of the Holocaust, has engendered monumental changes in Reform Judaism, including a heightened sense of Jewish peoplehood and a greater openness to tradition. Reform Jews are fiercely loyal to Israel. Reform institutions look to the Jewish State as a source of inspiration, and as an educational resource of unprecedented magnitude. And yet Reform Judaism as a religious expression and guide to a Jewish life-style continues to be perceived, even by its strongest adherents, as being tied inextricably to the western Diaspora, where its flexibility in matters of liturgy, education, and religious practice make an indispensable contribution to Jewish survival in an overwhelmingly non-Jewish environment. In Israel, where the simple fact of residence insures a large measure of Jewish identity, Reform Judaism would seem to be virtually irrelevant.

In fact, this conclusion may turn out to be the final one. Thus far, however, it has not been tested. Certainly, a *Yahadut Mitkademet* drawn along North American lines will attract few Israelis beyond a handful of western *olim* drawn by nostalgia. But, despite extensive talk about developing a truly indigenous expression of Israeli Reform, the rabbinic and lay leaders of *Yahadut Mitkademet* have done little in this direction. While it would be unreasonable to blame Diaspora Reform Jews for this failure, the chilling effect communicated by their lack of interest does take its toll. More critical, however, is the absence of a serious effort to involve leading Diaspora Reform thinkers in a cooperative enterprise with their Israeli counterparts to study the nature of Reform Judaism, the nature of the Jewish State, and the possibilities for creative interaction in developing a meaningful *Yahadut Mitkademet,* as well as a Diaspora Reform enriched by a new appreciation of its potential as a force in the total Jewish community.

Because they are Zionist organizations, ARZA, Kadima and their counterparts in four other countries are in a unique position to initiate this process. Zionism, more than any other movement in Jewish life, affirms the indivisible unity of the Jewish people. The concept that a major branch of religious Judaism may be irrelevant in Israel is an anathema to that affirmation. Reform Zionists must also challenge a working hypothesis that writes off as unreachable a growing community that currently numbers some 3.5 million Jews, and which will soon become the largest Jewish community in the world. Conversely, Reform Zionism might learn and teach a lesson from the history of its Orthodox counterpart, Mizrachi, concerning Zionism's potential for inspiring theological advances. The dynamism of modern Orthodoxy would be unthinkable without Zionism's earlier challenge to reevaluate traditional notions of messianic redemption.

The specifics of where this process might lead Reform Judaism are beyond the scope of this paper, as are the logistics of its implementation. But several aspects can be briefly noted. There is a need to look beyond the policies and programs of Diaspora Reform to identify a set of organizing principles that is both transcendent and motivating. Whether principles of this nature exist, other than a commitment to individual autonomy, is an open question. However, because the Diaspora environment in general, and America in particular, tolerates and even encourages an ad hoc approach, it is a question that can be forced only by endeavoring to define an expression of Reform suited to an entirely different environment. Reform Judaism as a movement has been content to leave the question alone; Reform Zionism cannot.

Inherent in the process is an attempt to formulate what constitutes a Reform Jewish life-style. When the founders of Kibbutz Yahel set out to build their community on the principles of Reform Judaism, they were immediately frustrated by the absence of role models. They knew, of

255

course, that there were no antecedent full-time Reform communities. But neither could they find guidelines or even a loose consensus on what Reform Jews do to manifest their Reform Judaism other than a very few basics such as lighting Shabbat candles. A more energetic definition is essential not only in Israel, where it is needed immediately, but also in the Diaspora, where a growing number of Reform Jews are becoming increasingly aware of the need for consensus, direction, and content.

The search should not be for a universal Reform Judaism, an analogue to Orthodoxy's *mitzvah* system, which, with a few exceptions, applies equally in Israel and the Diaspora. It would be folly for Reform to forfeit its adaptability to fit the contours of particular environments. Rather, the search should be for those principles and practices that inform implementation in every instance, so that they can be applied both in the development of a truly indigenous *Yahadut Mitkademet* and also to strengthen Reform's various manifestations in communities throughout the Diaspora.

In his presidental address to ARZA's first National Assembly in September 1978, Rabbi Roland B. Gittelsohn noted that Reform Zionism's potential lay in the fact that it represented an encounter of Zionism and Reform Judaism, the two ideological movements that have had the greatest influence on modern Judaism.

In a real sense, that encounter has yet to take place.

Susan Schaalman Youdovin is Rabbi Herman and Lotte Schaalman's older child. She holds two master's degrees, one in speech therapy, the other in child psychology. Herself a rebbetzin, *married to Rabbi Ira Youdovin, she is director of education at Temple Beth El in St. Petersburg, Florida. Her essay is a personal recollection of the life of the Schaalman rabbinical family.*

A Kid's Eye View: Remembering Our Family

Susan Schaalman Youdovin

Milestones have always been important in the Schaalman family. Guided by our parents, we always took great care to mark the festivals and celebrations that make up the rhythm of the annual cycle, as well as those events that note the passage of years.

When my brother and I were little, the return to school each September was an occasion not only for a "last fling" before the rigors of academic discipline, but also, perhaps more importantly, for a special *b'racha* with all the family participating. Similarly, family celebrations were no less a part of our childhood birthday rituals than the annual cake and ice cream party with friends.

The Schaalmans' abiding fascination with time would have, itself, been a sufficient stimulus for a *Festschrift*. This year we celebrate our parents' seventieth birthdays, their forty-fifth wedding anniversary, and the forty-fifth anniversary of Dad's rabbinical ordination.

But this is also the year our father retires from the active rabbinate, which adds special impetus to the project. Throughout the many years they have served the Jewish people, our parents have touched countless lives. This book is a symbol of their achievement. Indeed, because books have been such an integral part of our lives, and because covenant theology has long been at the heart of Dad's monumental faith, the volume is especially fitting.

Moreover, this *Festschrift* is an opportunity for some of the many people who care about our parents to express their profound feelings. Some have contributed their talents, others their material resources. All

259

have given of their love, admiration, and respect for Mom and Dad.

Last but not least, for us, their children—Mickey and Roberta, Ira and me—this undertaking has been another way of telling our parents how much we love and admire them, and how much they mean to us.

*　　　　*　　　　*

Milestones. The important milestones in our parents' lives are incredibly numerous and varied. By the time they arrived at their first pulpit, the event many rabbinical couples count as the beginning of their adult lives, both parents had already experienced the horror of Hitler's rise to power, crossed a vast ocean, and begun the difficult process of building a new life in an environment that was very new and strange to them. While they had met only after they had been in this country a few years, and although they came from radically different upbringings, the shared experience of growing up in Germany during the twenties and thirties linked my parents, influencing their perceptions and uniting their lives.

Cedar Rapids, Iowa, in 1941 must have been a different world to two immigrants to the United States. They no doubt delighted in a clean town, far from the horror of Europe. The large house, too, must have been a pleasure. Perhaps they were a bit disappointed that the cultural life was less stimulating than what they had known in Germany, or even in Cincinnati. But on the whole, the Schaalmans were very comfortable in Cedar Rapids. They were, however, "greenies." A story that is still told whenever we gather with friends from Cedar Rapids concerns heroic efforts by some of Dad's cronies to help the young rabbi with his sermonizing: they joined the local Toastmasters' organization to learn the fine points of speech making themselves.

My own happy memories of Cedar Rapids (I "arrived" in 1943!) are reinforced by black-and-white photographs and grainy eight-millimeter home movies of our life then. Foremost among my recollections is a 1948 visit from Aunt Ilse, a mysterious traveler from the new State of Israel. Coming ostensibly to help Mom through the birth of a new baby, Ilse wound up being the personal companion-psychologist every firstborn needs in adjusting to the intrusion of an uninvited newcomer. While everyone else was admiring my new brother, my aunt showed me how to make a wonderful paintbrush by snipping locks of my own hair. I had a short-lived (but significant!) career in art. Ilse provided my first opportunity to hear English spoken with an exotic accent (I did not know my parents' speech was tinged with umlauts and odd grammatic constructions until I was older). Indeed, Ilse always brings a little excitement with her. To this day, we await her visits eagerly so that we can dispute her definitive view of world and human affairs.

But Ilse's first visit to our new home also brought a note of sadness, for it reminded my parents that their family, like so many other Jewish families, had become scattered across the face of four continents. Only our mother's mother, Grandma Gussie, was with us; Mom's sister, Aunt Ilse, lived in Palestine. Dad's parents and brothers were in Brazil.

I remember an on again-off again trip to Brazil in 1947, just before my brother was born. It was the first time my Dad had seen his parents since they had left Germany in 1937. One can imagine his excitement, his anticipation as he flew to São Paulo, with his wife of six years and a four-year-old daughter.

I do not know how my parents, or others during that time, managed to live without an unquenchable anguish. With one's parents, sister, and brothers in foreign countries, unable to share holidays, milestones, how could people go about the ordinary business of living? Perhaps as loving grandparents they are making up for the ghastly holes in their early adult years. I don't know how they did it.

*   *   *

Our move to Chicago in 1949, when our father became regional director for the Union of American Hebrew Congregations (UAHC), brought major changes to our lives. Even without the buildings that now punctuate its skyline, Chicago was the Big City to us. Our parents quickly became part of the Jewish community, establishing the pattern that was to shape our lives: whenever there was a need, expressed or perceived, that my parents could fill, they were there. In a city as large as Chicago—and, later, in a congregation the size of Emanuel—this dedication entailed, and entails, a major commitment in time.

Yes, Mickey and I occasionally felt "neglected," and we were vocal in our outrage. Mom and Dad understood this, and endeavored to make us part of their calling. They included us in any activities where our presence was appropriate, engendering in us the priceless feeling that we, too, were somehow contributing to the well-being of the Jewish community. In small but meaningful ways, we "worked" alongside our parents. To maintain the pre-Shabbat tranquility of our home on Friday afternoon, Mickey and I took turns answering the telephone so that our parents were spared having to deal with the outside world to some extent. This might strike some as being antithetical to child-centered modern child-rearing practices. To us, it was a marvelous opportunity to "protect" our parents. Besides, these and other assigned tasks were often genuine fun.

Schaalman "togetherness" even served to make the kids at least a footnote in American Jewish history. When Dad began exploring sites for what was to become the first Reform youth camp, (now called the Olin-Sang-Ruby Camp–Institute for Living in Oconomowoc, Wisconsin), I tagged along on the adventure.

Arguably, Mickey and I were also America Reform Judaism's first "faculty brats" during those dreamlike summers on Lac La Belle. We were (an undersized) part of the workforce that dug post holes for the benches in the magnificent outdoor chapel. We coughed and sneezed with Mom and the other rabbis' wives as they beat dust and mildew from the campers' mattresses. We eavesdropped on the counsellors' sophisticated conversations, and learned things our parents would never have taught us!

Other idyllic summers were spent in Eagle River, Wisconsin. What glorious times those were . . . once we got there. I can still see us straining to shoehorn everything into the trunk of the car. Books in, record player out. Record player in, Mickey's suitcase out. Susie's things in, Mickey's things consolidated with Mother's . . . Somehow, nothing was left behind.

Like most American kids, we swam and played and had fun at Eagle River. But as a family, we also read each day (and I mean every day!) from a book selected by our father. One summer's "light reading" was a tome by the contemporary Catholic theologian Teilhard de Chardin, an exercise that stood me in good stead once I reached college.

*   *   *

The task of succeeding the great rabbi, Felix Levy, dominated the early years at Temple Emanuel. Additional challenges came from the Jewish migration from city to suburbs following the Korean War, which cast doubt over the future of inner-city congregations such as Emanuel. Moreover, the casual attitude toward religion that pervaded America in the fifties assaulted Jewish commitment. The task of leading a congregation, never easy, became a monstrous undertaking.

Mom and Dad addressed this challenge in the only way they knew how, by lavishing their intelligence, talents, dedication, and enormous amounts of their time on the congregation. We used to joke that if an emergency forced postponement of Dad's Tuesday morning Study Group, we would reschedule it for Wednesday morning by bumping the Wednesday Public Affairs Forum to Thursday morning, if, of course, the Thursday morning Bible Class wouldn't mind meeting Thursday afternoon in place of the Thursday afternoon Holiday Workshop, which could meet Friday before breakfast . . . .

Unknown to all but family and our closest friends, this pace, and the commitment that motivated it, did take its toll in an odd way. Every year as the Yomim Nora-im approached, Dad developed a high fever. By Rosh Ha Shana, it had blossomed into a raging virus. Each Yom Kippur passed with Dad refusing water to soothe a burning sore throat. Stage fright? Not really. The sight of a capacity crowd shouldn't trouble an experienced preacher. To this day, I believe that Dad's anxiety stemmed from his unique sensitivity to the enormity of both the challenge and the opportunity the High Holidays presented: trying to reach hundreds of Jews who were unreachable during the rest of the year.

Beginning with the time Mickey and I went away to school, memories take on a different texture. We had become accustomed to seeing our father mentioned in Jewish publications, but now we began noticing his name and picture in the Chicago press. I was surprised one day to open the *Chicago Sun-Times* and to see a photo of Herman speaking to a group of students on the steps outside a North Side high school. Fearful of violence and confrontation, the principal had asked Dad to do what he could to reduce the tension between whites and blacks, Jews and Chicanos.

Dad's rabbinical colleagues also called upon him for leadership, appointing him to a series of progressively more prominent positions within their rabbinical association, culminating in his election as president of the Central Conference of American Rabbis in 1981.

Mom has never permitted Dad to take his new prominence all that seriously. When his turn came to receive the honorary Doctor of Divinity degree Hebrew Union College awards all its graduates on the twenty-fifth anniversary of their ordination, Mom wanted to know whether the new "doctor" was entitled to prescribe headache remedies! Of course, Mom's chiding is both good-natured and superfluous. Dad is blessed with a unique combination of humility and inner strength available only to a truly religious human being.

In recent years, Dad has discerned in colleagues a need to find for themselves the spiritual underpinnings that have sustained him through the years. Rabbis who had become ensnared in the "business" of running a congregation have benefited from Dad's example, his open door to them, and seminars he conducts to help them rediscover the core of what inspired them to become rabbis in the first place. For a time, "spirituality" threatened to become a gimmick, the latest fad. But Dad has resisted "franchising" spirituality, and those who listen to him, participate with him, realize that spirituality alone is of relatively little value unless it becomes an enabling force, as it is in his life, in his service to his congregation and the community.

*   *   *

Through these recollections, one message shines above all others. What makes our parents so special, so unique, is their undeniable authenticity, which shows us how to live our own lives and affects us with the profound depth and genuineness of their ideals. This authenticity has enabled them to strike a delicate and complex balance between often conflicting forces. They have shown, as have Jews throughout the centuries, that it is possible for an individual to behave morally, ethically, Jewishly . . . while at the same time enjoying success as defined in contemporary terms.

So to Lotte and Herman Schaalman we lovingly present this *Fest-schrift*.

Susan Schaalman Youdovin, together with my husband, Ira, and step-grandchildren, Joshua and Julie, sister-in-law, Roberta, and brother, Michael Schaalman, and grandchildren, Johanna, Keren, and Jeremy.